HO[illegible] GET WHATEVER YOU WANT

X+

Above is your personal success symbol. This book will reveal its meaning and explain how to use it.

UBSPD®

UBS Publishers' Distributors Pvt. Ltd.

New Delhi • Lucknow • Bhopal • Ahmedabad • Mumbai • Pune
Bangalore • Chennai • Coimbatore • Ernakulam • Hyderabad
Bhubaneshwar • Kolkata • Guwahati • Patna

UBS PUBLISHERS' DISTRIBUTORS PVT. LTD.

5 Ansari Road, Daryaganj, **New Delhi**-110 002
Phones: 011-23273601-4, 23260232, 23273552

(Export Division)
First Floor, MPL No. 4948, Plot No. 47, Opposite Hindi Park,
Daryaganj, **New Delhi** - 110 002 (India) • Phones: 011-23266646-47

9, Ashok Nagar, Near Pratibha Press, Gautam Buddha Marg, Latouche Road,
Lucknow-226 018 • Phones: 0522-4025124, 4025134

Z-18, M.P. Nagar, Zone-I, **Bhopal**-462 011
Phones: 0755-4203183, 4203193, 2555228

1st Floor, Shop No. 133-134, Aust Laxmi, Apparel Park, Outside Dariyapur
Gate, **Ahmedabad**-380 016 • Phones: 079-29092241, 29092248, 29092258

2nd Floor, Shree Renuka Plaza, Tilak Road, Mahal, **Nagpur**-440 002
Phones: 0712-6457909, 2736010

2nd Floor, Apeejay Chambers, 5 Wallace Street, Fort, **Mumbai**-400 001
Phones: 022-66376922-23, 66102067, 66102069

680 Budhwar Peth, 2nd Floor, Near Appa Balwant Chowk, **Pune**-411 002
Phone: 020-24461653

Crescent No. 148, 1st Floor, Mysore Road, **Bangalore**-560 026
Phones: 080-26756377, 26756362

60 Nelson Manickam Road, Aminjikarai, **Chennai**-600 029
Phones: 044-23746222, 23746351-52

2nd & 3rd Floor, Sri Guru Towers, No.1-7 Sathy Road, Cross III,
Gandhipuram, **Coimbatore**-641 012 • Phones: 0422-2499916-17

No. 40/8199A, 1st Floor, Public Library Building, Convent Road,
Ernakulam-682 035 • Phones: 0484-2353901, 2363905

3rd & 4th Floors, Alekhya Jagadish Chambers, H.No.4-1-1058, Boggulkunta,
Tilak Road, **Hyderabad**-500 001 • Phones: 040-24754473-74

1st Floor, Plot No. 145, Cuttack Road, **Bhubaneshwar**-751 006
Phones: 0674-2314446-47

8/1-B Chowringhee Lane, **Kolkata**-700 016
Phones: 033-22529473, 22521821, 22522910

1st Floor, House No. 4, Kanaklata Path, Lachit Nagar, Bharalupar,
Guwahati-781 007 • Phones: 0361-2461982-83

Ground Floor, Annapurna Complex, Naya Tola, **Patna**-800 004
Phones: 0612-2672856, 2673973, 2686170

Visit us at www.ubspd.com & www.gobookshopping.com

Reprint 2012

ISBN 978-81-85944-41-8

Printed at: Ram Printograph, Delhi

× +

When You Bought This Book, You Bought Stock In Yourself!

The best investment you can make is in YOU.

You can make more money or acquire more of whatever you want—by investing in YOU than in any other investment.

When you bought this book, you bought stock in YOURSELF.

Nobody buys stock in anything unless he or she has *confidence* in it. Because, in buying this book, you really bought stock in YOURSELF, you have proved that you have *confidence* in YOURSELF.

Now that you have bought stock in YOURSELF and proved that you have *confidence* in YOURSELF, you have taken the first step in getting *whatever you want in life.*

This book now will tell you *how* to do it.

× +

YOURSELF STOCK CERTIFICATE

This certifies that you own

1,000,000 shares

of

STOCK IN YOURSELF

This is your certificate of confidence in yourself and your agreement to begin at once and constantly use proven success methods to get whatever you want as a worthy life goal.

× +

HOW TO GET WHATEVER YOU WANT

Contents

71 chapters on *how* to do it:

× +

Chapter 1

YOU Were Born To SUCCEED!

You were born to succeed!

Success is Nature's Law.

Success is a *natural instinct.* Everything in nature has a *success instinct.*

Plants instinctively seek and obtain the nourishment, moisture and all of the elements needed for successful growth. If it were not for the *success instinct,* there would be no plants.

Animals instinctively seek and obtain food, water, mates. Without their *success instinct* to GET WHAT THEY WANT, there would be no animals.

People, being more highly developed than plants and animals, have a *much more highly developed success instinct.* They are *born* with this natural *success instinct,* the urge, the drive to GET WHAT THEY WANT.

Yet some people fail.

Why?

Certainly not because *Nature intended* for

them to fail. *Nature intended for them to succeed*—to GET WHAT THEY WANT in accordance with Natural Law.

People fail ONLY because they have not USED the natural *success instinct* with which they were born.

The fact that YOU *want* to succeed (which is why you are reading this SUCCESS COURSE) is positive proof that *your* success instinct is intense and ready to GET WHATEVER YOU WANT . . . *now!*

There is a famous proverb which states, "*When the student is ready, a teacher arrives.*"

YOU are ready *now* to succeed in GETTING WHATEVER YOU WANT.

The teacher (this book) has arrived—as promised in the proverb—to tell you exactly HOW to do it.

This Book Is For You ... Yes, YOU!!!

It is the purpose of this book to tell YOU how to get whatever YOU (*yes, YOU!!!*) want.

Let's get it clear:

When this book says: "You", it means YOU (*yes, YOU!!!*)

This book is a complete SUCCESS COURSE specifically for YOU—to enable YOU to get whatever YOU want.

This book is written *for* YOU . . . *whoever* YOU *are* . . . *wherever* YOU *are* . . . *whatever* YOUR *age* . . . *whatever* YOUR *skin color* . . . *whatever* YOUR *present education* (or *lack* of education) . . . *whatever* YOUR *present situation* (whether YOU are *employed* or *unemployed*) . . . *whether* YOU *are rich* or *only in the middle income bracket* or *poor* . . . *whether* YOU *live in a ghetto* or *in a mansion* . . . THIS BOOK IS FOR YOU (*yes, YOU!!!*)

The success methods in this book can be used

by YOU—*whoever you are.* It is not WHO YOU ARE . . . but IF YOU USE the success methods in this book, which will enable YOU to get WHATEVER you want!

The success methods in this book can be used by men and women of *every age*—starting with *teen-agers* (*all teen-agers*) and continuing through *every age,* including *senior citizens past seventy* and many in their *eighties.* The author knows many men and women in their *eighties* who, not only personally will use the methods in this book, but who will derive a lot of satisfaction from giving copies to their children, grandchildren, relatives and friends, and also to worthy organizations—just as they give the author's book: *Thoughts To Build On.*

The author frequently receives letters from men and women in their *eighties,* telling how much *they are being helped* by his books. But the letters from older readers often add, "I wish I could have had these books years ago."

So *whatever* YOUR age—be glad YOU have *this* book NOW!

This book is for YOU—*wherever* YOU are—in city, town or country. Success is not a matter of LOCATION—success simply is a matter of YOUR DOING certain things (using the success methods in this book). Success does not depend primarily upon WHERE you use success methods—success depends upon IF you use proven success methods and HOW EFFECTIVELY you use them!

This book is for YOU—*whatever the color of your skin. It is long past time that ALL people got over being sensitive and self-conscious about their own skin color—and stopped over-reacting to the skin color of others!* The success methods in this book are for EVERYBODY *and they will work equally well for EVERYBODY regardless of skin color.*

This book is for YOU—*whatever* your present education (or *lack* of education)—whether you are a high school drop-out or a Ph.D. As Dr. Walter Scott, famous psychologist and President of Northwestern University taught, "Success or failure is caused more by mental ATTITUDES than by mental CAPACITIES." And YOU control your mental ATTITUDES, *whatever your education!*

If you can *read* this book, YOU can *use* and *succeed by using the simple, easy success methods* which this SUCCESS COURSE teaches.

It is the purpose of this book to make it *simple* and *easy* for EVERYBODY (*whatever* his or her education —or *lack* of education) to SUCCEED . . . *fast!*

This book is for YOU—*whatever* your *present situation* (*whatever* your present job, or if you are unemployed). The success methods in this book are used by the presidents and top executives of the nation's largest corporations—which is *why* they *are* presidents and top executives! (Before he retired, the author of this book was president of eight corporations and success counsel to 102 companies—so he has had considerable personal experience in *using* and *teaching* these success methods.)

But YOU do not have to be an executive (the author started using these success methods when he was an *office boy*). Whatever YOUR present position, the success methods in this book will enable YOU to get WHATEVER you want!

Getting WHATEVER you want by using this SUCCESS COURSE does not, in any way, depend upon WHO you are, or upon WHAT you are, or on WHERE you are—but *ONLY* on *IF YOU CONSTANTLY USE* the success methods on the following pages.

This SUCCESS COURSE is based on a great, old proverb: *"The tide lifts ALL the boats."* The tide does not lift only *some* boats or only *special* boats—it lifts ALL the boats.

It is the purpose of this book to *lift* ALL its readers—whoever they *are* . . . whatever their *age* . . . whatever their *skin color* . . . whatever their *present education* (or lack of education) . . . whatever their *present situation* (whether they are profitably employed or unemployed) . . . whether they are *rich* or *only in the middle income bracket* or *poor* . . . whether *they live in a ghetto or in a mansion*—this book is for EVERYBODY.

"The tide lifts ALL the boats."
This book will lift ALL its readers.

Chapter 3

How To Get WHATEVER You Want!

It is the specific purpose of this book to enable *you to get WHATEVER you want.*

If WHATEVER you want is *attainable—you CAN GET IT by using the simple, easy success methods in this book,* which really is a SUCCESS COURSE consisting of seventy-one chapter-lessons.

For example, by using the simple, easy success methods in this book, *you can get:* HAPPINESS . . . LOVE . . SUCCESS . . . WEALTH . . . INFLUENCE . . . POWER . . . POPULARITY . . . FAME . . . WHATEVER YOU WANT!

It actually is simple and easy to get WHATEVER you want!

There is not *anything* difficult or complicated about it. Anybody can do it.

Getting WHATEVER you want merely requires three very simple things:

(1) That you know WHAT to DO—and this

book teaches you WHAT to DO in *clear, simple, easy-to-understand* explanations.

(2) That you know HOW to DO it—and this book teaches you the *simplest, easiest, fastest* success methods.

(3) That you *constantly* USE the simple, easy success methods in this book. You will find it is easier and a lot more fun—*to USE the simple success methods in this book—than it is to suffer the unpleasant consequences of being unsuccessful!*

Actually, that's ALL there is to being SUCCESSFUL: (1) Knowing WHAT to DO . . . (2) Knowing HOW to DO it . . . (3) DOING it! . . . *And, there isn't any other way.*

This big book is devoted *exclusively* to: (1) Teaching you WHAT to DO . . . (2) Telling you HOW to DO it . . . (3) Inspiring and motivating you to DO WHAT YOU MUST DO in the simplest, easiest, quickest possible way . . . so that you will SUCCEED in *getting WHATEVER you want . . . fast!*

This is a "how-to-do-it" SUCCESS COURSE. It gives you *no magic power*. It gives you *personal power!*

This SUCCESS COURSE gives you the *personal power* of proven, practical, easy-to-learn, easy-to-use success methods of *Motivational Psychology, Personal Improvement Psychology* and *Personal Influence Psychology.*

This SUCCESS COURSE enables you to *get whatever you want* by simply telling you *exactly* HOW to do it—so that YOU can do it easily, quickly, confidently.

Chapter 4

The Power of Knowing WHAT!

The first requirement for getting WHATEVER you want is to know WHAT!

You must know WHAT you want.

Not knowing WHAT you want is like starting out on a trip without knowing the name of your destination . . . or what direction it is in . . . or what road to take . . . or how far away it is.

Your chance of reaching an unknown destination in an unknown direction by driving on an unknown road for an unknown length of time—is practically zero!

"WHAT YOU WANT" is your destination in life. It is your life-goal.

"WHAT YOU WANT" is your life-target. You cannot aim at NO target!

You must know WHAT.

The *first* reason that people do not succeed is that they do not know WHAT they want. So they wander aimlessly through life looking for *something*—but they do not know WHAT! They go hopelessly around in circles—only to come back to where they started. They rush boldly—in the wrong direction! They think they are going up—when they really are sinking down. What they start as a wonderful high—turns out to be a sickening low! They know they want *something*—but they don't know WHAT!

Start *thinking* NOW about WHAT you want. You don't have to *decide* now. But keep *thinking* about it while you read this book. Not just *when* you are reading, but in between times, too. Frequently—almost constantly—ask yourself: "WHAT do I want?"

When you ask yourself: "WHAT do I want?" think only in terms of a *life-goal.*

WHAT do *you* want? . . . *Happiness?* . . . *Love?* . . . *Success?* . . . *Wealth?* . . . *Influence?* . . . *Power?* . . . *Popularity?* . . . *Fame?* . . . WHAT?

You CAN have *any* or *all* of those things . . . and *more!* But you *must* decide WHAT.

And, if you keep asking yourself: "WHAT do I want?". . . *you will know exactly WHAT you want by the time you finish reading this book*—because this book is a SUCCESS COURSE consisting of seventy-one chapter-lessons which help you decide WHAT you want in life and then tell you HOW to get it! WHATEVER you want!

Knowing that *you CAN get it,* makes it easy to choose WHAT you want.

And . . . knowing WHAT YOU WANT is the first step in *getting* it!

Chapter 5

The Power of Knowing WHICH!

Getting WHATEVER you want in life is simply a matter of *making the right choices—deciding* WHAT and WHICH . . . and then *knowing* HOW.

Consciously or subconsciously, your mind constantly is confronted by the necessity of making choices—of deciding WHICH. You must decide if you will do *this* . . . or if you will do *that* . . . or if you will do *nothing*. There is no such thing as *not* deciding.

Deciding to do *nothing* is making a *choice* just as is deciding to do *something*.

Choosing to do *nothing* is a *choice* which may well determine whether or not you will GET WHAT YOU WANT. *Ask any drop-out!*

You cannot avoid the necessity of constantly making choices. If you try to avoid or delay making a choice, you are choosing to do *nothing*—and *that*, as just stated, is a *choice* which can affect your life as much, or perh. *more,* than deciding to do *something*. If you DO *nothing*—you will BE *nothing!*

Having chosen to BE *something,* you must decide to DO *something*—and that confronts you with choosing WHICH among life's tangle of pathways.

You must choose *which* action to take . . . *which* group to join . . . *which* cause to advocate . . . *which* job . . . *which* city . . . *which* neighborhood . . . *which* person . . . *which* life-goal . . . *which?* . . . WHICH?

This book cannot make those decisions for you because they are personal choices which only you can make.

But this book is a SUCCESS COURSE which gives you seventy-one chapter-lessons filled with success principles, methods and techniques to use in making the constant choices of life.

This book gives you the *power of knowing* WHICH!

With *that* knowledge and power you can successfully decide HOW to get WHATEVER you want.

The next chapter introduces you to the Power Of Knowing HOW!

Chapter 6

The Power of Knowing HOW!

The two preceding chapters emphasized the need for your knowing WHAT and WHICH.

Unless you know WHAT you want, you have no life-target at which to aim.

Unless you know WHICH of many choices will produce success, you are lost in your search for a rewarding life.

But only knowing WHAT and WHICH will *not* get you whatever you want in life.

You've got to know HOW to do it!

This book is a HOW-TO-DO-IT *Success Course*. It tells you *simply, clearly* and *exactly* HOW to GET WHATEVER YOU WANT.

And this book—this *Success Course*—tells you HOW TO DO IT the *sure, proven, easy* way . . . by using simple *Success Psychology*.

You will learn to use all three kinds of *Success Psychology:*

(1) You will use *Motivational Psychology* to propel you into dynamic, successful *action*—and to enable you to motivate others to act in your behalf to help you get WHATEVER you want.

Motivational Psychology is what *turns you on* and gives you the personal power to *turn others on!*

Motivational Psychology will give you *lift off* from your present condition and send you soaring to higher goals!

(2) The methods taught you in the following chapters also will enable you to use *Personal Improvement Psychology* which is the easiest, fastest way to *improve yourself*. There are techniques in the following chapters which will improve you *instantly!*

Your family, your friends, your employer, and everyone you want to impress will notice your personal improvement beginning with the *very first time* you start using the amazing techniques of *Personal Improvement Psychology*.

Only by *self-improvement* can you *earn, deserve* and *get:* HAPPINESS . . . LOVE . . . SUCCESS . . . WEALTH . . . INFLUENCE . . . POWER . . . POPULARITY . . . FAME . . . or WHATEVER are the BIG DESIRES in your life.

No one can *give* you the BIG REWARDS. You must personally *earn* them and convincingly *deserve* them! The following chapters use *Personal Improvement Psychology* to enable you to *earn* and *deserve* the BIG REWARDS . . . *fast!*

(3) To positively assure your success you will learn the powerful methods of *Personal Influence Psy-*

chology which will enable you to smoothly influence others to willingly—and *enthusiastically*—help you get WHATEVER you want.

You cannot obtain the help and win the necessary cooperation of others by pressure or by force. *Pressure creates resistance. Force creates enemies.* And . . . resistance and enemies you don't need!

But you can always obtain the *willing help* and the *enthusiastic cooperation* of others by using *Personal Influence Psychology* to influence them to WANT to do WHATEVER *you want them to do!* The following chapters tell you exactly HOW to do it.

Beginning right NOW—as you read this book, you will begin to radiate the enthusiastic, confident glow of *Success Psychology.* You will *look* like a success! You will *act* like a success! You will *be* a success! And, by using the methods of *Success Psychology* clearly described in this book, *you will attract more and more success like a magnet!*

You will become *magnetized to attract to you* WHATEVER YOU WANT!

This book—this SUCCESS COURSE—tells you HOW . . . in its seventy-one chapter-lessons.

And you start by being a VOLCANO!

Chapter 7

Be A VOLCANO!

A mountain is an impressive sight—when you see a mountain for the *first* time.

But after you have seen a mountain, or a lot of mountains, with what becomes a sort of monotonous frequency, even a mountain becomes just part of the landscape. A mountain . . . is a mountain . . . is a mountain.

There it is. Another mountain. Just there. *Doing nothing.*

Not so, a VOLCANO!

When a mountain becomes a VOLCANO, it *turns on!* It *comes alive!* It becomes a *shaker* and a *mover!* It *lights up!* It *radiates a glow!* It is a *something!* It is a *happening!* It is *somebody!*

So, be a VOLCANO!

Don't just be part of the landscape. Or just part of a crowd. Or just a member of a group. Or just one of the employees.

Be something *special!* Like a VOLCANO!

People *pay attention* to a VOLCANO! It is a *one-mountain spectacular!* If you want people to pay attention to you, *you are going to have to be a one-person spectacular!*

Turn on! Come alive! Be a *shaker* and a *mover! Light up!* Heat up an *inner glow* so that you can *radiate* an *outer glow!* Be *something!* Be a *happening!* Be *somebody!*

People respect a VOLCANO! It simply is *too hot to handle!* A VOLCANO does more than flame and glow. *It spreads heat!* Molten, red-hot lava *spreads out* from the blazing center. Nothing can stop it! Woe unto any person or any thing which dares to stand in its way! It is nature's proof of the devastating power of *ever-expanding, uncontainable heat!* So people *respect* it. No one dares to oppose the oncoming, unstoppable, constantly spreading, all-consuming *heat*.

Do you want to *attract attention?*

Do you want to *command respect?*

Do *you* want to be *unstoppable?*

Then, be a human VOLCANO!

And remember the source of its power . . . HEAT!

Get HOT!!!

Chapter 8

Don't Be A COLD FISH!

The last chapter described a VOLCANO. Read it again—before reading this chapter.

I want you to compare that VOLCANO . . . to a COLD FISH!

That comparison may make a lasting impression on your personality!

VOLCANO—or—COLD FISH!

Have you looked at a COLD FISH lately?

Have you looked at a COLD FISH—a *real fish,* cold, frozen—looked the COLD FISH *in the eye* and tried to *relate* to it?

Do you feel a *glow of togetherness* with a COLD FISH?

Perhaps you should have a more intimate aquaintanceship with a COLD FISH . . . so rush to your nearest fish market and choose the COLD FISH that seems *most friendly* to you!

Don't just *look* at a COLD FISH . . . *buy*

one—select the most *friendly* COLD FISH you can find!

Hold the COLD FISH in your hands. Look it in the eye. Try as hard as you can to *relate* to it. Build up a *meaningful relationship* between you and the COLD FISH.

If you are unwilling to actually buy your very own COLD FISH to relate to . . . then at least *imagine* that you have done so, and visualize—*mentally picture*—the *physical awareness* and the *deeply personal emotions* you would feel if you were *holding* a COLD FISH . . . looking it steadily in the eye (establishing *"eye contact"* as the top personalities do) . . . and developing a *meaningful, personal relationship* with your own special COLD FISH!

If you do this—actually or mentally—*you will get the message:*

DON'T BE A COLD FISH!

Chapter 9

Be A GEYSER—
Not A Little Squirt!

In the two preceding chapters, which compared a VOLCANO to a COLD FISH, I hope you found a lesson in personality development.

Now let's turn from *heat* and *cold,* and let's examine *FORCE* and *POWER*—or the lack of them.

Imagine that you are in Yellowstone National Park with the huge crowd waiting to see the *spectacular geyser,* Old Faithful, erupt in its tremendous exhibition of irrepressible water power!

At the same time, imagine that you are holding in your hand a *toy water pistol.*

Then, in all of its sensational, awesome power, the great geyser bursts skyward in a towering display of steaming water—one of the most amazing *natural power* spectaculars man has ever seen!

The huge crowd of viewers from all over the

world gasps at the magnificent demonstration of *unleashed power!*

Then you look at the toy water pistol in your hand. You boldly pull the trigger . . . and out of the muzzle of your toy water pistol comes a *little squirt* of water which diminishes to an even smaller *dribble* . . . and ends weakly in a *drip.*

Well?

Well, you have just seen the difference between a *powerful geyser* and a *little squirt.* Both used the *same material* . . . water. *But what a difference!*

It is a difference worth remembering because Life gives you that *same* choice: *To be a powerful geyser —or a little squirt!* With the same material . . . YOU!

You can acquire the spectacular power and skyward thrust of a *great geyser*—or you can be a *little squirt* which soon ends in a dribbling, downward *drip.*

The choice is *yours!*

If you choose *greatness*—you will find the methods and techniques in the following chapters.

Chapter 10

There Is NO Excuse For NOT Getting WHATEVER You Want!

People who haven't succeeded to the full extent of their capacities *always have an excuse*. Like any law-breaker (and they are breaking the Law of Success) they have figured out what they believe to be an iron-clad alibi for not being more successful.

They have a *handicap*—real or imagined—which is holding them back. And, of course it isn't their *own* fault. (It never is!)

This is not to say that people don't have *real* handicaps. Certainly they do! *Everybody has handicaps—only some handicaps require more effort and will-power to overcome than others.*

Nor are imagined handicaps any less real than those which are entirely physical. A pain is a pain and it hurts just as much whether it results from a physical injury or a mental defense mechanism. A headache is just as painful if it is a subconscious alibi for avoiding a disagreeable task as if it is the result of eye-strain. Either way it hurts just as much.

And a headache is a mild example. People actually go blind, become partial or entire invalids, suffer every conceivable disability, *because their subconscious minds are using these physical means to give them an alibi for not doing what they should do,* for not living up to the expectations of others.

Sometimes these mentally or emotionally caused pains or illnesses are a means of self-persecution for some real or imagined sense of guilt submerged deep in their subconscious—so deep that the sufferers often do not realize the cause and so blame something else. At least half of *all* illnesses have *some* mental cause.

Real or imagined, physical, mental or financial—handicaps are something everybody has and it isn't the purpose of this book to underrate them.

In fact, it is the purpose of this book to tell you how to *overcome any handicap* you may have! More than that, this book will tell you *how to use your handicap as a springboard to success!*

Starting right now this book is going to tell you how poor boys became multimillionaires, how cripples became world champions, how weaklings became the strongest men in the world, how a deaf man composed some of the world's greatest symphonies, how "old men" past retirement age amassed huge fortunes!

Well . . . what's YOUR excuse? So YOU'VE

got a *handicap* that's holding you back? *Congratulations! You can use it to be a lot more successful than if you didn't have a handicap at all!*

Of course you can't be a track star if you have no legs. But you can be a champion athlete even if, in the beginning, your legs are weak—even if your legs have been crippled by accident or disease. And *that* applies to *all kinds* of handicaps! *The record books are filled with the names of champions who overcame supposedly insurmountable handicaps!*

A HANDICAP CAN BE YOUR GREATEST ASSET. Many handicapped people are *so determined to overcome their handicaps* that they *over-compensate* for them and thus *accomplish far more than normal men and women!*

Annette Kellerman was *lame and sickly*—yet she became the World Diving Champion and was judged one of the world's most perfectly formed women!

Sandow started life as a *sickly weakling*. He exercised until he developed one of the most perfect bodies in history and became the strongest man of his time!

Some years later, George Jowett, *lame and weak* until he was eleven years old, built such a perfectly muscled body that, in just ten years, he became the world's strongest man!

If you are physically handicapped you can do one of two things: (1) you can feel sorry for yourself and expect others to feel sorry for you, or (2) you can overcome your handicap by will-power and mind-power (which are described in this book) and if you are willing to pay the price in vigorous exercise, systematic training and hard work, you even can become a *champion* as so many other handicapped people have.

But suppose you are not *physically* handicapped. *Suppose your handicap is that you don't have much school education and you are very poor.*

Let's have a look at some of such *poor* people:

Let's start with poor Andrew Carnegie. Andrew Carnegie, *poor?* Why he was the great steel tycoon—who made so many millions he couldn't give them away fast enough, even though he endowed free public libraries in cities all over this nation! *Well, Andrew Carnegie was so poor he had to start work at $4.00 a month!*

John D. Rockefeller, who later became one of the richest men in the world, started out much more highly paid than Carnegie. *Rockefeller made $6.00 a week!*

He also was more highly paid than Henry Ford *who started at $2.50 a week!*

Then there was Thomas Edison who started as a newsboy on trains and became *the world's greatest inventor* by conducting more experiments that *failed* (yes, *failed!*) than anybody else in the world! *Of course, every time he failed, he found out what wouldn't work until finally all that was left was what would work!* That's an easy way to achieve greatness—*just fail your way to success!* (A later chapter will tell you how *YOU can fail your way to success!*)

And, another failure: Babe Ruth struck out more times than any baseball player in the Major Leagues —1,330 strike-outs! He also hit more home runs—714. *You'll never become a batting champion if you're afraid to take your bat off your shoulder!*

But back to the *poor* folks: A man named D. A. Thomas was born poor, in a tiny Welsh village. Not only was he poor, but he was a very delicate boy. *So, naturally, as all delicate boys should (and many of them do) he trained himself to be a strong athlete.* He became a good walker, swimmer and cyclist. He was a good boxer, too, the middle-weight champion of Cambridge, in spite of his bad eye-sight. *He also trained himself well in business by building more than thirty companies and becoming a multimillionaire!*

There was another delicate boy who had so little schooling that he had to be taught by his mother. *He also read books, lots of good books.* And, he liked to experiment—which resulted in his inventing the steam engine that changed the industrial world! His name? James Watt.

Of course you've heard of the worthless farm boy whose father died before he was born and *his mother had to rear him on a total income of $400 a year.* You will remember him as Sir Isaac Newton, discoverer of the Law of Gravity.

George F. Johnson was poor, too. He earned *$20 a week* working in a small shoe factory—which went bankrupt. The principal creditor was a man named Endicott. Admitting that he had *no money,* Johnson gave Endicott his personal note for $150,000 for half interest in the bankrupt factory. It became the Endicott-Johnson Company and grew to be the largest manufacturer of shoes in its time.

A good many years ago, there was a *frail, lame little chap* named Elias Howe. *He was so poor that he and his family were starved most of the time.* He invented the sewing machine but nobody would buy it. His garret workshop burned down. His wife died. He still *kept on trying.* Finally his sewing machine began to sell. *Elias Howe became a millionaire in twelve years, because, in spite of every discouragement, he kept on trying!*

Michael Faraday was born over a *livery stable,* the son of a poor blacksmith. Not a promising start for the founder of *electrical science and one of the foremost scientists of his day!*

Joseph Fels was born in a tiny cottage in Virginia. *His parents were poor. His education was poorer.* He started his business career as a soap salesman. By great personal sacrifices and utmost thrift he saved $4,000 with which he bought a small soap factory. *It grew into a large soap factory and made him millions.*

Alice Foote MacDougall served coffee and waffles from a little stand in Grand Central Station in New York. As a matter of fact, she didn't just serve waffles, *she gave them away* with her coffee—*and built a $5,000,000 restaurant business!*

King Camp Gillette was born in a small town in Wisconsin. *When he was seventeen his father lost everything by fire, so young Gillette had to make his own way.* How? *Ever heard of a safety razor?*

A young man named Stewart came to New York with *$1.50 in his pocket. The only way he could get more capital was to earn it.* And earn it he did! He started what became the John Wanamaker Store, one of the greatest department stores of its time!

Andrew Jackson and Abraham Lincoln, both

great presidents of the United States, *started life in the poorest and humblest of homes* with *little education* and *no advantages.*

Ulysses S. Grant at first *failed* as a business man. *Finally, at 39, he was chopping cordwood for a bare living.* Nine years later he was President of the United States!

And so we can go back through history and learn one of Life's greatest lessons: *Nobody is holding you back but YOU!*

A German named Elbert *started out as a saddle maker* and became the first President of Germany after World War I.

Mustapha Kemal was an *unknown officer* in the Turkish army and became Ruler of Turkey!

Reza Khan started as an *ordinary trooper* in the Persian Army and became the fabulously wealthy and powerful Shah of Persia.

Julius Caesar was epileptic, but he conquered the then-known world!

Demosthenes *stuttered*—so he filled his mouth with pebbles and shouted over the roar of the waves until he became the greatest orator in all of ancient Greece.

Darwin was neurasthenic. *His nerves were so shattered that even writing a letter on a subject that excited him made it impossible for him to sleep that night!* Yet he found within himself the enormous energy and vitality required for the vast scientific research and exacting writing which gave the world: *The Origin of the Species.*

Do you think "old age" is a handicap? I put

"old age" in quotation marks because there is considerable disagreement among scientists and writers concerning when this alleged period of increasing disability is supposed to begin. *There now seems to be a growing conviction that we shall learn to live to be at least 150, with quite adequate mental and physical capacities.*

In the meantime, it might be interesting to note a few items of accomplishment by men of considerable "*age*" according to present actuarial tables.

After World War I, there was a conference in France to draw up the *Treaty of Versailles.* It was attended by the world's most important and powerful men. The one man most powerful and dynamic in the entire group was Clemenceau, the "Tiger of France." *He was seventy-five years old.*

Andrew Mellon, one of the nation's greatest financiers, retained vigor, endurance and extraordinary energy throughout his *eighty-two years* of outstanding accomplishments.

Vanderbilt planned and constructed most of his railroads when he was over seventy. *He made most of his millions at an age after lazier men have retired!*

When he was *seventy-five,* Walter Damrosch wrote and personally conducted one of the finest operas of our age.

Kant wrote some of his greatest philosophical works *after he was seventy!*

Monet, the great French artist, was still painting his magnificent pictures when he was *eighty-six!*

Von Humbolt began work on his famous "Kos-

mos" when he was seventy-six and completed it at ninety!

Goethe wrote the second part of *Faust* when he was *eighty* years "old."

Also at *eighty*, Victor Hugo produced *Torquemada.* Should "mandatory retirement" be based on *age?*

Titian painted his incomparable "Battle of Lepanto" when he was ninety-eight!

So much for "old age"! But suppose you are *really* handicapped?

Beethoven, composer of immortal symphonies, was *deaf!*

Milton wrote *Paradise Lost* when he was *blind!*

Audubon *rose from poverty and disgrace* to lasting distinction through his contribution to our knowledge of bird life.

Alexander Pope was so crippled he could hardly move yet he was a giant of English literature.

Joan of Arc, *an illiterate and penniless peasant girl,* became the heroine of France in that nation's crisis.

Theodore Roosevelt was *sickly and weak* as a young man, yet by great will power and strenuous exercise he gained such strength and vigor that he rode at the head of the rugged Rough Riders up San Juan Hill and later became President of the United States!

Franklin D. Roosevelt also became President, even though he was *severely crippled by infantile paralysis!*

John Bunyan, *in a prison cell,* wrote a book that will live forever as an epic of English literature: *Pilgrim's Progress.*

Robert Louis Stephenson *never for one hour*

was free from pain and a hacking cough, suffered from fever and tuberculosis—yet gave to generations yet unborn the adventures of *Treasure Island,* the genial philosophy of *Travels With A Donkey,* and countless hours of pleasure and inspiration from his versatile pen.

It is clearly evident, from the experiences of courageous men and women in all walks of life, that the so-called "*handicaps*" of lameness, sickness, poverty, misfortune, lack of schooling, and "old age" can be overcome by will-power and mind-power and success methods which are described later in this book.

If you are "handicapped," you can use what psychologists call over-compensation to lead to ever greater accomplishments and success than normally would be achieved!

To put it simply: SUCCESS IS AVAILABLE TO EVERYBODY!

This book—this SUCCESS COURSE—tells you *how.* It teaches you all of the success methods you ever will need to GET WHATEVER YOU WANT.

The next chapter gives you some keys which you can use to open the doorways to the Treasure Room of Success!

Chapter 11

Keys To The Doorways To Success

You can have SUCCESS in *unlimited abundance, you can have the good things you want in life*—just by unlocking any ONE of the *many* Doors To Success!

There are many *keys* to the many Doorways To Success, and it is the purpose of this book to use those keys to bring SUCCESS to more people, more easily and more quickly. The success methods which are clearly described in this book require *no formal education, no unusual talent, no exceptional ability, and no personal influence.*

This book makes SUCCESS easily and quickly available to EVERYBODY—not just to a fortunate few.

There are few services which can be rendered to this nation which are more important than to fill this entire country with successful people who are quickly and easily obtaining all the good things in life!

That's why this book was written—to put SUC-

CESS within *easy* reach of EVERYBODY. That's why you should use this book to start getting the good things in life for yourself and your family NOW!

This book will give you many keys to SUCCESS. In this world of *unlimited abundance*, SUCCESS is a Treasure Room with *many* doors! Let's look at a few of the keys which will unlock the Treasure Room:

The "*Hollywood and T.V.*" Key to Success

For example, there is the "*Hollywood and T.V. Personal Magnetism Method*" of achieving success. This is the way movie and television actors and actresses are taught to acquire *the powerful personal magnetism* by which they attract crowds, win fame and earn fabulous wealth.

This success method is simple because it is based upon doing *only three things!* Try it yourself:

(1) Maintain a magnetic INNER-glow!
(2) Radiate a magnetic OUTER-glow!
(3) Smile with your EYES!

If you can do *those three things*—with the *right* people, in the *right* places, at the *right* times—you have a key which will unlock one of the many doors to the Treasure Room of Success.

Lots of men and women have used this method of achieving success—and not just movie and television stars either—but all kinds of people who took time and trouble to learn, practice and use this secret of personal magnetism. (It is taught in detail in my book: THOUGHTS TO BUILD ON.)

The "*Make Friends and Use Influence*" Key to Success

Now let's look at what we'll call the "*Make Friends and Use Influence*" key to success. This method has two desirable qualities:

(1) It is pleasant to use.

(2) Properly used, it gets good results.

I highly recommend it although, personally, I feel that it omits some of the powerful success techniques which will be described later in this book.

Certainly there is much to be said in favor of making friends—especially the right kind of friends—although *too much time spent in "making friends" can greatly limit your degree of success.* Often, people have learned to their dismay that many friendships do not have the permanence upon which to build substantial and lasting success.

Nor is the influence based on friendship by any means the most powerful. *There are deep, psychological influences which are much more dependable sources of power for you to use in getting what you want.* These deep, psychological powers will be given you later in this book as an important part of this SUCCESS COURSE.

Nevertheless, as I said at the beginning, I also recommend the "*Make Friends and Use Influence*" technique, although it is a little like being for "God, Mother and Country." However, it produces good results and that's what counts. So, use it!

The "*Overwhelming Service*" Key to Success

"*He profits most, who serves best.*" That's one of the best-known slogans in business. It also is one of the most sensible keys to success. *It works if you understand that the words "serves best" mean OVERWHELMING SERVICE, not just expected service or regular service or good service.*

Everyone in business, more or less tries to give expected, regular, good service. And, that's exactly why it doesn't produce extraordinary results. *There just isn't anything extraordinary about doing the ordinary, expected services. It may make you a living—but it won't make you rich.*

One of the purposes of this book is to tell you how to get rich. *And, one of the surest ways to get rich is to give OVERWHELMING SERVICE!*

The secret is to do *much more* for those you want to influence than any one else is willing or able to do. If you *can't* do that—you need to make some changes! If you *won't* do it—move over—who wants you?

I'm talking about *personal* service—constantly (day and night) thinking of *new and more ways to help those whose help you want in return.* And then *doing* these personal services continuously without thought of *immediate* benefit to yourself. The less you *directly* benefit, the more impressed those you want to influence will be that you sincerely want to help *them,* and the more obligated they will feel that they should help *you* in return!

But remember: expected, regular, routine service will get you exactly nowhere. You've got to really OVERWHELM others with service (including services not *directly* connected with what you want). Of course, you have the good sense not to make a nuisance of yourself—but it's very hard to be a nuisance when you are constantly helping your friends and associates be a lot more successful themselves!

Long ago, I heard an inspiring speech on the subject of "*What's Your Plus?*" What *extra* are you putting into your cooperation with others? What EXTRA are you willing to do that other people are not doing? It's your *extra* that attracts attention, makes you stand far above the crowd, gets you what you want, makes you rich!

So there you have another key to the Treasure Room of Success: The "*Overwhelming Service* method."

The "*Human Dynamo of Unlimited Energy*" Key to Success

What is the one characteristic found in almost all tremendously successful persons throughout history?

It is unlimited energy! These tremendously successful people are human dynamos of super-energy!

To have this key to success you must develop and continuously use personal energy which is so intense, so terrific, so much *greater* than that of your associates and others that *you simply overcome all obstacles by your unlimited capacity to get things done!*

The "*haves*" and the "*have nots*" can be traced back to the "*dids*" and the "*did nots*"!

One of the great labor-saving inventions of today is—*tomorrow!* Putting off action until tomorrow not only will save you labor today, but it will save you the future effort of making deposits in your bank account.

Don't think the world owes you a living. The world owes you nothing. It was here first!

But you're always so tired? Why? Because you

work so hard? Because you never really feel energetic? Maybe you can sell those excuses for failure to yourself because you want desperately to believe them—but you'll never sell them to a psychiatrist, or to your family doctor, or even to your own family or friends, although some may politely pretend to believe you.

Every psychiatrist will tell you that chronic fatigue (except in very rare cases of glandular or other physical malfunction) is caused by boredom, anxiety, annoyance, irritation, worry, resentment or a sense of guilt hidden deep in your subconscious.

This is not a book on how to eliminate chronic fatigue and I shall not pursue the subject further except to recommend that if you have chronic fatigue, first see your doctor, then read some of the good books specializing in that subject, or see a psychiatrist. (And, by all means, thoughtfully study the next paragraph.)

This is a book on the many keys to success, one of which is *the effective use of unlimited energy*. If you haven't got unlimited energy take the advice of William James, one of America's leading psychologists, who said that *feeling follows acting—so to FEEL energetic, ACT energetic!* Do the things you ought to do, even when (*especially when*) you don't feel like it—and you'll find you have plenty of energy to do them. *To FEEL energetic —ACT energetic!* Do it NOW!

The "*Mind Power*" Key to Success

This method utilizes the unlimited power of continuous positive thinking. *There is no doubt that certain deliberate uses of your subconscious mind can amazingly influence your life and perhaps even the circumstances surrounding it!* There is growing evidence that your own Mind Power may even influence the lives and circumstances of others.

A detailed discussion concerning Mind Power as one of the most important keys to success would require a whole book. In fact, much of *this* book is devoted to the use of Mind Power through various kinds of *Success Psychology*. Although the *success methods* of using Mind Power are clearly and simply taught throughout this book, the *exact means* by which Mind Power produces such *astounding results* is still somewhat of a mystery.

This is no reason why Mind Power should not be used to achieve success any more than we should refuse to use the benefits of electricity and many other wonders of this world which we cannot trace to their ultimate source.

Basically, the technique of using Mind Power is to mentally intensify a specific desire to such a focus of white heat in your conscious mind that it burns its image deeply into your subconscious mind. There it maintains such a continuous influence on your own thoughts and actions (and perhaps even on your environment and outer circumstances) that it materializes your desire into reality!

Some psychologists believe that your subconscious mind is connected with, and is *your personalized part of, a superconscious or universal MASTER MIND which controls the entire universe.*

Theologians think of intensifying a desire in your conscious mind as prayer, which is imparted through your subconscious to a universal mind—the MASTER

MIND which they call the God Mind or, simply, God.

No matter what the terminology, *Mind Power produces such amazing results that they border on and perhaps should be called miraculous!* Definitely, Mind Power should be considered a major key to success and I strongly recommend your detailed study of it as it is clearly and simply explained in later chapters.

The "*Will Power*" Key to Success

There is a key to another of the doors of success which in some aspects is like the key of Mind Power, but in many respects it is different. One of the elements of difference is that this method is as old as some of the uses of Mind Power are new. This key to success is as old as success itself.

It is called "Will Power." *Will Power is the relentless, driving, irresistible determination to obtain what you want, to reach a desired goal regardless of everything!*

Nature says, "You can have anything you want! Pay the price—and take it."

Will Power is the willingness to pay the price —whatever it is—in sacrifice, in money, in time, in effort, in any way in which the price of success must be paid. Will Power will pay it!

Psychologists have devised an interesting test. You are told to visualize a straight walkway which will take you directly to a desirable goal. You imagine yourself walking determinedly along that walkway when suddenly it is blocked by an obstacle of unknown substance, height, width and thickness.

You then are asked what you would do:

(a) Would you *return* to your starting point and resume life as it was?

(b) Would you *stop* at the obstacle and start life anew there?

(c) Would you attempt to force your way *through* the obstacle and continue toward your goal, fully realizing that you might never reach the other side of the obstacle?

(d) Would you attempt to climb *over* the obstacle and continue toward your goal, fully knowing that you might never reach the top?

(e) Would you attempt to walk *around* either side of the obstacle and continue toward your goal, fully realizing that the obstacle might be so wide you might never reach the end?

Well, what would YOU do?

Your answer to that question would tell a psychologist quite a lot about the kind of person you are. It also would give him a clearer insight into your degree and use of Will Power, one of the keys to success.

President Calvin Coolidge said, "*Nothing will take the place of persistence.* Talent will not. Nothing is more common than unsuccessful men with talent. Genius will not; unrewarded genius is almost a proverb. Education will not; the world is full of educated derelicts. *Persistence and determination alone are omnipotent.* The slogan, '*Press On,*' has solved and always will solve the problems of the human race."

A survey some time ago showed that very few millionaries had much money to start with. In fact, just about all they had was the Will Power to keep trying! That same survey showed that *only one out of seventeen* sons who had inherited large fortunes from their wealthy parents *retained* his wealth throughout his own lifetime. *The other sixteen had everything but the need to get out into the world and go to work!* Thus, they not only failed to improve, but they lost what they had. They did not have the incentive to build Will Power.

Don't feel discouraged when you're so low you have to reach up to touch bottom. Many men have succeeded without formal schooling. Many have succeeded in spite of occasional poor judgment. *But none has succeeded without Will Power.*

Perhaps you have heard the inspiring story of the group of war refugees who were planning to escape by traveling over very rough terrain. Since they had to walk, they pondered long over whether they could take a mother and her little girl. Finally they decided to try, with the strong men in the group carrying the child. For three weary days they trudged along and their path became more and more difficult.

Finally, unable to keep up, an old man collapsed. He begged the group to go on without him and leave him to die, that they might save themselves.

The group sadly started forward and then the mother of the little girl took her child and returned to the old man. She gently placed the little girl in the old man's arms and calmly said, "You can't quit now. It's *your turn* to carry my little girl." Then she turned and followed the group of refugees.

A little later they looked back and there was the old man walking determinedly after them with the little girl snuggled in his arms.

A great historian, having written the history of the world, was asked what he had found to be the greatest lesson in history. He replied simply, "When it gets darkest . . . the stars come out."

Sometimes the key of Will Power is handed us in our darkest hour. But whenever and however we get it, the key of Will Power will surely open one of the doors to the Treasure Room of Success!

Next . . . you will learn the *easy* way to GET WHATEVER YOU WANT!

Chapter 12

EASY SUCCESS Begins With A Three-Letter Word!

In the preceding chapter, you were given some of the keys to the Treasure Room of Success.

The success methods described in the preceding chapter all WORK! *There is not the least doubt about their positive effectiveness!* Each of the success methods described will definitely make you successful!

That is *why* they are given to you. Because they *are* success methods which will enable you to GET WHATEVER YOU WANT, and *that's* what this book is about! It is a complete SUCCESS COURSE!

This SUCCESS COURSE contains seventy-one chapter-lessons filled with methods which you can use to succeed. Naturally, some success methods require more effort than others.

The success methods in the *preceding* chapter not only *work*—but they *are work!* Hard, tiring, time-consuming *work!*

It is not the purpose of this book to mislead you into thinking that *all* success methods are quick, simple and easy. The fact is that *all* success methods are *not* quick, simple and easy. That is why many people do not succeed. *They just can not or will not pay the price of success* in terms of the success method *they have chosen to use*—because *that* success method requires more knowledge or more experience, or more patience, or more effort than they have—or that they are willing to pay as the price of success.

Nevertheless, *all* of the success methods described in this book are worth the time and effort they require because *they are sure to make you successful* and they will *positively* enable you to GET WHATEVER YOU WANT! And, that is better—*at any price*—than suffering the consequences of being unsuccessful!

In those terms, let us briefly *re-examine* some of the success methods described in the previous chapter:

The "*Personal Magnetism*" success method requires the *hard work* of self-training and constant practice to develop a magnetic personality which attracts people, opportunities, success, wealth and fame. But one doesn't hear the millionaire movie and television stars complaining about it! Nor the other million-dollar personalities complaining about this success method which they used to achieve their own famous careers!

The "*Make Friends and Use Influence*" success method takes a lot of time and demands a very active, busy life—often all day and far into the night. But it is exciting and fun—and an altogether pleasant way to acquire influence, power and great wealth.

The "*Overwhelming Service*" success method

requires continuous effort, long hours, and personal skill in dealing with people. It takes a lot of cooperating on your part to win the necessary cooperation of many others—but the result is that you succeed in GETTING WHAT YOU WANT.

The *"Human Dynamo of Unlimited Energy"* success method, by its very name and nature, describes the enormous and continuous output of energy required to *power* your way through all obstacles by the sheer force of your capacity *to do more* and *do it better!* It's hard work but *it assures that no person and no barrier can block your power-drive to success!*

Yes, each of the foregoing success methods requires *work.* But each is worth its price in time and effort because each success method (or a combination of several or all) will *assure your success* and enable you to get WHATEVER YOU WANT.

But what about the promise of this book to tell you how to get WHATEVER YOU WANT by using *quick, simple, easy* success methods?

Well, the *quickest, simplest, easiest, surest* way for you to succeed in getting WHATEVER YOU WANT . . . is to use a "magic" *three letter word!*

This "magic" *three-letter word* EASILY will do the following things for you:

(1) It will enable you to *influence people* to do what you want them to do.

(2) It will give you the power to *arrange events* for your personal advantage.

(3) It will employ the *Law of Averages* to assure your success.

(4) It will *put at your service* almost *any* per-

son, facility, resource or advantage needed to help you get WHATEVER YOU WANT.

(5) It will enable you to *obtain the advice of the leading experts* in any field in which you need facts and counsel.

(6) It will get you *more* of everything you want—*quickly, simply, easily, surely.*

(7) *It will enable you to avoid most of the disagreeable things in life, to protect yourself against unknown dangers, to guard against preventable illnesses!*

(8) This "magic" *three-letter word* will be the key to your *easily* attaining: HAPPINESS . . . LOVE . . . SUCCESS . . . WEALTH . . . INFLUENCE . . . POWER . . . POPULARITY . . . FAME . . . WHATEVER YOU WANT!

This "magic" *three-letter word* is revealed in the next chapter which describes some of the almost *unlimited things it will EASILY accomplish for you!*

Chapter 13

This "Magic" Word Will Get You WHATEVER You Want!

There is a "*magic*" *word* which will produce *miracles* in your life!

This "*magic*" *word* is the secret of getting others to DO what YOU want them to do!

This "*magic*" *word* will enable YOU to get WHATEVER you want!

Who says so?

The Bible says so. And the teachings of ALL of the great religions are based on the use of this "*magic*" *word.*

The entire medical profession uses this "*magic*" *word.* Yes, your own family doctor, ALL medical specialists, ALL mental specialists; psychiatrists, psychoanalysts and psychotherapists use this "*magic*" *word.*

Educators, business leaders, researchers, scientists, salesmen—ALL people whose success depends upon obtaining information or cooperation from others—use this *"magic" word.*

Actually, this "magic" word really isn't magic —but it produces such miraculous results that it *seems* like magic!

This *"magic"* word is: ASK!

Here are some of the things it will do for YOU:

"ASK . . . and you shall receive," promises the Bible.

"ASK . . . and every human being has been trained from childhood to do what he or she is ASKED to do," assures the psychologist.

"ASK . . . and according to the Law of Averages you'll get enough 'yes' responses to guarantee your overall success," teaches the sales manager.

"ASK . . . and people in all walks of life will come forward and surrender themselves to your salvation crusade," preaches the evangelist.

"ASK . . . and you'll be surprised by the number of people who will be anxious to improve your education," asserts the educator.

"ASK for the order and you'll increase the results of advertising ten times," states the experienced advertiser.

"ASK and you won't get blocked by a road under construction," warns the Automobile Club.

"ASK and maybe the girl will marry you," thinks the man (or the girl).

"ASK, and prove you deserve it, and you'll

get that raise in salary," advises the employment counselor.

"ASK for more" has been the principal basis of the success of the union movement since its very beginning.

"ASK through testing" is the basis of scientific research and progress.

ASK the expert and you'll get expert advice and perhaps even expert training in almost any subject in which you are interested. It's just as easy to ask an expert as it is to ask a novice—so don't settle for less than expert advice.

ASK the news editor for deserved publicity and you'll be surprised how easy it is to get. After all, he's looking for interesting information to print in his paper. I know because I was president of one of the largest publicity organizations in the nation. We got millions of dollars worth of publicity by ASKING for it and furnishing interesting material. But we wouldn't have gotten a penny's worth if we hadn't ASKED.

ASK for a discount. ASK for a better deal. ASK for a "refigured competitive quotation." You'll be surprised at how much money you'll save.

ASK more than one seller before you buy. As president of eight corporations I have seen our buyers frequently get price quotations varying over 40% on identical specifications.

ASK for the job you want. I once was president of a large employment agency. Amazing as it seems, unemployed people were either afraid to or didn't know how to ASK for jobs for themselves—so they paid us a big fee to ASK prospective employers to give them the jobs for which they were obviously qualified. We built the biggest employment agency in our part of the nation just by ASKING for jobs for people who could more easily have obtained the same jobs *themselves* by ASKING the employers personally.

ASK strangers impersonal, pleasant questions while you are waiting for the elevator or the bus or anytime you are together for a few minutes with nothing to do. ASK the stranger what he or she thinks about the weather, the crowded conditions in which you find yourselves, or any general, casual question. The key is "casual." Don't be aggressive. Don't cross-examine. Don't be impertinent. Don't be offensive. Just start a pleasant, casual conversation with a *question*. In the first place, it's a lot more enjoyable than staring at each other in glum silence. And then it's one of the best ways to start to learn the delightful art of pleasant conversation. Don't miss an opportunity to do this! It's interesting and it's fun!

ASK important people any sensible, pertinent question—for their opinion, for their advice, for a favor, for anything which will enable you to meet and know them. Be sure they remember you and be sure you maintain your contact. *Make a list of one hundred of the most important people you want to meet and use this "ASKING method" to meet them.* Don't you think it will help you be more successful if you personally know the one hundred most important people in your city?

ASK yourself, "How can I do it *better?*" (*Improve quality.*) ASK yourself, "How can I do *more?*" (*Increase quantity.*) *The success combination in business is the answer to those two questions.* If you don't know the answers, find someone who does and ASK him. Keep ASKING until you get those answers. You *must* have them to succeed. Do *better*—do *more!*

ASK your doctor. You might prevent a serious illness or an operation.

ASK your dentist. You might prevent a painful toothache at an inconvenient time. You might save a tooth.

ASK your eye specialist. You might improve or even save your vision.

ASK your lawyer. You might avoid a lawsuit or legal loss. Or you might obtain a legal gain.

ASK your banker or investment counselor. You might prevent a financial loss or make a substantial financial gain. I have, many times—by ASKING *experts.*

ASK your insurance agent about new policies with more benefits and lower rates. Insurance is taking on a merchandising complex to meet modern competitive conditions. The deals are better if you know where and how to shop for them. ASK!

ASK the best tax accountant you can find to prepare your income tax and other tax forms. There are lots of legal ways to save tax expenses. The taxes you save and the trouble you avoid will easily offset the expert tax accountant's fee.

ASK major business executives how the top leaders got on top and how they stay there. They will tell you that the top leaders spend a lot of time ASKING for facts. *There is no substitute for getting the facts!*

ASK *expert* opinions about your own plans. *Do not announce your plans as though they had been handed down with the Ten Commandments.* Test them first by ASKING people who will judge them impartially and critically. *Polish your plans with other people's ideas.*

ASK! It is dangerous to travel in a fog—*especially a mental fog!*

ASK for favors. *People get a satisfying sense of pleasure out of doing favors for those who ASK for favors courteously and properly*—and if you thank them sincerely afterward, they will be glad to do other favors for you later. Don't make a nuisance of yourself—*but do give others the satisfaction of being helpful.*

ASK . . . to increase your knowledge of people and places. This will increase your familiarity with them. *People and places often seem to be unfriendly when they are merely unfamiliar.*

"ASK," says the experienced raiser of funds for charities. Hundreds of millions of dollars are contributed to charity every year because people are ASKED for them. Only a small amount would be contributed unless people were *directly* ASKED.

"ASK," says the Finance Committee of every church as it ASKS for pledges. ASK is what every preacher does before the offering is taken each Sunday. By ASKING for pledges and ASKING for Sunday contributions, hundreds of millions of dollars are freely donated to maintain the churches of this nation.

ASK any politician how he gets votes and he will tell you he ASKS for them. Watch any political campaign and you'll see the candidates shaking as many hands as possible and ASKING for votes.

I could give you hundreds of other examples to

prove that ASKING is unquestionably one of the most important—and the quickest, easiest, surest—of *all* success methods. *The very act of ASKING can, by itself, guarantee that you eventually will be a success!*

Why is this so? Why do people—often people who do not even know you—tend to do what you ASK them to do?

Why do people—often people who have no interest in you at all—use their time and sometimes go to a lot of trouble to furnish you information just because you ASK them for it?

You will find out WHY in the next chapter.

In the meantime, start ASKING! *Make ASKING a way of life! You will find that it pays . . . and pays . . . and pays . . . and pays!*

Chapter 14

Why People Will Do What YOU WANT

"ASK . . . and you shall receive!" ASK . . . and others will do what you WANT!

Know why?

People are taught from earliest childhood to do what is ASKED of them. This training to do or say what they are ASKED to do or say starts in the home as soon as little children are first able to understand anything.

When the child begins to learn, he or she is expected—and I do mean *expected*—to answer promptly and correctly a continuous bombardment of questions.

The dialogue begins something like this:

Mother: "Who is this? Is it Ma-ma?"

(Note: It doesn't really start out so easily, but gradually the child does proudly answer the question to an even prouder "Ma-ma.")

Then the same routine is repeated for "Da-da."

So begins conditioning to responding favorably to what is ASKED and it goes on through life. It progresses to such questions as:

Mother: "What does the little doggie say?"

Little child: "Bow! Wow!"

Mother: "And what does the pussy cat say?"

Little child: "Mee-ow!"

Later, more questions, *always questions*—ASKING for action or information in the form of a favorable response and getting the response wanted—*or else!*

"What is the name of the little girl next door?"

"What did you learn at Sunday School?"

"Where were you all afternoon?"

"When did you see the red bird?"

"How would you like to go on a picnic?"

"What do you want for lunch?"

"Will you please hand me your socks?"

"Will you pull your wagon off the driveway so Daddy can drive in?"

Always more *questions*—always ASKING and always requiring a response. *Not just requesting a verbal reply, but increasingly requiring compliance.*

Then comes school—consisting of at least half of the time being taken up with required answers to what is ASKED by the teachers. If there were no ASKING and answering, there would be no measurement of learning. And unless there is a measurement of learning, there can be no evaluation of teaching methods. The *value* of what is *learned*, establishes the *value* of the *teacher*—not what the *teacher knows,* as certified by *academic* degrees, but what the *teacher implants into the mind and personality of each student.*

While this ASKING is continuing day after day . . . month after month . . . year after year . . . *the result is mental (conscious and subconscious) conditioning—the "learned response" to complying with what is ASKED.* It becomes an unconscious habit—a way of life.

And after you graduate from school, you have not finished your training in responding to ASKING. In fact, your mental conditioning to replying with a *favorable* response to what is ASKED of you has just begun.

School's out!!! But then comes the business world. It's a world of bosses . . . bosses . . . bosses. At first, everybody is your boss. Finally, if you study this book carefully, you may become president of a big corporation —and then only the stockholders (perhaps 10,000 of them!) and your Board of Directors and your company's customers and regulatory agencies of government will be your bosses, along with an unlimited number of other people and organizations whose authority may be questionable, but whose intentions of ASKING *you to do things are quite vocal!* So, you always will have bosses and you might as well get used to the boss-employee relationship.

In business, it is the boss' job to ASK you to *do* things. And it is your job to *do* what you are ASKED to do. That's how business is run and it applies to all levels of management and employees.

You *do* what you are ASKED to do—and you do it promptly, courteously and correctly—or you find yourself holding a pink termination slip!

The technique of succeeding in business has changed and you had better study these next few facts carefully because if *you* haven't changed to meet the new requirements of business leadership you are headed for the nearest trash can.

No longer can anyone become a business leader by fighting his way to the top. The days of ruthless battles for leadership are gone. And so are the days when one could climb the ladder of Success by kissing the feet on the rung of the ladder above and kicking the face of the fellow holding the rung of the ladder just beneath.

No, you can no longer fight your way up to Success. You have to be LIFTED up by your fellow men! The Secret of Success today is making yourself EASIER TO LIFT!

To begin with, that means *cooperating with everybody!* It means responding to what you are ASKED —and doing it courteously, promptly and efficiently. It means doing more . . . more . . . more than you are ASKED to do! And it means doing some ASKING yourself, such as ASKING management *how you can make yourself more useful.*

Note this well: *One of the nation's business leaders says there is only a four-word procedure for Success: "MAKE YOURSELF MORE USEFUL."*

Business is a continuation of *doing* in response to being ASKED. For example:

Executive: "Will you come in and take my dictation now, Miss Jones?"

"Miss Jones, will you tell Mr. Brown that I can see him now?"

"Miss Jones, will you bring me the file on the Smith case?"

"Miss Jones, will you get me Mr. Black on the phone?"

Miss Jones, will you do this, will you do that, will you come here, will you go there? And all day long, day after day, Miss Jones and every employee *is being consciously and subconsciously conditioned to respond to being ASKED—and to respond courteously, promptly and efficiently—or else.*

Meanwhile the executives, at all levels, *are equally being conditioned to the benefits of doing what is ASKED*—courteously, promptly and efficiently. All executives have bosses—and when *you reach the top* you will find that the *public* is your most demanding boss of all!

All of us, from early childhood throughout all our lives, are constantly, continuously and irrevocably being taught and trained to do what is ASKED of us, and the doing becomes a "conditioned response."

Frequently, we willingly do what is ASKED just as a matter of course without giving it a serious thought.

Even if we do stop and seriously think about whether we should do what is ASKED of us, *the forces of a lifetime of teaching, training and conditioning bear heavily upon our decision, urging us to comply.*

To refuse to do what is ASKED of us is like trying to swim against the tide. It is unnatural, difficult and often dangerous.

You can be sure that the person you ASK to do something for you or to give you information already has had a lifetime of teaching, training and conditioning which will strongly favor his (or her) doing it. So ASK!

And there are other powerful forces ready to help you get what you want by ASKING.

Psychologists say that the one factor which motivates people to act—more than any other—is their desire to be IMPORTANT. In fact, psychologists even go so far as to say that everybody should have to wear across his chest a big sign printed in capital letters reading, "I WANT TO FEEL IMPORTANT." *This constant reminder would greatly improve our relations with each other and would enable us to get a lot more cooperation and avoid a lot of unnecessary friction!*

When you ASK people to do something or to give you something or for some information you need, *they will have a strong tendency to do what you ASK because, by so doing, it demonstrates THEIR importance.* It makes *them* feel superior to you and gives them that warm inner glow of having been helpful.

At the same time you, too, have gained. *You got what you ASKED for.* And, you, also have the inner satisfaction of having helped someone else feel important and helpful.

On the negative side, *the other person would lose his sense of importance by refusing to do what you ASKED because it might indicate his inability to do so.* Or it would be rude, discourteous and probably antagonizing for the other person to respond unfavorably by declining what you ASKED if your request were logical, courteous, friendly and appropriate. *Most people would not want to put themselves in that unpleasant position.*

Perhaps a few people would, and you might as well get used to meeting them in this imperfect world of ours.

Marcus Aurelius, one of the wisest men who ruled the Roman Empire, wrote in his diary, "I am going to meet people today who talk too much, people who are selfish, egotistical, ungrateful. But I won't be surprised or disturbed, for I could not imagine a world without such people."

Yes, you, too, will meet people like that. You will meet people who not only will refuse to do what you ASK, but they will not even civilly answer your reasonable questions.

But don't let those few stubborn, neurotic people bother you. Joyfully ignore them and get on your way to success. *Remember that Success is like a bicycle—when you stop pedaling (ASKING) you will fall!*

Encourage others to talk by ASKING:

"What do *you* think should be done about . . . ?" (This is an irresistible conversation-starter!)

"What has been *your* experience in such a situation?" (Avoid making contrary pronouncements.)

"What is *your* opinion?"

"How would *you* do it?"

As Will Rogers said, "There is still a lot of monkey in us. Throw anything you want into our cage and we will give it serious consideration." That applies to ASKING questions or ASKING for favors. All but a few abnormal people just can't ignore a logical, courteous request for action or information. As Will Rogers said, "They will give it serious consideration." *It is a natural instinct—and also a "conditioned response."*

It is the scientific finding of psychologists that *a favorable response to ASKING is a "conditioned response" developed in everybody* starting in early childhood, continued constantly during all the years of schooling, and established as the principal business procedure for getting things done.

That is WHY people will do what you ASK.

That is why the "magic" three-letter word—ASK—is the *quickest, simplest, easiest, surest* way for you to GET WHATEVER YOU WANT.

So let us begin, in the next chapters, to explore some of the many "magic" ways of ASKING which lead to the Land of Abundance!

Chapter 15

Make It EASIER For Others To DO What You Want—Than NOT To!

Until you learn and *use* the success-methods of ASKING, as taught in this book, you will find it difficult to realize how *easy* it is to get what you want just by *properly* ASKING for it!

The proper success-method is for you to make it *easier* for others to *do* what you reasonably ASK—than *not* to do it. Here's how:

As explained in the previous chapter: *Why People Will Do What YOU WANT*, *all* people have been taught, trained, and "attitude-conditioned" to *do* what they are ASKED. This "*doing what is ASKED*" is a form of "*learned response*" which is begun in early childhood, and continues throughout life. Without it, civilization could not function smoothly and the result would be chaos, total conflict and the ultimate destruction of organized society.

ASKING is a *psychological push-button!* You

push the psychological button of ASKING—and others respond by *doing* what you ASK!

Of course, *all* persons you ASK are not going to give you *every* thing you ASK for, or do *every* thing you ASK them to do—the *first* time you ASK . . . and perhaps they *never* will. *Nor is a high percentage of compliance necessary for your success.*

The ASKING technique is based on the *Law of Averages.* This is described in a later chapter which explains how to apply the *Law of Averages* to ASKING in such a way as to GUARANTEE your success! Not your success in getting a favorable response *every* time you ASK, but *enough* of the times to make you a *sure success!*

The other psychological "push-button" techniques of ASKING will be discussed in various other chapters in detail as they apply to other success methods. However, in order for you to begin using the success method of ASKING right now, here are some principles of *Personal Influence Psychology* applied to ASKING:

(1) ASK *courteously*—not merely by using such courteous words as "please," but ASK in an *extremely courteous manner.*

(2) ASK *expectantly*—in the voice and attitude that *of course* the other person will *gladly* do what you courteously and expectantly ASK.

(3) ASK *reasonably.* This applies to *what* you ASK and *how* you ASK.

Obviously, people are not going to do *unreasonable* things just because you ASK them to. If you go about, ASKING *unreasonable* things, you will reap a harvest of undesirable consequences.

Not only must what you ASK *be* reasonable, but it must "*sound*" reasonable. The more *reasonable* your request *is* and "*sounds,*" the more readily it will be granted.

(4) ASK *persuasively*. The success method of ASKING depends upon using the *Personal Influence Psychology* of *influence-by-persuasion. Never* DEMAND! *Never use the word:* "DEMAND." *Never even "sound demanding."* (More about this in the next chapter.)

(5) ASK *pleasantly—without pressure*. Do not let your voice or manner imply *pressure*. Pressure creates *resistance*—and *resistance* is the *exact opposite* of what you *want*. What you *want* is agreement, cooperation and friendly compliance.

(6) ASK *positively*. Let your voice and manner, in *every* way, imply that, *of course*, the other person will be *agreeable* and *cooperative* by *gladly doing* what you ASK. (More about *Positive Power* in later chapters.)

(7) ASK *firmly*. This is the most difficult (and probably the most important) technique of ASKING successfully—because you must give the *firm* impression that *what you ASK is so reasonable, logical and just—that you shall pleasantly persist until you get it!*

The *needed skill* is to ASK *firmly—with the implication of continuing persistence*—BUT to do it courteously, reasonably, persuasively, pleasantly, *without any offensive pressure* and *without threatening argument*. Develop the skill of *implying persistence—without pressure.*

When you master *that* skill, *you will make it easier for others to do what you want—than not to do it!*

And your success is thereby assured!

This applies to your dealings with *everybody*

—individuals, groups, businesses. But let's use businesses as an example:

The most successful businesses have learned that it simply requires *too much valuable time* to *argue* with a customer or a prospect. At today's high wage-rates, executive and employee time probably will cost much more than whatever could be gained or saved by *arguing*.

The most expensive element in business is time! Time is too costly to waste in *arguing*. The usual business policy now is: If what a customer or prospect ASKS is reasonable and if the cost of *doing* it does not greatly exceed the cost of *arguing* about why the business may not do it—then *do* it pleasantly and agreeably. *Do it promptly —do not waste time arguing!*

This policy began many years ago, when the more intelligent businesses started using the now famous slogan: "*The customer is always right!*" Their sales skyrocketed—and so did their profits! *So now almost all businesses have adopted this policy,* even though they may no longer visibly display the slogan: "*The customer is always right!*" Arguing costs too much.

Arguing with customers and prospects not only wastes costly employee and company time, but it loses sales and it incurs ill will. So every cost-conscious, public-relations-minded business acts on the proven principle that *it is less costly, as well as good business,* to *agree* with its customers and prospects, and *promptly comply* with their reasonable requests.

The author, who has been sales counsel to 102 companies, has found that one of the most effective lessons in sales training is to teach salesmen to *HELP the prospect*

BUY in his or her OWN way—not to try to *sell* the way the salesman wants to sell, but to *HELP the prospect BUY the way the PROSPECT wants to buy.* With *unobtrusive guidance* by the salesman, *the prospect will sell himself or herself!* This makes selling *easy* and *pleasant.*

Yes, businesses have learned that it pays to operate by the slogan: *"The customer is always right!"* Businesses have learned *the high cost of not doing what people reasonably ASK!* So you can be sure that most businesses *will respond favorably* to what *you* ASK.

In fact, almost *all* people will *do* what you reasonably ASK—for the very *practical reason* that it probably will be *easier* to *do* what you ASK, than to *risk* the *time-consuming* explanations, discussions and possible arguments which might result from refusing your reasonable, logical, courteous request. Also, agreeably *doing* what you ASK will win your *goodwill* which is preferable to incurring your *ill will* by *refusing to do* what you pleasantly and expectantly ASK.

You *psychologically underscore* the *advantages* of *doing* and the *disadvantages* of *not doing* what you request—when you ASK *firmly* with *"implied persistence."*

Next to applying the *Law of Averages* to your success method of ASKING, the use of *"implied persistence"* will most greatly increase the favorable responses to what you ASK.

Remember, *"implied persistence"* must be friendly, courteous, reasonable and persuasive—*without offensive pressure* and *without threatening argument.*

Simply give the impression that a "No" reply *will NOT send you scurrying out the nearest door* but, on the contrary, you will not have moved an inch and will calmly be inquiring. "Why?". . . and *unhurriedly* waiting for a logical answer. Your attitude must never show a trace of belligerency. You must not be argumentative. You must exert no pressure. You must give the clear impression that you are *pleasantly patient*—unhurriedly awaiting *an understanding of the reasonableness* of what you ASK, and expecting *ultimately* a favorable response.

Make it amicably obvious that it will be easier, more pleasant, more agreeable to *do* what you ASK than to *risk* the time-consuming and other undesirable consequences of *unreasonably* refusing!

Yes, there is a *skill* to ASKING—and *it is a skill worth developing to the greatest degree!*

As you proceed through this SUCCESS COURSE, you will learn many techniques of *Personal Influence Psychology* which will improve your ASKING methods *until the results you get will seem miraculous!*

Chapter 16

NEVER Use The Word: "DEMAND"

HOW you ASK—often is as important as WHAT you ASK!

HOW you ASK—often will determine whether or not you will *get* WHAT you ASK!

Therefore, it is essential that you learn *how* to ASK. And, also, that you learn *how not* to ASK.

The briefest, clearest way to express the basic teaching of this chapter is in its title: *NEVER Use The Word: "DEMAND."*

That states a rule to which there are *no exceptions*. It is easy to remember—and remembering it is so essential to GETTING WHATEVER YOU WANT that you must memorize it and remind yourself of it *whenever you are tempted to use pressure: NEVER Use The Word: "DEMAND."*

Arrogant DEMANDING his become a misguided method tried by many would-be pressure groups and especially their leaders in seeking to impose the will of a minority upon a majority.

Next to *ensuring permanent failure by using actual physical violence in acts of dissent, defiance or revolution*—DEMANDS (usually accompanied by *threats,* real or implied) are the surest way to create *instant, hardened resistance* which GUARANTEES that *whatever* is DEMANDED will be *delayed, reduced* or *denied*—with sullen resentment and varying degrees of hostility.

It is not the purpose of this book to judge the justice or the possibility of attainment of any of the DEMANDS made by any one group (usually a minority) upon any other group (usually a majority).

But since what is so vehemently DEMANDED obviously is what *some* people want, it is consistent with the purpose of this book, in teaching *how to get what you want,* to emphasize that DEMANDING it—is NOT how to get it easily, simply and surely. *Or even how to get it at all!*

In fact, many of the desired actions or desired things which are DEMANDED—*are DENIED solely because of the MANNER in which they are DEMANDED!*

And, many of those desired actions or desired things often clearly are *deserved*—and *would have been granted—if they had not been arrogantly DEMANDED!*

It is a fact of human nature that people do not like to be *forced* to do anything.

If, for whatever reason, resistance *already* exists—then *any* attempt to use DEMANDS to *force a humiliating SURRENDER, only increases the resistance*—and enflames the hostility which accompanies the resistance.

DEMANDS are counter-productive. Instead of making it easier to get whatever is wanted, DEMANDS *make it much more difficult.*

It is a law of psychology, as well as a law of physics, that *pressure creates resistance.* If you want to give the impression that you are trying to *force* others to give you whatever you want by your applying *pressure*—just say, "I DEMAND!" The response of others to *whatever* you DEMAND (*no matter how worthy*) will be instant, hardened RESISTANCE.

Then, if you want to blow the whole deal, just add: "And my DEMAND is NOT NEGOTIABLE!" *That* will blow it!

Just consider a few (*deliberately extreme*) examples of DEMANDS, and imagine the *response* to each:

A husband comes home from work. Instead of his usual greeting, he shouts at his wife: "I DEMAND that you serve me my dinner NOW!" (Imagine the wife's reaction!)

A salesman walks up to his prospect and shouts: "I DEMAND that you give me an order NOW . . . on MY terms . . . and MY terms are NOT NEGOTIABLE!" Well, he not only will get *one* order, but *two* orders: "Get out!!!" and "Get lost!!!"

In your own *imagination,* apply the "I DEMAND" approach to all sorts of situations. *Then imagine the response!* The response may be overt and violent, or the response may be silent hatred, or the response may be sullen resentment and hardened resistance.

Yet people, in all walks of life, from those who have no power at all, to those who represent large power-seeking organizations, incur resentment, resistance, hostility and hatred by saying: "I DEMAND!". . . "We DEMAND!"

You see them at meetings or on television—their faces contorted with contempt and hatred—shouting "I DEMAND!". . . "We DEMAND!". . . "And our DEMANDS are NOT NEGOTIABLE!"

The use of such resistance-assuring and hostility-provoking statements brand those using them as insolent, arrogant, ignorant people—pretenders of power—who, any psychiatrist will tell you, are *over-compensating for an inferiority complex* hidden deep within their subconscious. They really are *unsure of themselves* so they consciously or subconsciously try to cover up their *unsureness* by shouting DEMANDS. *The more unsure they are the louder they shout!*

In their show of bravado, they *imagine* that their DEMANDS demonstrate that *they have POWER*—when just the *opposite* is true: *Those who really HAVE POWER never NEED to DEMAND!* And never do!

People and organizations with the POWER to get what they ASK, *never* DEMAND. They REQUEST. That is all *they need* to do. A DEMAND is an admission of WEAKNESS *magnified by threats!*

All you need to do to GET WHATEVER YOU WANT is to *use the success methods taught in this book.* One of the easiest of these success methods is to ASK (*never* DEMAND). This book will teach you *how* to ASK so that *you never will incur resentments which will cause resistance.*

Chapter 17

How To Get Others To Help YOU Succeed

Few people can succeed just by themselves.

In fact, so very few people have succeeded without the help of others that we shall ignore that possibility and devote this chapter to emphasizing the absolute necessity of YOUR obtaining the *willing help of others* to enable YOU TO GET WHATEVER YOU WANT.

As explained throughout the first part of this book, the quickest, easiest, surest way to get *anything* is to ASK for it.

That applies to obtaining the *willing help of others* to enable you to get whatever you want.

You simply ASK for the help you need.

You ASK *courteously*—do not demand.

You ASK *forthrightly*—do not beg.

You ASK *expectantly*—with the confidence

that others will *do* what you ASK or *provide* what you ASK. Confident *expectation* makes resistance difficult.

You ASK *persistently*—with the calm patience that implies that you are prepared to devote as much time as necessary to *ultimately* obtaining what you ASK.

WHOM should you ASK to help you get whatever you want?

Of course, that is determined by *what* you want, but there are basically *two* principal sources of help: PEOPLE and BOOKS.

Since BOOKS simply are *people in print*, books can be considered almost as people when you decide WHOM to ASK for help.

However, PEOPLE must be *influenced* with appreciation, gratitude, admiration, cooperation and friendship—plus their desire for their *own* personal gain, and the entire range of *Personal Influence Psychology* taught throughout this book.

A BOOK *does not need to be influenced* because a BOOK is your *total and constant servant!* You *own* a BOOK and *all that's in it!*

To GET WHATEVER YOU WANT, it is necessary for you to make *full use* of PEOPLE and BOOKS. The reason most people are not a lot more successful is that they *use* only a *small fraction* of the *total* help that is available to them for the ASKING!

They do not ASK *enough people,* and they do not ASK (by reading) *enough books!*

Incredible as it seems, most people simply do not ASK even a *few* of the *hundreds* of PEOPLE who could (and, if properly ASKED, *would*) help them GET WHATEVER THEY WANT!

Most people DO so few of even the simplest things which would make them many times more successful—that it almost seems that they are deliberately *trying* to fail!

How *many* PEOPLE have *you* ASKED to help you get what you want? Any? A few? A dozen? A hundred? How *many?* How *often?*

WHY HAVEN'T YOU ASKED *more* PEOPLE? Don't *wait!* Take the *initiative!* ASK!

How *many* BOOKS have *you* ASKED (by reading them) to help you get what you want? Any, besides the one you now are reading? A few? A dozen? A hundred? (I have *three personal libraries* filled completely with books on how to succeed. I read these books *every night until past midnight*. So I am not asking you to do anything which I have not done *all my life*—and *still do every night.*)

WHY HAVEN'T YOU ASKED (*read*) *more* BOOKS? Read or re-read a book *every* month.

Not knowing what *you personally want*, obviously I cannot tell you *which* PEOPLE or *which* BOOKS you should ASK to help you succeed. YOU will have to choose the PEOPLE and BOOKS for your *own* needs.

I only can tell you that there are *hundreds* of PEOPLE and there are *hundreds* of BOOKS *ready, willing, and able* to help you GET WHATEVER YOU WANT —if you will just ASK them!

You have a *lot* of ASKING to do! Why not start NOW?

Chapter 18

Many "Best Buys" Do Not Cost Any Money!

ASKING is the quickest, easiest, surest way to get what you want. It usually is the most inexpensive.

But it isn't FREE!

Successful ASKING has a *price tag.*

You have to *pay*—before, during, or after—you get whatever you want, even though you get it simply by ASKING.

That is as it should be. Success should not—and does not—consist of going around begging: "Gimme, gimme, gimme."

There are too many people trying *that* now—and it isn't getting them anything! Perhaps a few tokens, but that's all.

Let's take a good look at the *price tags* on GETTING WHATEVER YOU WANT by the success method of ASKING. Actually, there are *many* price tags and *different* price tags, but that fact will not confuse you once you learn how to read the prices on the price tags of success. And that is easy.

Obviously, some ASKING really is no more than *expert purchasing*. All you do to get the BEST BUY is to use your skill in ASKING to be sure you always get the best value at the lowest possible price But since in actual purchases, the "*price*" means "*money,*" we shall not discuss it here—except to emphasize that perfecting your skill and persistence in ASKING will enable you always to get the BEST BUYS.

In this chapter let us consider getting many of the things you want *without paying any MONEY at all!*

The price tags are there—but they don't have DOLLAR marks!

Instead of DOLLAR prices, the price tags on many of the things you want have such prices as: appreciation, gratitude, admiration, cooperation and friendship.

You see, *other people don't just want money.* Many people don't want or need *any* more money. But *everybody wants and needs:* appreciation, gratitude, admiration, cooperation and friendship. So you often can pay for many of the things you want *with what other people want MORE THAN MONEY!*

And, if you try, you can cultivate and possess in *unlimited abundance:* appreciation, gratitude, admiration, cooperation and friendship with which to pay others for providing you with many of the things you want and need most.

If you ASK a powerful and wealthy person to help you get what you want—you wouldn't offer to pay in *money*. You would *pay* in *admiration* of his achievements, *appreciation* of (in the meaning of holding in esteem) his accomplishments, sincere *gratitude* radiant with the warmth of *friendship*, and the assurance of *your total cooperation* in any of *his* activities where your services might save *his* valuable time for *his* more important endeavors. *If you are genuinely and obviously sincere, this will get you the help you want—plus valuable goodwill which may last a lifetime!*

Even in those cases where you should and do pay with money—*always add an extra bonus payment* in appreciation, gratitude, admiration, cooperation and friendship. This *may* get you special consideration, service or other tangible benefits—*but always it will get you a bonus of goodwill in return.*

And, as you go through life, you will find that you need all of the goodwill you can accumulate.

You should start an imaginary GOODWILL INVESTMENT ACCOUNT and invest in it all of the goodwill you can acquire so that you will accumulate an *unlimited abundance of goodwill!* The best investment you can make in that imaginary GOODWILL INVESTMENT ACCOUNT is the goodwill you will receive in return for *your adding an extra bonus payment* of appreciation, gratitude, admiration, cooperation and friendship—*whenever you ASK anyone to help you get what you want!*

That will make your success method of ASKING *doubly profitable!*

Chapter 19

Why Be Afraid? . . . You CANNOT LOSE!

Are you AFRAID to ASK for WHATEVER YOU WANT?

Are you AFRAID that those whom you ASK will say, "NO!"

Would being told "NO!" hurt your feelings? Wound your precious ego? Would you be personally offended? Are you *afraid* that the person you ASK would be offended? Why are you *afraid* that someone will tell you "NO!"?

Many people are so *afraid* of being told "NO!" that they do not *persistently* ASK for WHATEVER THEY WANT (sometimes they are *afraid* to ASK at all!) and so they do not get what they want.

Silly isn't it? Imagine going through life being *afraid* to ASK for what you want! Are YOU doing *without* WHATEVER YOU WANT, because you are *afraid* to ask for it?

Let's put an end to that silly *fear!*

In the first place, you simply *cannot lose* by ASKING! Obviously, you do not NOW *have* that for which you ASK—or you would *not need* to ASK for it. Since you do not NOW *have* it, you *cannot lose* it by ASKING for it—if the other person says "NO!" to what you ASK. *You did not have it anyway!* So how could you *lose* it?

You *cannot lose* that which you do *not have.* So by ASKING for what you do *not have*, you *cannot lose!* You can get *more* by ASKING, but you *cannot lose anything!*

Be like the salesman who timidly approached the door to the big buyer's office. The salesman was *afraid* to go in and ASK the buyer for an order because the salesman was *afraid* the buyer would tell him "NO!"

Then the salesman gave a silent talk to himself, which went like this:

"I do *not NOW have* the buyer's order.

"The *only way I can get* the buyer's order is to ASK him for it.

"If I ASK the buyer for an order, what is the *worse possible thing* which could happen to me?

"The *worse possible thing* which *could* happen *only* would be that the buyer would say 'NO!'.

"Then I *still* would not have the buyer's order, but I do *not have it NOW, either—so I cannot lose by asking!*"

So the salesman went in, ASKED for the order, *got* the order, thanked the buyer, and left to go ASK more buyers for more orders!

But if the buyer *had* told the salesman, "NO!",

the salesman *would not have been ANY worse off* for having ASKED for something he didn't *already have* anyway!

In fact, he would have been *better off*--because *one of the most effective ways* to get what you want is to *start* with getting a "NO!" response to what you ASK! (Maybe you ought to read the preceding statement again! *Two or three* times!)

Most people think a "No!" reply is the *end*—when a "No!" reply to what you ASK is *only the beginning* of one of the most *successful* methods for *getting* what you want!

Many of the most successful people use the technique of *almost inviting a "NO!" reply* so that they can use the success methods described in the next two chapters which take the *fear* out of ASKING.

Let's start with the next chapter, which tells you: *What To Do And Say When The Answer Is "NO!"*.

Chapter 20

What To Do And Say When The Answer Is "NO!"

Your success in using the success-factor: ASK —will depend upon *how often* you ASK, *whom* you ASK, and *how effectively* you ASK. *Most important is how often you ASK!* The *Law of Averages* will more than offset any deficiencies you may have in the "*whom you ASK*" and "*how effectively you ASK*" categories. Naturally you should try to improve your entire ASKING technique, but in the meantime, *start ASKING now and depend on the reliable Law of Averages!*

When you ASK—*many people will say "Yes"—and they will readily give you the information you want, or give you what you want, or do what you want.* People will do what you reasonably ASK, because they have been "conditioned" by training since childhood to do what they are ASKED to do. Re-read the chapter: *Why People Will Do What You Want* (Chapter 14).

But, some people will reply "Maybe"—which simply means that they need a little more *assurance* before they will say "Yes." This enables you to use one of the many techniques of *Personal Influence Psychology which enables you to influence others to do whatever you want.*

Usually the *only* real reason people do not instantly do what you ASK is that they are *not sure* that doing what you ASK is *best for them!*

All you need do is *assure* them and *re-assure* them until they *are sure.* The very instant that they *are sure* that doing what you ASK will in no way detract from *themselves,* but actually will be best for *them,* they *immediately* will do what you ASK without a moment's further resistance. So you easily convert "Maybe" responses to "Yes" responses.

A "Maybe" response is an *invitation* and a *challenge* to provide assurance.

Now let us apply *Personal Influence Psychology* to the people who will say "NO"—and there may be quite a few of them. If you don't *enjoy the friendly confrontation* of people telling you "NO"—if you don't *get a lift out of the challenge* of a "No" response—then you just are not mentally and emotionally mature enough to successfully ASK others to do what you want or to engage in the business of dealing with people at any level which requires personal influence.

But before you panic at a series of "No" responses, and give up the *Personal Influence Psychology* of ASKING for whatever you want, let's see what a "No" response *really* means.

When a person replies "No" to what you have ASKED, it could mean one, or a combination of several things:

(1) Most "No" people are just like "Maybe" people, only they are less timid and more direct. Like the "Maybe" people, the "No" people are simply telling you that they are *not sure* that what you ASK *will benefit them more than it will cost them.* They are telling you that it's up to you to *assure* and *re-assure* them, furnish them more proof, more testimonials, positive guarantees, whatever is necessary—to make them *sure.* Just as soon as you can make them *sure* that what you ASK *will benefit them more than it will cost them*—they will be *eager* to do what you ASK. Don't think, for a moment, that they will be too proud to change their minds. Once they are *sure* that *they cannot lose* but, in fact, *will benefit by doing what you ASK,* they'll say "Yes" without the faintest blush! Of course, you can help by assuming that they didn't *really* say "No," but that they simply were using good, practical judgment by insisting on positive *assurances.* This enables them to "*save face*" which always is desirable in dealing with sensitive people.

(2) Some people say "No" just to stall for time to think it over. They've been rushed into decisions before —which they later regretted and they don't want to develop the habit—so they instinctively say "No." It's a self-defense mechanism. They are slow thinkers and slow deciders—and they don't want to be rushed or high-pressured, so they say "No" just to stall for time. *Don't show any sign of rushing them or high-pressuring them.* In fact,

assure them that you want to *help them* reach *the best decision for them.* This gives you the opportunity to use the "WHY?" technique described later in this chapter. This will enable you easily to turn many of these types of "No" responses to "Yes" responses.

(3) Of course, some people say "No" for good and valid reasons. When you positively have determined (*by using the following Personal Influence Psychology techniques*) that these "No" reasons are genuine and unchangeable, then just ring up "No Sale" on your ASKING-cash-register, courteously leave, and *hurry* to see the next person whom you will ASK to give you what you want or to do what you want—enthusiastically *believing* that, by the *Law of Averages,* he or she will say "Yes." Just *keep on* ASKING, and the *Law of Averages* will GUARANTEE you enough "Yes" responses to get you what you want.

You will greatly increase your average of "Yes" responses by using the following techniques of *Personal Influence Psychology.*

When a person says "No" to what you ASK, *you should be surprised and show it.* Note that I didn't say *act* surprised. Most people are not good enough actors. If your reaction to a "No" response is not genuine, the other person will sense it and deeply resent your trying to put over an "act."

The way to look surprised, is to really *be* surprised. You don't have to fake anything. *You must intensely believe that the person will do what you ASK.* You must ASK *expectantly.* (That's part of the *Personal Influence Psychology* technique of ASKING.) Then if you get a "No" response, you will be *genuinely* surprised. Let your surprise show on your face, in your manner and in your voice. But don't *act*—just let your genuine surprise show. *Your genuine surprise will cause the other person instinctively to wonder if perhaps he or she was wrong in saying "No."*

Then use the "Why?" technique which is one of the most powerful and effective methods of *Personal Influence Psychology.* Here's how to use the "Why"? technique:

While *showing surprise* that the other person said "No," ASK *in a surprised tone of voice* "Why?" Then look *expectant* and wait. *The other person just simply has to tell you why!* There is nothing else he can do without being unreasonably rude.

He will tell you "Why" in one of three ways:

(1) *He will frankly and honestly tell you* why he *thinks* he cannot do what you ASK. Or . . .

(2) *He will give you a "rationalized" reason*—which he may even believe himself—but which isn't the *real* motivation for telling you "No." Or . . .

(3) *He will just plain lie about it,* saying whatever he thinks would appear to be his strongest justification for refusing to do what you ASK. For example, he might say, "I don't have the money right now"—when he does, in fact, have much more than enough money. (He's really afraid that you will use the money unwisely, lose it, and be unable to repay him—thus causing not only the loss of his money, but putting a severe strain on your friendly relationship).

When you use the "Why?" technique, you will uncover the *real reason:* whether it is the *truth,* or is a *rationalized excuse,* or is an *untruth* (which may be felt to be justified). It is *useless to proceed* until you learn the *real reason* for a "No" response.

Your *effective* use of the "Why" technique of *Personal Influence Psychology* is so important to you that we shall first review it—and then analyse it in more detail.

When a person says "No" to what you ASK—you simply ASK *again,* only *this time* you ASK "Why?"

The other person will almost *be compelled to give you his reason* for saying "No." He may have *several* reasons, but *he will lead with his strongest reason,* which may be what he *honestly thinks,* or what he *rationalizes,* or what is an *untruthful excuse.*

Thus—by ASKING "Why?"—*you will cause the other person to reveal to you* (out of perhaps *dozens* of possible reasons) the *real reason* to be *overcome, modified, negotiated, turned into an advantage,* or otherwise effectively handled *before* you can get a "Yes" response.

People fail to get whatever they want because they waste too much time—and create irritation—by ASKING (*even arguing!*) about things which are not VITAL in influencing others to respond favorably.

The *only* thing which is *vital* to getting what you want is *why* the other person is *reluctant* to give it to you. So when the response is "No"—you *pleasantly* ASK "Why?"—and learn the *real reason.*

Thus by ASKING "Why?"—you narrow the field of objections from *dozens* of possible objections to the *real reason* . . . and *that* is the *vital* objection to be overcome.

When you feel that you have overcome *that*

objection, you *again* ASK for what you want. If the other person says "No" *again*—you are *more* surprised, and ASK "Why?" . . . *Again.*

Since many people may not have had a very logical reason for saying "No" the *first* time, they will have an increasingly difficult time explaining their *subsequent* "No's" when *each* of their "No's" *instantly* is followed by your *sincerely interested* (*not argumentative*) question "Why?"

Do not be *argumentative* when ASKING "Why?" to a "No" response. Do not *argue* in your reply. Do not *argue* at all! *Ever!* You are not engaging in a debate; you are using *Personal Influence Psychology!*

Just be *sincerely interested in learning and understanding the other person's point of view,* and the REAL REASON for his or her refusing to do what you courteously, *reasonably,* confidently, expectantly *and persistently* ASK.

Then, using the *real reason,* as revealed in answers to your question "Why?"—you can ASK for what you want in *specific* terms of *benefiting the person more than he or she possibly could lose!*

You happily will discover that this technique of *Personal Influence Psychology will get you whatever you want* from almost *all* people who can be shown that *they* will *benefit* in complying with your *reasonable* request.

Obviously, if what you ASK is *not reasonable* —you should *never ask it!*

Of course, there will be instances when your ASKING (including your ASKING "Why?") will reveal that the person you ASK *actually can not* or *reasonably should not do what you ASK.*

Usually, you cannot be *sure unless* you ASK. But, as soon as a person sincerely *convinces* you that he or she *actually can not* or *reasonably should not* do what you ASK—then you should give *genuine assurances* that you *understand* and *completely agree.* Do not pout. Do not be sullen. Above all, do not be irritated or angry. *Change the subject and do not return to it!*

No matter how reasonable *you* think your request is, do *not* unrealistically expect that *everybody can* . . . or *should* . . . or *will*. . . . do *whatever* you ASK. Pleasantly handling a "No" response is a natural, routine part of the success method of ASKING. Agreeably accept the fact that you *will lose some*—confidently depending on the *Law of Averages* to produce *enough* "Yes" responses to assure that you will GET WHATEVER YOU WANT.

The *Law of Averages* will GUARANTEE that YOU WILL GET WHATEVER YOU REASONABLY WANT if you *constantly* use the *Personal Influence Psychology* of ASKING and the *other success methods* taught by this book!

We shall devote an entire chapter (Chapter 22) to: *How To Use The Law of Averages To GUARANTEE Your Success.*

But to enable you to use the *Law of Averages* most effectively, you first will learn: *How To Discover And Remove The HIDDEN REASON For Refusal*—which is the next chapter . . .

Chapter 21

How To Discover And Remove The HIDDEN REASON For Refusal

In the previous chapter you learned how to handle a "No" response by ASKING "Why?" . . . with additional help from *Personal Influence Psychology*.

There are two more questions which you may need to use to isolate the objections causing a "No" response. They are: "*For example?*" or "*For instance?*"

Use one of these two questions (which really mean the same thing) whenever the person saying "No" gives you a *vague, general excuse* when you ASK "Why?"

For example: When the other person says, "There are a lot of reasons why I can't do what you ask," the next question you should ASK is "For example?" or "For instance?" These questions will bring out *specific* objections which you can overcome by using the ASKING techniques described in this book.

Let me repeat for emphasis: You have to know

exactly why the person you ASK *resists* doing what you want. You know, in general, that the resistance is caused by the person's *not being sure* that he or she will *benefit* (directly or indirectly) by doing what you ASK—or that he or she is *afraid* that doing what you ASK will result (directly or indirectly) in a *loss* of some kind.

So . . . you have to *find out* what the person you ask *wants*—and *offer* what he or she *wants* as the *benefit* of doing what *you* ASK.

And . . . what is even *more important,* you have to make the person you ask *sure* that he or she *cannot lose anything* (directly or indirectly) by doing what you ASK.

The reason it is *more important* to *assure* the person *that he or she cannot lose anything*—is that psychologists have learned that *people are much more interested in preventing losses than they are in making gains.* A person who wouldn't show a flicker of interest in *getting* an additional $10, would go to great lengths to *prevent losing* $10.

That is because FEAR is one of the most powerful of all emotions and EVERY FEAR is a fear of LOSING something!

If you psychologically dig deep enough, you will find that *the very root of every FEAR is the fear of LOSS* . . . *loss* of confidence . . . *loss* of status . . . *loss* of health . . . *loss* by death . . . *loss* of money . . . *loss* of time . . . *loss* of security . . . *loss* of job . . . *loss* of love . . . *loss* of admiration . . . *loss* of one or more of a thousand different things!

Be sure that you ASK in such a way that you

make the other person *feel secure against any possibility* of LOSS—because LOSS is the *main thing* the person you are asking *doesn't want!* This is the *key* to successfully getting WHATEVER *you* want!

So be sure you learn *specifically* what the person *doesn't want,* in addition to finding out what he or she *does want.*

Therefore, bring out the *specifics* by ASKING "For example?" or "For instance?"

You cannot ASK in *generalities.* You must *know exactly* what the person *wants* and *doesn't want.* Find out by ASKING "For example?" or "For instance?" Then—and *only then*—can you ASK for what *you* want in such a way as to make the person you ask *sure* that he or she will *benefit* and *not lose* by doing what you ASK.

Getting WHATEVER you want by *effectively* ASKING for it—is sure and simple when you use the two following principles:

(1) Whenever the person you ASK is *sure* that he or she will *not lose anything* by doing what you ASK, then that person *will not resist doing it.*

(2) Whenever the person you ASK is *sure* that he or she *actually will benefit* by doing what you ASK, then that person *will be eager to do it.*

Getting WHATEVER you want by ASKING for it is just as simple and easy as *that!*

Chapter 22

How To Use The Law of Averages To GUARANTEE Your Success

When you ASK *enough* people for *whatever* you reasonably want—the LAW OF AVERAGES will GUARANTEE your success. It will make you successful, rich, popular and famous!

You start with a simple rule of success: "A *wise man knows everything—a shrewd man knows EVERYBODY!*" At least everybody who is *worth* his knowing. And *everybody* is *worth* knowing.

How do you get to know everybody who is worth your knowing?

One thing you can count on, they probably aren't going to seek you first . . . so you are going to have to contact them first!

The best way is to write them—or if they and the reasons you are using to establish your contacts are sufficiently important, send them telegrams. Either letters or telegrams, using the ASKING techniques of *Personal Influence Psychology* almost always will be read and usually acted upon. (I say "usually acted upon" because that's where the LAW OF AVERAGES comes in. We'll discuss that later.)

Telegrams are almost always sure-fire attention getters and action getters. *The longer the telegram, the more attention it gets!*

I know because I once needed the help of the federal government. I believe in starting at the top. (You get better action when *the head man assigns your request,* even if he does not act on it personally.) So I sent a five-page telegram to the President of the United States. Result? A government official came to see me the next day! My cost? Merely several dollars! Had I written a letter, it would have been one of thousands, but my telegram probably was only one of a relatively few *five-page telegrams* the President got that morning. And it used the ASKING techniques described in this book, so even if the President did not see it personally, it was assigned to someone who gave it prompt—and favorable—attention.

What about telephone calls? They are a fast and excellent means of communication. *But for establishing initial and permanent contacts, use letters and telegrams which give your name and address as a clear, permanent record.* Letters and telegrams also are more complete and convenient for forwarding by the important recipient to a subordinate who actually will do the work. *And they can be proudly shown to others if they contain a deserved commendation.*

For example: A department of my city government had promptly and efficiently complied with my request for a special service. So I wrote the Mayor a letter of glowing commendation and appreciation, asking *him* to pass along my compliments to the department involved. I could have not bothered to thank anybody. Or, I could have directly thanked the department. But by writing the Mayor, I maintained a friendly contact with him. Naturally, he was pleased that his Administration was so profusely complimented. Obviously, he showed my complimentary letter to others as evidence of citizen (voter) approval. (More favorable contacts!) Then, of course, he passed along my letter to the department involved, probably adding some commendation of his own, which would gain for me additional goodwill from the department. *All this from just one easily-written letter!*

So, in constantly enlarging your field of contacts with more and more important people, write or telegraph using the *Personal Influence Psychology* taught in this book.

Be sure to *compliment. Secretaries and subordinates don't dare throw away a letter or telegram glowingly complimenting and commending their bosses!* And your COMPLIMENTS always will make a favorable impression.

Then, offer *cooperation* if, by any stretch of your imagination, you can do so. Even the most important people will welcome sincere *cooperation* from *anybody* who will help *them* to get what *they* want. In any event, they will consider your offer of *cooperation*—and thus you will have *intensified your contact.*

Most important, ASK the person whom you

write or telegraph to *do* something! This greatly ***intensifies your contact*** because it gets him ***involved*** with ***you***. First, he has to consider and decide *if* he will do what you ASK. Then if he decides to do it, he has to consider and decide how and when to do it. And should he decide not to do what you ASK—if you have used the *Personal Influence Psychology* in this book—he will feel obligated to advise you and explain *why*. A person just cannot ignore a letter or telegram which uses ASKING methods in the courteous, complimentary manner described in this book.

Finally, be sure to *confidently express* your BELIEF that he will *do* what you ASK.

That's how to use the *Personal Influence Psychology* of ASKING to establish your initial contact with people whom you should know and whom you want to know you!

*You personally should know and be well-known by at least the one hundred most **important** people in your city*. The bigger you want to **succeed**, the more you must expand that list to include your industry, your state and nation. *Don't get stuck in one place!* **Expand** your contacts—*everywhere!*

The wider and more important are your contacts, the bigger will be your reputation **and** the more valuable you will be to other people. When you can casually say, "*I am in contact with the President* (or the Governor, head of a large organization, or others of *known* importance) on *another* matter, and I shall be glad to see if *I can get his help* in what *you* want to do" . . . *when you honestly and confidently can say that—you establish yourself as a positive power source!*

Remember this: Establishing contacts will do you little good unless you follow the techniques on the preceding pages to get *important* people *involved* with you so that *you* will be *well-known* to them. This also requires that you *constantly, consistantly* and *deliberately maintain* all of your important contacts. This means constant follow-ups by letters, telegrams, telephone or personal calls. All of this takes time—a lot of time—every week, every month, year after year.

But, you will say that I wrote that *success is easy!* Let me assure you again: Success *is* easy! Success *is* simple! Success *is* certain—if you use the success methods in this book. But I do not promise that achieving success will not be time consuming—because it is. The success methods taught in this book are the *easiest, simplest, surest* way to success, wealth, popularity, fame, love—WHATEVER you want in life—in *unlimited abundance!* But you still have to thoroughly *learn* and constantly *use* these success methods. And I *do* mean *thoroughly learn* and *constantly use all of them!* You cannot *read* this book *just once* and expect that by some hocus-pocus you suddenly will be successful. Nor can you expect to succeed the *first* time you try, *every time* you try.

That's why using the LAW OF AVERAGES is a necessary part of your Success Plan!

The LAW OF AVERAGES simply means that when you ASK *any* number of people (using the ASKING methods taught in this book), *some percentage of those people will do what you ASK.* The *more often* and the *more effectively* you use ASKING methods of *Personal Influence Psychology,* the *greater will be the number of people who will do what you ASK.*

It therefore follows that to achieve the *greatest possible success* you must do *two* things:

(1) Thoroughly learn, practice and *use* the ASKING methods and all the success techniques taught in this book. This will assure your getting the *greatest percentage* of people to *do* what you ASK.

(2) ASK more and *more* people! Always have an *abundance* of contacts. The LAW OF AVERAGES is based on the *number* of people you ASK. *The more people you ASK, the more you will get of WHATEVER you want!*

Thus by combining the ASKING methods taught here with the LAW OF AVERAGES *your success is assured!* If you do this, *you can't lose! You can't fail!* You are *sure* to be *successful!* Not *all* of the time of course—but *enough* of the time to GET WHATEVER YOU WANT!

By knowing that the LAW OF AVERAGES will *assure* the *success* of your use of *Personal Influence Psychology*, you don't panic at a "No" reply to what you ASK. You naturally expect *some* "No" replies. *Everybody* is *not* going to do what you ASK the *first* time you ASK them! Some people *never* are going to do what you ASK—because it actually is impossible for them to do so. This should not disturb you in the least, because you know that if you *constantly use* the ASKING methods on *more* and *more* people, the LAW OF AVERAGES will *guarantee* that *enough* people will *do* what you ASK to make you a *great success!*

The LAW OF AVERAGES will produce *more* and *more abundance* for you as you *increase* the *number* and *quality* of the people you ASK for whatever you want.

To increase the *number* of your contacts you must "*go where the people are*" . . . you must write *more* people *more* ASKING letters and send them *more* ASKING telegrams . . . you must make *more* ASKING phone calls . . . you must meet *more* people personally (by being introduced by a mutual friend or by introducing yourself). Whenever you make a contact (new or follow-up), you must use your ASKING methods to get the other person *involved* in *cooperating* with you in helping you achieve what you want to accomplish.

To increase the *quality* of your contacts, do everything suggested in the preceding paragraph, but *concentrate* on making and maintaining contacts with *successful people* who have *influence, money* and a wide range of *important contacts of their own.* In the words of the financial counselors, "*Go where the success and money is!*" Go in person . . . go by mail . . . go by telegraph . . . go by telephone . . . but GO! As all success trainers advise, you've got to *throw your body around! Which means you've got to get up, get out, and get among 'em!*

Remember the wise words of the Chinese sage, How Tu Du: "*Man who sits in chair, always on bottom.*"

If you want to completely eliminate forever the fear of failure—*keep your success production line always filled with valuable contacts.* Then if it should happen that one of your contacts positively cannot help you get what you want—*you can turn to any of several hundred other important contacts,* many of whom can and will *cooperate* with you when you *compliment* them . . . ASK them . . . intensely *believe* that they will cooperate with you (*after you first offer to cooperate with them*).

Then you can be *sure* that one success after another will come continously to you from your SUCCESS

PRODUCTION LINE which you keep always *filled* with *valuable contacts* and *from which you manufacture success* by your constant use of the ASKING methods and other *Personal Influence Psychology* techniques taught by this book.

When you read, in the preceding paragraph, that "*one success after another will come continuously to you from your* SUCCESS PRODUCTION LINE" . . . that is a *fact*. But it does not mean that, among the successes which will flow continuously to you, there will not *also* be *some* failures.

Of course you will fail *some* of the time! You should not expect to succeed the very *first* time in *every* thing you attempt.

If you do not fail some of the time, you are attempting too little! And will accomplish nothing worthwhile!

There are some timid people who will urge you to prepare yourself so well that it is *impossible* to fail. That will condemn you to the *mediocrity of endles preparation and instill a fear of failure which, itself, will prevent your even attempting—and therefore ever achieving—the big, important, worthwhile goals in life!*

As they say in sports: "*You win some and you lose some.*"

We shall devote the next several chapters to the *certainty*, the *necessity* and *especially the advantages* of *losing some!*

Beginning *right now*, we shall ELIMINATE FOREVER YOUR FEAR OF FAILURE!!!

Chapter 23

Not ALL . . . Not Even MOST . . . Just ENOUGH!

In the preceding chapter, you learned how to use the LAW OF AVERAGES to GUARANTEE that *you will get WHATEVER you want.*

You learned how to get WHATEVER you want by using the simple and easy ASKING method of *Personal Influence Psychology.*

You also learned that, according to the LAW OF AVERAGES, many people will readily do what you reasonably ASK—but that some people will refuse at first until you make them sure that they will benefit and cannot lose, and then they also will do what you ASK.

Then you learned *the necessity of accepting the inevitable routine failures in life* (including a lot of people *refusing* to do what you ASK) and *continuing, completely unperturbed by temporary failures, to cheerfully and confidently ASK until you get whatever you want in life.*

Knowing that the **LAW OF AVERAGES** will **GUARANTEE** your *ultimate* **success**, enables you to conquer your fear of failure.

YOU MUST **CONQUER YOUR** FEAR OF FAILURE ***in order to get whatever you want*** . . . *happiness* . . . *love* . . . *success* . . . ***wealth*** . . . *influence* . . . *power* . . . *popularity* . . . *fame* . . . *whatever you want in life.*

The first step in conquering your fear of failure is to realize that *failure is simply a routine event* which happens to *everybody* in *some degree* almost *every day*—and often *many times a day!*

As they say in sports: *you win some* and *you lose some!*

The biggest reason for permanent failure—or even for prolonged failure—is that tender, timid people think of failure as something to be *avoided!* They try to *avoid* failure by *never attempting to accomplish anything!* And, of course, *that assures failure!*

Even if you are one of those tender, timid people, *you cannot avoid failing some of the time!*

If YOU now *are* one of those tender, *timid* people, that fact alone will *assure* your failure, because *being AFRAID OF FAILURE attracts failure like a magnet! Fear of failure assures failure!*

This is why *tender, timid people FAIL:*

(1) Tender, timid people think of failure as something to be *avoided.*

(2) Tender, timid people are *ashamed of* failure.

(3) Tender, timid people feel that they are *disgraced* by failure.

(4) Tender, timid people are *disappointed* by failure.

(5) Tender, timid people are *discouraged* by failure.

(6) Tender, timid people *panic* when confronted by failure.

(7) Tender, timid people *fear* failure.

(8) Tender, timid people *quit trying* because of failure.

It is obvious that tender, timid people who are AFRAID OF FAILURE, actually *assure* their own failure by being afraid *to really try to succeed, and thus in seeking to avoid failure, they miss unlimited opportunities which lead directly to success!* They actually *avoid success!*

Every time you FAIL in trying to accomplish something—you simply have taken another step on the road to SUCCESS! Yes, it may be a *stumbling* step—but this book will teach you to STUMBLE *FORWARD!* Even if you should *stumble* and *fall* on your way to *success*, this book will teach you to FALL *FORWARD!*

SUCCESS is largely a matter of STUMBLING *FORWARD* . . . FALLING *FORWARD* . . . and GETTING *UP* whenever you fall down!

Failure is an *inevitable* . . . a *necessary* . . . and a *useful* . . . part of being *successful.*

You learn more from failing than from succeeding because failure *impresses* you with what *not* to do—and it *impresses* you more memorably than succeeding (for *succeeding* soon will become *routine* to you). *A sock on the jaw is more impressive and more memorable than a pat on the back!*

FAILURE CONDITIONS YOU FOR SUCCESS! It strengthens you to overcome adversity.

You've got to learn how to fail successfully! It is through *failing* that you learn to *succeed!* It is important to learn the valuable lessons taught by failure. Failure teaches you *what won't work,* so if you fail *often* enough you will know *all* of the things *which won't work.* Then just *eliminate* what won't work and you have your Master Success Plan which you know *will* work!

What is equally important in learning the *lessons* of failure, is to obtain the *mental-emotional conditioning* of failure! FAILURE teaches you to *"take it!"*

Did you ever hear of a boxing champion who never had been *hit?* And hit *hard?*

Or a star football back who hadn't been tackled? *Hard?*

Or a salesman who sold *every* prospect?

Having been sales counsel to 102 corporations, let me tell you how salesmen FAIL their way to SUCCESS. In selling (depending upon the cost-profit ratio) *a salesman can FAIL to sell 9 out of every 10 prospects—and still make a fortune!* A salesman does not have to sell ALL prospects . . . or even to sell MOST prospects . . . *but only to sell just ENOUGH prospects to get rich!*

In some businesses, a salesman can get rich if he *fails* to sell *every* prospect *except one a week!* I know of successful businesses which give each salesman a sales quota of *only three sales per week,* which means that the *acceptable rate of FAILURE is to FAIL to sell every prospect except THREE every week!*

There are some instances when only *one sale in a lifetime made a millionaire!*

The point to remember is: *You do not have to succeed ALL of the time . . . you do not even have to succeed MOST of the time . . . but you ONLY have to succeed ENOUGH of the time—to get WHATEVER you want!*

You can FAIL your way to SUCCESS!

Consider the "*99-failures-to-one-success*" *failure ratio in advertising*. You can get *very rich* in advertising by *failing to sell 99% of the time!*

Huge fortunes are invested daily in advertisements which are *certain to FAIL even to attract the ATTENTION of 90% of the time!*

Huge fortunes are invested daily in advertisements which are *certain to FAIL even to attract the ATTENTION of 90% of the possible readers!* So the advertiser *starts* with an *expected* 90% FAILURE rate! Then of the 10% of the people who actually LOOK at the ad at all, only a small percent READ it—and a *very small percent actually BUY what is advertised.* But *that* is ENOUGH!

So, in advertising you can FAIL 99% and only SELL 1%—and *get very rich!*

So what is all this foolishness about FAILURE being something to AVOID?

FAILURE is an *inevitable* . . . a *necessary* . . . and a *useful* . . . part of being SUCCESSFUL!

You do not have to succeed ALL of the time . . . you do not even have to succeed MOST of the time . . . you ONLY have to succeed ENOUGH of the time—to get WHATEVER you want!

In the next chapter you will learn HOW TO FAIL YOUR WAY TO SUCCESS!

Chapter 24

How To FAIL Your Way To SUCCESS!

Those of us who have FAILED actually *thousands* of times in the necessary process of *finding out* what *would not work* in order to be *sure what would work*—wish we could explain the *necessity of failing hundreds or* perhaps *thousands of times*, to those "INSTANT FAILURES" who whine and gripe because they have FAILED a *few* times!

The "INSTANT FAILURES" get discouraged and *quit trying* before they find out that *failing is a necessary learning process in order to succeed!* It is impossible to be a *big* success without failing sometimes.

To hear their complaints, one would think that their *entire future was ruined* because they FAILED in their *few half-hearted attempts* to accomplish some minor objective! So they *quit trying* after only a few—or a few dozen—failures!

These "QUICK QUITTERS" start looking for excuses as soon as they *fail* a *few* times. They are so disappointed and discouraged that they *mentally panic* in FEAR that *they never can succeed* (in the kind of system in which *millions of people are succeeding every day!*).

Do these "INSTANT FAILURES" try to change (*improve*) *themselves*—to do what this book teaches, for example—*so that they will succeed as millions of others are succeeding?* No! Certainly *not! They don't want to change themselves!*

They want to change the *system!* "Down the Establishment!!!", they shout (to distract attention from *their* failure).

It is far easier for an *unsuccessful individual* to *change himself,* than it is for that *unsuccessful individual* —*or any group of such unsuccessful individuals*—to *change* the *world* (or any substantial part of it).

The root of much—perhaps most—of the social, civil, student, racial unrest (and its disruptive manifestations) is a "*failure psychosis*" which results initially from FEAR OF FAILURE.

We could go into more complex detail by explaining that FEAR OF FAILURE threatens the sense of "*personal adequacy*" which thus undermines a "*hypersensitive ego*" and starts a chain of "*overcompensating responses*" resulting in exaggerated kinds of "*radical behavior.*"

But there is no need for complex explanations.

All that is required is the simple knowledge that *FAILURE is not something you should FEAR*—but just the opposite: *FAILURE is something you USE TO SUCCEED!*

To put it even more simply: YOU CAN FAIL YOUR WAY TO SUCCESS!

In fact, FAILURE is one of the *most effective methods* which you can use to *succeed!*

FAILURE should *not* be *feared* and *avoided;* FAILURE should be *accepted* and *used!*

Let's learn how—from the man who FAILED *more times* than any other person who ever lived!

Thomas Edison FAILED more than anyone else. As a result, he knew more things that *wouldn't work* than anyone else. So with that kind of information, naturally he SUCCEEDED more than anyone else! He patented 1,093 inventions.

These were not insignificant discoveries, either! He first invented a stock ticker and printer which he marketed for $40,000. Then he used this money to make a business of inventing things by employing any expert who could add specialized knowledge to his own so he could invent more and better things—faster. As he received more and more money he spent it all on salaries, equipment, experiments—and, more often on FAILURES through which he learned what *would not work* so he could perfect an invention which *would work.*

Have you ever FAILED? Congratulations! Now you know *one* thing which *won't work*. Edison, after a long series of FAILURES once remarked, *"Now we know 1,000 things that won't work, so we're that much closer to finding what will."* Edison actually FAILED his way to SUCCESS!

Edison even deliberately blew up expensive machinery which would require all his capital to replace. Why? To find out how much stress it would stand *before* it blew up! Then he could build a better machine which would stand up under much more stress.

Are you worried about FAILURE? Perhaps you aren't FAILING enough to find out enough things that won't work so you can learn what will work and thus succeed more rapidly! Remember, you've got to *try!* You can't get a hit with your bat on your shoulder!

And remember that *because* Edison *tried 18 hours a day,* he invented 1,093 items worth patenting—and worth millions of dollars to him and incalculable benefits to mankind. Thomas Edison invented the phonograph which captured sound on records. He invented the incandescent light bulb which lighted the world. He invented the movies, the microphone, mimeograph, and medical fluoroscope.

These inventions were the result of hard work, not flashes of inspiration! As he said, "Genius is 1% inspiration and 99% perspiration." And he proved it by *working 18 hours a day!*

He worked *ten years* to invent the nickel-iron-alkaline storage battery!

He and his staff tested and classified 17,000 varieties of plants before they succeeded in extracting latex in substantial quantities from just *one* of them! When YOU are willing to FAIL *17,000 times* in order to *succeed* ONCE—you'll be beginning to learn the VALUE of FAILURE!

Thomas Edison patented 1,093 inventions even though he attended school for *only six months!* Did YOU attend school for longer than *six months?* What have YOU accomplished lately?

Edison succeeded because he used the success principles given you in this book. In fact, he INVENTED many of them! But instead of ASKING *people,* he ASKED *actual tests.* And, as this book has taught you, when the answer was "No," he immediately asked "Why?" his *test failed.* When he learned "Why"—*he succeeded!*

And, in dealing with people, if you answer their "No" by ASKING "Why," sooner or later you will find out *why*—and that answer will lead you straight to your success in getting *whatever* you want!

Thomas Edison *intensely believed* in FAILING his way to SUCCESS! You will not be willing, in just one experiment, to make 17,000 tests that FAIL unless you *intensely believe* that *even after 17,000 failures you still will succeed!* The LAW OF AVERAGES *guarantees* that if you learn from your failures and *continue to try*—you ultimately will succeed.

YOU, too, can FAIL YOUR WAY TO SUCCESS when you *accept* failure for what it is—*a means of learning* (what *not* to do!).

Then you will accept failure, not as a disgrace, but merely as one of life's lessons. You should *eagerly learn* from failure, realizing that *failure is the best teacher* because it is convincing and often very impressive (like losing a lot of money, for example).

When you fail . . . and learn from your failure . . . *and try again*—YOU OUTLAST DEFEAT!

That is one of the most important success lessons. Learn it. Live by it. It *guarantees* your success!

We shall devote the next section of this SUCCESS COURSE to teaching you—through real life stories:

(1) How to fail your way to success
(2) How to outlast defeat
(3) How to succeed in spite of *all* obstacles
(4) How to GET WHATEVER YOU WANT

Chapter 25

How To Get WHATEVER YOU WANT In Spite Of All Obstacles!

Here is the power which will enable you to succeed—to GET WHATEVER YOU WANT—in spite of *all* obstacles, *all* handicaps, *all* failures, *all* defeats.

It is the POWER OF BELIEVING!

Without it, you are doomed to *constant* failure.

With it, your success is assured—YOU WILL GET WHATEVER YOU WANT.

The POWER OF BELIEVING will:

(1) *Enable you to BE whatever you want to BE!* What you ARE helps determine what you GET.

(2) *Enable you to DO whatever you want to DO!* What you DO helps determine what you GET.

(3) *Enable you to HAVE whatever you want to HAVE!* Intensely BELIEVE and RECEIVE!

On what authority can I make such statements? I make those statements on the authority of the Bible and of the Holy Scriptures of ALL of the great religions, past and present, and ALL of the greatest thinkers, philosophers and psychologists throughout the entire history of mankind.

ALL of the great teachings and ALL of the greatest thinkers throughout ALL of history cannot ALL be wrong!

Here is the POWER—not just to conquer your fear of failure (which it instantly will do)—but *to enable YOU to BE whatever you want to BE . . . to DO whatever you want to DO . . . to HAVE whatever you want to HAVE!*

THIS . . . is what the POWER OF BELIEVING will *do* for YOU:

"As a man thinketh in his heart [as he INTENSELY BELIEVES] so IS he," says the Bible.

The Bible also says, "ALL things are possible to him that BELIEVETH." That's a strong statement, but it comes from a reliable source—God.

In fact, the power of INTENSELY BELIEVING is the basis of ALL of the great religions.

Study the great religions and you will find the ONE thing they ALL have in common is the need for and the power of INTENSELY BELIEVING.

Buddha taught, "ALL that we *are* is the result of what we have *thought* [INTENSELY BELIEVED]."

Confucius taught, "The way of a superior man is three-fold: virtuous, he is free from anxieties; wise, he is free from perplexities; bold, he is free from fear." Through this wisdom of that great thinker runs the golden thread of INTENSE BELIEF.

The Koran of Mohammedanism emphasizes the *need* for and *power* of BELIEVING.

The book you now are reading is not a book about religion. I do not intend to intrude upon your personal beliefs. I just respectfully want to point out that the deepest convictions of *all* mankind in *all* religious faiths are centered in the *need* for and the *power* of BELIEVING. *Everybody throughout all history can't be wrong!*

Therefore, I am sure we can conclude that INTENSELY BELIEVING is one of the greatest forces in the world! From the quotations just given, we are told on the highest authority that *we* actually *become* what we INTENSELY BELIEVE!

"As a man thinketh in his heart [INTENSELY BELIEVES] so IS he."

"ALL things are possible to him who *believes.*" This is the teaching of *all* religions.

"ALL that we *are* is the result of what we have *thought* [INTENSELY BELIEVED]."

Here is *Universal Power* in *your own* hands! You can *become* what YOU *want* to become . . . you can *be* what YOU *want* to be . . . you can *achieve* what YOU *want* to achieve—by INTENSELY BELIFVING that YOU can!

Study the *miracle cures* and you will find *one* motivation . . . INTENSE BELIEF!

Study the *lives of all great men and women* and you will discover *always* the *same* motivation . . . their own INTENSE BELIEF in their personal abilities, INTENSE BELIEF in their *ultimate success.* (You will find many actual examples in the next chapters.)

Psychologists have proven that whatever the mind of man can conceive and BELIEVE—man can achieve!

William James, famed philosopher and psychologist of Harvard University, who is acknowledged as probably the greatest thinker of modern times, constantly taught that: "BELIEF CREATES THE ACTUAL FACT." He said, "In any project, the *important factor* is your BELIEF. *Without BELIEF there can be no successful outcome.* That is fundamental."

And William James further wrote: "If you only care enough for a result, you will almost certainly attain it. *If you wish to be rich, you will be rich; if you wish to be learned, you will be learned; if you wish to be good, you will be good.* Only you must, then, *really* wish [INTENSELY BELIEVE] these things, and wish them *exclusively*, and not wish at the same time a hundred other *incompatible* things just as strongly." IF YOU INTENSELY BELIEVE THAT YOU WILL GET WHAT YOU WANT—YOU WILL GET IT!

Dr. Walter Scott, famous psychologist and President of Northwestern University, said, "*Success or failure in business is caused more by MENTAL ATTITUDES than by mental capacities.*" In other words, your success in business is the result of YOUR INTENSE BELIEF that you will succeed—*and is not dependent upon superior brainpower.*

Then, what about will power? Many leading psychologists have no faith in will power alone. Their experiences prove that *it is a person's DESIRE and INTENSE BELIEF that he or she will achieve that desire—which determines the success of that person.* INTENSE BELIEF must be *reinforced* by will power, but it cannot be *replaced* by it.

As Bruce Barton said, "Nothing splendid has

ever been achieved except by those who dared BELIEVE that *something inside them was superior to circumstances.*"

And Emerson, one of the wisest men this nation has ever produced, said, "No accomplishment, no assistance, no training, can compensate for lack of BELIEF." He also wrote that every man reveals in his eyes the exact indication of his rank. You can just look at a man and tell how much he BELIEVES in *himself* and what he stands for.

Now let's take our case for BELIEF all the way to the United States Supreme Court. The decision . . . by the late Justice Cardozo: "*We are what we BELIEVE we are.*"

Or let's ask a great American thinker and poet, Henry Wadsworth Longfellow. He wrote: "Perseverance [based on INTENSE BELIEF that you will succeed] is a great element of success. If you only knock long enough at the gate [of Success] you are sure to wake up somebody."

The famous preacher-psychologist-writer, Dr. Norman Vincent Peale, says, "Think success, visualize success, and you will set in motion the power force of the realizable wish [INTENSE BELIEF]. When the mental picture or attitude [INTENSE BELIEF] is strongly enough held, it actually seems to control conditions and circumstances."

Yes, you are or you become what you INTENSELY BELIEVE. You never can be better, more successful or bigger than you BELIEVE you can!

A farmer exhibited at a County Fair a pumpkin grown in the exact shape of a two-gallon jug. "When this pumpkin was no bigger than my thumb," he explained, "I stuck it in the jug and just let it grow. When it filled the jug, it quit growing." *What the walls of the jug did to the pumpkin, our BELIEFS do to us!*

Our INTENSE BELIEFS shape—and *limit*—our lives just as the jug shaped and limited the size of the pumpkin. We can never be bigger than we INTENSELY BELIEVE.

So let me repeat—so that you never will forget it: *All of the great religions and the greatest thinkers, philosophers and psychologists in the entire history of the world agree that we are or will become exactly what we INTENSELY BELIEVE!*

The principle of BELIEVING is like dialing a telephone. You get what you dial. If you dial the wrong number (fear, sickness or failure) that's what you will get. You will get it automatically—not as a trick of Fate but because *you dialed it yourself.* If you dial (by INTENSELY BELIEVING) happiness, success, health, love, riches, popularity, power, fame—you will get exactly what you dial—not because you are lucky, but because *you dialed it yourself* by INTENSELY BELIEVING.

BELIEF in their ability to succeed is the one basic, essential characteristic of all successful people!

You become what you BELIEVE to the exact extent of the INTENSITY of your BELIEF. That's why it is so important to BELIEVE INTENSELY. You cannot achieve your goal by a casual, indifferent, occasional belief. Your BELIEF must be INTENSE. "As a man thinketh *in his heart* so *is* he," says the Bible. You have to think [BELIEVE INTENSELY] *"in your heart."* The Bible didn't emphasize that you must BELIEVE INTENSELY "*in your heart*" just to teach meaningless words. No, the Bible meant to state, as a definite *requirement*, that YOU MUST BELIEVE INTENSELY.

As we shall discuss in later chapters, your conscious mind must BELIEVE with such white-hot intensity that the exact image of what you want will be burned *deeply* into your subconscious mind *which then will use its unlimited powers to achieve for you your greatest desires!* YOU MUST BELIEVE INTENSELY.

In this connection it might be well to repeat the instructions of philosopher and psychologist William James: ". . . *not to wish at the same time for a hundred other incompatible things just as strongly.*"

You will deepen your BELIEF by *concentrating* INTENSELY on *one desire* or, at most, *several compatible desires.* And when I say "*concentrate,*" I mean deeply thinking about your INTENSE BELIEF, not just a few times a day, but *hundreds* of times a day!

Remember you are a living advertisement of the contents of your mind . . . and "heart." "As a man thinketh *in his heart* [INTENSELY BELIEVES] so *is* he."

Remember, too, that if you are not accomplishing what you should, it is because you do not really "*think in your heart*" that you can do it. You do not INTENSELY BELIEVE you can do it. Therefore, you do not do it.

I gave the following illustration in my book, *Thoughts to Build On:* A little boy who lived in the mountains found an eagle's nest high on a rocky crag. In the nest was just one eagle's egg. The boy took the egg home and placed it in a hen's nest under a setting hen. The eagle's egg hatched along with the chicken eggs and the baby eaglet played with the baby chicks and of course thought he was just like them—a chicken.

Since he BELIEVED he was a chicken he, of course, lived and acted like a chicken. He did not try to fly but remained with the chickens in the fenced-in chicken yard. Yet as the eagle grew bigger and stronger there seemed to be something inside him that made him feel he was not just a chicken—and he felt the urge to fly. Because he BELIEVED he *could*—he COULD!

So he stretched his mighty wings and began to fly . . . higher . . . higher . . . higher . . . until he reached his new home on top of a lofty mountain. Because he BELIEVED in a greater destiny—he knew he was not a chicken, confined to a dirty chicken yard. *Because he BELIEVED—his belief released his real powers!* He now lived on the highest pinnacle and soared through the bright, blue sky as the proud symbol of courage and freedom—the American Eagle!

The most powerful forces of nature are the invisible ones: heat, sound, electricity, gravity—just as the most powerful forces of man also are invisible: love, thought, desire, BELIEF. You see and feel *only* their powerful *effects*.

In the next chapters, you will learn what a mighty force is this invisible power of INTENSELY BELIEVING that YOU CAN SUCCEED. We shall examine the exciting, inspiring, real-life stories of men and women *whose achievements were so great as to almost be miracles* —because they used their tremendous POWER OF BELIEVING!

Chapter 26

Special Section

The Miraculous Power Of INTENSELY BELIEVING That You Will Succeed

This *Special Section* has been included so that you have for your own inspirational reading the real-life stories of men and women whose INTENSE BELIEF that they would SUCCEED enabled them to accomplish *miraculous* achievements—in spite of the great handicaps which they had to overcome.

The people, their life stories and accomplishments already are well known. They were selected from thousands of similarly inspiring examples partly because they are so familiar that you will not be overly distracted by the WHO and WHAT—but can concentrate on the HOW.

It is HOW such miraculous achievements were accomplished in spite of seemingly insurmountable handicaps—which should become the motivating power in your own life!

There is in each story a constant demonstration of the *invincible power of persistence* in moving toward a life-goal.

But the compelling purpose of the real-life stories which follow is to give you motivating examples of the *miraculous power of INTENSELY BELIEVING that you will succeed!*

The power of these inspiring, real-life stories to motivate *your own life* is illustrated by the example of the effect of the first story on a little boy during the last century. The story is repeated here in the belief that it will inspire and motivate you.

The little boy's name was Samuel Clemens. He was just an average little boy who lived in a small river-town.

One day he noticed a torn sheet of paper being blown across the street by a sultry breeze. With the natural curiosity of a little boy with nothing special to do, Sam Clemens picked up the piece of paper and read the story printed on it.

Reading that inspirational story was the turning point in little Sam Clemens' life!

That *one* story, picked up by mere chance (or was it Fate?) so inspired little Sam Clemens to INTENSELY BELIEVE that he could achieve success and fame that *he became the great American humorist . . . whom we now know as Mark Twain!*

The story was about a little girl, tending a flock of sheep, who suddenly began to INTENSELY BELIEVE that *she was appointed by God to save France!*

That story is the *next chapter* . . .

Chapter 27

She BELIEVED She Was Appointed By God To Save France!

Anyone who has the slightest doubt about the tremendous power of INTENSELY BELIEVING should study this amazing story of Joan of Arc. Joan was a peasant shepherdess tending a small flock of sheep. There was nothing unusual about her. She was just a plain little girl of twelve.

Suddenly, she was filled with an INTENSE BELIEF! She had a vision that she was appointed by God to lead the armies of France to victory over England in the Hundred Years' War which had been going on for seventy-five years before she was born! *A poor, little shepherd girl to lead the armies of France!* Her BELIEF became an obsession—she INTENSELY BELIEVED!

If we could believe in our ability to SUCCEED as INTENSELY as Joan of Arc BELIEVED—*we would succeed at ANYTHING we attempted!* Just as Joan of

Arc did! Nothing could stop us! Just as nothing could stop Joan of Arc—not even the thirty-foot walls of the supposedly unconquerable bastion of Orleans.

She had her first intensive vision of victory when she was twelve. Then for the next five years she believed—INTENSELY BELIEVED—that she heard voices of Saints assuring her of her divine appointment with destiny.

When she was seventeen Joan went before the Dauphin Prince Charles and so INTENSE was her BELIEF in her divinely-appointed mission to save France that he outfitted her with a suit of shining armor and raised an army to follow her into battle!

So with her sword flashing and her personal banner flying she led the attack and conquered heavily fortified Orleans. A seventeen-year-old shepherd girl who INTENSELY BELIEVED she could do it!

And here is the place where we must emphasize that only INTENSE BELIEF in SUCCESS brings SUCCESS . . . *and just as surely, BELIEF in TRAGEDY brings TRAGEDY!*

Joan of Arc, the conqueror, *began to BELIEVE that she would be captured, betrayed and executed.* And that is exactly what happened! She was burned at the stake as a heretic, sinner, idolator—this saintly young girl who had saved her country!

But betrayal, torture and death could not destroy the eternal glory of her years of divine belief. The Church made Joan of Arc a Saint.

Imagine a plain, little, peasant girl of twelve, tending a flock of sheep—INTENSELY BELIEVING that *she could lead the army of France to victory in a war France had failed to win in seventy-five years before she was born!*

Yet, at the age of only seventeen, because Joan of Arc INTENSELY BELIEVED that she could—she SUCCEEDED in doing exactly that!

Before YOU decide that your lack of something is keeping you from succeeding—your lack of education, lack of training, lack of money, lack of influence, or whatever "lack" you are using as an alibi—remember that Joan of Arc was a poor, unknown, uneducated, peasant girl of seventeen, who obviously *lacked* any military training—yet, because she was *obsessed* by an INTENSE BELIEF, she led the previously unsuccessful army of France to victory!

Her *only* qualification was INTENSE BELIEF that *she could succeed!*

Think what YOU can achieve if your BELIEF that YOU CAN SUCCEED *is so intense that getting WHATEVER you want becomes such an obsession that you activate your BELIEF with SUCCESS TRAINING!*

In a later chapter, this book will teach YOU how to develop *that* kind of INTENSE BELIEF!

Chapter 28

He BELIEVED In Self-Improvement So He Improved Himself To Become One Of The Greatest Americans!

Benjamin Franklin was America's first self-made man. The early settlers may have come here seeking freedom, but they retained the rigid class system prevalent in England. Ben Franklin changed that, as he changed so many other things!

If he was to learn anything, he had to teach himself! If he was to achieve anything, he had to do it himself! He INTENSELY BELIEVED that he could—*so, of course, he did!*

Born in Boston in 1706, Ben Franklin was the fifteenth of seventeen children of a poor candlemaker. *He had little more than one year of actual schooling! He taught himself: philosophy, four languages, the classics, writing for publication, science, finance, politics, diplomacy!*

He did all this while also devoting long hours to the urgency of making a living. And urgent it was. *He had to go to work when he was twelve!* When he was seventeen, he left Boston, couldn't find a job in New York, and went on to Philadelphia—*walking most of the way!*

He arrived with only a few pennies in his pocket, got a job as a printer, soon went into business for himself as a publisher—first of a newspaper, then a magazine—and, by the time he was only forty-two, had made a fortune and retired from business. *Which just goes to show what you can do with self-education and self-help if you INTENSELY BELIEVE you can do it!*

And succeeding in business was only one of Ben Franklin's many achievements. After retiring from business at forty-two, he spent the next forty years serving his government, including twenty-five years negotiating important matters in England and France.

He debated the British about mishandling their American colonies and obtained the repeal of the hated Stamp Act, thus postponing the Revolutionary War for 10 years and giving the American colonies necessary time to organize and prepare.

Then when the Revolutionary War finally came, Ben Franklin went to France and first secured supplies for the colonies and, later, the open declaration of war by France as an ally of the colonies.

Franklin's *powers of persuasion were so important* in the history of this country and the founding of the original United States—being more responsible than any others in getting the Constitution ratified by the quarreling States—*that we might profit here by learning how he did it.* So here's how:

As a boy, he argued belligerently for his causes. *Then he learned what I have emphasized so strongly in this book: Argument and pressure create resistance! He found that the more he argued and the harder he pressed his views, the fewer people he convinced!*

In exactly the same way as now explained in this book, Ben Franklin began to ASK *questions which would lead to negotiable responses* and finally to the action he wanted. *As soon as he stopped arguing and started ASKING, he became one of the greatest persuaders of all time!*

Franklin was the foremost advocate of self-improvement. He INTENSELY BELIEVED: "God helps those who help themselves." When he was a young man he started a notebook with a page headed by each desirable quality he wished to develop in his character and personality. Then he devoted a week to concentrating on each one, recording his failures in emphasizing that quality, and deciding how to improve still more. When he no longer had any personality or character failures to record in his notebook, he discontinued using it. *He later attributed the great success he achieved to this character-building and personality-development technique. I highly recommend it to you!*

At the early age of fourteen, Franklin INTENSELY BELIEVED he could be a great writer. *So naturally he set about to become one!* He copied the great essays of famous writers and memorized them to improve his style. He worked constantly to improve his vocabulary. And so, in his time, Benjamin Franklin was the best known writer of the English-speaking world. His first great publishing success was *Poor Richard's Almanac*(*k*) which he started when he was twenty-six and which later was credited with being the only printed matter in every American home.

Franklin's *Autobiography* is still one of the most widely read of all books.

He also was a noted scientist and inventor. A leading historian ranks Franklin with Newton as two of the most important scientists of the modern age. Every schoolboy knows that Franklin drew electricity from a cloud on a kite string but few people realize that Ben Franklin wrote one of the first text books on electricity. It was so important it was translated into foreign languages. He was the first to discover positive and negative electricity, without the knowledge of which there could be no electrical power today. He gave the world the concepts of the electrical battery, electrical charge, condenser and conductor. He invented a simple, safe, lightning rod which became almost a standard household item.

He didn't confine his scientific research and inventions to electricity. Franklin invented a wood-burning stove which contained a hot-air radiator. These efficient stoves were widely used for several centuries and still are used wherever coal or wood-burning stoves are needed today. He invented a kitchen stool that folded over to become a step ladder, and a mechanical hand for lifting objects from high shelves.

Franklin even invented bifocal glasses when he was seventy-eight years old and needed them himself.

He made a study of water and became the pioneer of hydrodynamics. He also discovered that storms rotate while traveling forward. He charted the Gulf Stream. He discovered that water will boil at a lower temperature in thinner air, as at high altitudes. He also discovered that light colored clothing repels heat and should be worn in the summer and in the tropics.

Franklin organized the first service club in America, In 1743, he founded the American Philosophical Society which really was a "scientific society," a national academy of science, the first national library and museum, and the first patent office.

He also started the first regular police force, the first fire department, the first fire insurance company and the great Pennsylvania Hospital. He founded the college which was later to become the University of Pennsylvania.

Benjamin Franklin did all these things—and many more—because he INTENSELY BELIEVED he could. *And, he greatly increased his achievements by becoming a master in the art of persuasion because he used the success principles which now are given you in this book!*

He early learned, and this book repeats for emphasis, that *arguing and pressure create resistance.* By ASKING questions which lead to *negotible* responses, you influence others *to do what you want them to do!* Franklin used the technique of ASKING to influence the decisions of great nations to make possible the very existence of our United States of America and to provide it with our Constitution which guarantees freedom and justice for all its citizens.

Benjamin Franklin proved how great is the persuasive power of ASKING! And he proved that INTENSE BELIEF can overcome all obstacles!

Chapter 29

He BELIEVED He Could Save Millions of Lives. So He Did!

Would you think that this little man with the scraggly goatee and crippled leg could *save millions of lives—and set up an institute to continue saving millions more?*

That's what the little man with the scraggly goatee and crippled leg did! *He declared a personal war on germs, microbes and infection. And he INTENSELY BELIEVED he could win it!*

His name . . . Louis Pasteur.

He developed *pasteurization*—which in the treatment of milk alone, *has saved millions of babies!* He developed vaccines to overcome the effects of deadly virus. He developed protective serums, anti-toxins, drugs, medicines—*to save more millions of lives!*

Prior to 1888, medical discoveries were made on a hit-or-miss basis by lone researchers. Louis Pasteur founded the Pasteur Institute in Paris where killer diseases were attacked by teams of trained scientists. He started a new era of scientific medical research.

He *saved millions of lives* and then established a medical research institute (which became the forerunner of many more) *to keep on saving millions more lives throughout the entire world*—because he INTENSELY BELIEVED he could!

And, because he converted his BELIEF into *action!*

If you BELIEVE you can, but *do nothing*—you will achieve nothing. Of course not! BELIEF is *power*. But power *unused*—accomplishes nothing.

Many people *imagine* that they BELIEVE, then do nothing but wait for success and abundance to happen! If they *really* BELIEVED, their BELIEF would *motivate them to acting* to fulfill their BELIEF!

BELIEF is not magic! BELIEF is *power*—power to be *used!*

So . . . *use* it! Start now to put your BELIEF into *action!*

INTENSELY BELIEVE that you *can* do it—and you will *have* the power!

Chapter 30

He Couldn't Read Music But Became America's Leading Song Writer!

If you INTENSELY BELIEVE you can do it—you CAN! *Handicaps and difficulties can't stop YOU anymore than they could stop Irving Berlin!*

During the Russian Revolution, Irving Berlin's parents and their six children had to flee Russia for their lives. Irving's only memory of Russia was seeing their home go up in flames in the darkness. His family arrived in America penniless. They lived in a dark cellar. But they found freedom and happiness in America, a feeling Irving Berlin was later to express in one of his most famous songs, "God Bless America!"

Irving Berlin had a song in his heart. In fact, as it turned out, *he had eight hundred songs in his heart!* He wrote more songs than any song writer of his time—*yet he attended school for only two years, never took a music lesson in his life and couldn't even read music!* But he INTENSELY BELIEVED he could give the world the happy, popular songs that seemed to fill his very being. So he hummed the melodies to a musical secretary who wrote down the notes in proper musical form.

He made *thirty-three cents* on the first song he wrote! But was he discouraged? Certainly not! He INTENSELY BELIEVED in himself as a great song writer so he just kept on writing songs. Three years later he wrote "Alexander's Ragtime Band," which was the beginning of a new era in American music. It also was the beginning of a new era in Irving Berlin's fame and fortune. *He was paid a fifth of a million dollars for that one song alone and the millions started pouring in!*

He still couldn't read music—but he still INTENSELY BELIEVED that he could create it. *And he did! And the millions kept pouring in!*

His most famous show probably was "This Is The Army." It earned more than twelve million dollars and Irving Berlin wouldn't accept a penny. He gave all the earnings to the Army Emergency Relief Fund.

The miraculous power of INTENSELY BELIEVING that you will SUCCEED—results not only in the personal satisfaction of success—but in *very tangible millions of dollars* if that's what you want!

The power of INTENSELY BELIEVING that you will SUCCEED will enable you to get WHATEVER you want in life.

What Irving Berlin *wanted* was not all those millions of dollars, most of which he gave away, but he wanted to give the world the happy, popular songs (*more than eight hundred of them!*) which he INTENSELY BELIEVED he could create—and DID!

Chapter 31

The Negro Whose BELIEF In Excellence Saved Millions Of Lives!

It should not be necessary to state that Dr. Charles Drew was *black*—anymore than it is necessary to state that another life-saving, scientific researcher, Louis Pasteur, was *white*.

The necessity arises because of the preoccupation of so many Negroes regarding *skin color*. Their time could more rewardingly be concentrated on studying proven success methods—in which *skin color is no more a factor than the color of one's hair or eyes*.

I have devoted a long life to the study of success—and *I do not know of even one Negro who constantly used proven success methods and who did not succeed.*

I do not know of *even one* superior Negro whose superiority has not been *promptly and fully recognized and rewarded*.

As in the case of Dr. Charles Drew:

Millions of people of every skin color owe their lives to this Negro scientist—who was no more interested in *their* skin color than he was in his own.

Dr. Charles Drew was not distracted by skin color, he INTENSELY BELIEVED *in achieving excellence.*

So he was a great athlete, an award-winning scholar, a famous research scientist and, finally, chief surgeon and chief of staff of Freedman's Hospital.

During the years when it was said that recognition and awards for Negroes were limited, Negro Charles Drew was awarded the Springarn Medal for Contribution to Human Welfare.

Dr. Drew was a native of Washington, D.C. As an Amherst College undergraduate, he was captain of the track team and a star halfback on the football team. He received the Mossman Trophy for having brought the most honor to the school over a four-year period.

At McGill University, he won first prize for research in physiological anatomy.

At Columbia University, he began his research into the properties of blood plasma and, subsequently, became a leading authority on that subject.

Dr. Drew was a pioneer in blood plasma preservation. Before his discoveries in that field, there was no efficient way to store large quantities of blood plasma for use during emergencies or war when thousands of lives would depend on the availability of blood for transfusions.

Dr. Charles Drew discovered how to preserve blood plasma in "blood banks" in time to save thousands of lives in World War II and millions thereafter.

The entire world will forever be indebted to the Negro scientist who, undistracted by skin color, INTENSELY BELIEVED in achieving *excellence* . . . Dr. Charles Drew.

Chapter 32

He BELIEVED He Could See The World; Tell Millions About It For A Fortune!

The man who has brought the adventure of far away places into the imaginations of more millions of people than anyone else is, of course, Lowell Thomas.

But to do that required two things: (1) the INTENSE BELIEF that he could surmount great travel difficulties, (2) the education to understand and appreciate what he saw in his travels, and the dramatic skill to describe what he saw and experienced.

The INTENSE BELIEF in his ability to SUCCEED, Lowell Thomas had in great abundance!

The education, he had to get the hard way. First, he wasn't satisfied with just *one* university degree; his career required that he had to have *four*, each from a different educational institution. But he didn't have the money to attend even *one* university, much less *four!*

So he went right on INTENSELY BELIEVING he could do it, *and backed his belief with hard work.* He punched cattle, pitched alfalfa, worked as a cub reporter, looked after furnaces, served as a waiter and short-order cook, sold real estate and even fed and milked a cow for one of his professors.

Did INTENSE BELIEF pay off for Lowell Thomas?

Well, he turned his education into profitable adventure . . . explored the most remote and interesting places in the world . . . made Marco Polo look like an average tourist . . . and dominated the stages of the world with his dramatic tales of travel and adventure!

He grossed a million dollars in one year while he was still in his twenties! And that, of course, was just the beginning! Because he INTENSELY BELIEVED.

Note that Lowell Thomas *materialized* his INTENSE BELIEF through *hard work.* He *worked* to get his education—*worked* his way through *four* universities to get the knowledge he needed.

He was not "*educationally deprived*"—because he would not permit himself to be "*deprived*" of an education *just because it was not free!*

Anyone—yes, *anyone*—can get all of the education he or she needs to succeed. All that is required is ambition, motivation, and using the success methods in this book.

Chapter 33

He BELIEVED He Could Make Lightning! He Did! Then Tamed It!

He was almost a dwarf, with a frail body deformed by a hump on his back. Oversized head. Poor eyesight. Threadbare clothes. No money. No job. A German immigrant who could speak almost no English.

His name, Karl Steinmetz, which he changed to Charles Steinmetz.

He had an INTENSE BELIEF in his ability as an electrical mathematician. So INTENSE was his BELIEF in his mathematical ability that he solved the most complex electrical problems—not like Edison by practical experiments—*but just with a box of pencils and an unlimited supply of paper—and his intense belief* in the infallibility of mathematics.

For example, it was impossible to make large electrical motors because of the effect of magnetism on the motors' iron cores. But Steinmetz so INTENSELY BELIEVED in his personal ability as a mathematician, that he devoted two years to the most complicated mathematical computations which he condensed into a 200-page report describing his discovery of the law which governs the loss of power by alternating magnetism.

He immediately was acclaimed a mathematical genius, and General Electric bought the company he worked for—*just to get Steinmetz, who refused a fabulous increase in pay, to stay with the employer who had given him his first job!*

He became the keystone of General Electric's brilliant engineering staff and was furnished unlimited laboratory and engineering facilities. *He used just pencil and paper and his INTENSE BELIEF in mathematics to solve problems*—then he used the elaborate laboratory *to prove that he was right!*

When Steinmetz first went to General Electric the only electricity then available was direct current *which could be transmitted only three miles!* He INTENSELY BELIEVED the problem could be solved by alternating current—which would alternate directions usually at the rate of 120 times a second and could be transmitted unlimited distances.

He not only INTENSELY BELIEVED he could solve this almost insurmountable problem—but he solved it with pure mathematics so involved that almost no one could understand his computations. *But they worked—and the electrification of the world was begun!*

However, electrical installations were constantly threatened by lightning. Steinmetz INTENSELY BELIEVED *he could produce lightning* and thus devise means to counteract it.

Produce lightning! Impossible! But not to a man who INTENSELY BELIEVED he could! It took two years of mathematical calculations and the construction of a monstrous, strange machine two stories high. When the switch was thrown there was a tremendous, blazing flash of *lightning* followed by a terrific crash of thunder!

Then Steinmetz calmly proceeded to produce a lightning arrester which harmlessly grounded lightning and protected electrical equipment everywhere.

Nothing is too difficult for the man who INTENSELY BELIEVES he can do it!

Nothing! Nothing is too difficult! Even for a dwarf with a frail body deformed by a hump on his back. Oversized head. Poor eyesight. Threadbare clothes. No money. No job. A German immigrant who could speak but a few words of the language of the strange land to which he had come.

What's YOUR excuse?

Chapter 34

He BELIEVED In Freedom And Justice For All

Historian John Fiske wrote: "William Penn was by far the greatest among the founders of the American commonwealth."

William Penn was even greater than that!

He INTENSELY BELIEVED in and proposed that there should be a *United States of America* although he died *70 years before it could be founded!*

He INTENSELY BELIEVED in and even drew up a plan for the *United Nations! This was in the 1600's!*

He INTENSELY BELIEVED in and proposed that there should be a *United States of Europe!* And this also was over 300 years ahead of modern ideas!

William Penn was born in London as a member of the class of nobility and high offices. He traveled widely and moved with ease in the courts of Europe, having close acquaintance with royalty and intellectuals. He was adviser to four consecutive British monarchs.

He could have lived a life of ease, luxury and pleasure—but he INTENSELY BELIEVED in freedom and justice, and he found neither in Europe. So he came to America and devoted his life to *working* to establish freedom and justice here.

King Charles I owed William Penn $80,000 and paid him by granting him all the land which now is Pennsylvania and there Penn began to build the city which now is Philadelphia.

But first, *he personally paid every settler* for each settler's property although legally the King had already given title to the land to William Penn. *Then he personally paid the Indians all over again!*

You see, William Penn INTENSELY BELIEVED in justice and freedom.

Because he INTENSELY BELIEVED, he built the greatest of the early American colonies with freedom of speech, freedom of worship, and the finest educational opportunities for *all* and—note this—William Penn worked hard to help *all people earn freedom from want!*

How these inspiring ideals came ringing down through our history and into our present!

Let us remember that they all started with the man who most INTENSELY BELIEVED in freedom and justice for *all* . . . William Penn.

And let us remember, too, that the real lesson of this chapter is that the power of INTENSE BELIEF can enable us to achieve much more than material success —*wealth*—which INTENSE BELIEF *assures.*

As it did in the life of William Penn, INTENSE BELIEF *can enable us to bring into reality our highest ideals!*

We can, in our own lifetimes, establish not just token civil rights, but *complete freedom of opportunity for all people of all races and all economic conditions!*

It is the principal purpose of this book to make available to ALL people of ALL races and ALL economic conditions—the success methods which will enable *them to attain complete freedom of opportunity and then to achieve their life-goals!*

The highly-paid, professional trouble-makers and their disruptive recruits have performed their "freedom" act on center stage for too long. In the name of "freedom" they have turned race against race, class against class, labor against management, generation against generation.

We have rewarded the disrupters with high positions in education, government, news media, and in all levels of our civic-social community—thus implementing their opportunities for divisiveness.

We got what we deserved. *And now it's time we gave the trouble-makers what they deserve!* It is time we re-establish American democratic leadership by majority—instead of by intimidation of divisive minorities.

It is time that we learn from William Penn that the noblest use of freedom is to *unite all citizens—not to divide them*—because it is only when *all citizens unite* that there can be freedom and justice and equality and abundance for ALL.

Chapter 35

He Built The Nations's Largest Negro Owned And Operated Business

When John Merrick and Dr. A. M. Moore founded what was to become the largest Negro owned and operated business, the North Carolina Mutual Life Insurance Company, the company's assets were a spare room and four chairs—and the indispensable assets of INTENSE BELIEF, courage and persistence . . . *and* Charles Clinton Spaulding.

Their insurance company began its operations by almost going bankrupt because it could not pay a $40 claim. But Merrick and Moore raised $39.71 and the company's janitor, C. C. Spaulding, put up the remaining twenty-nine cents—so the company was saved.

Charles Clinton Spaulding served as janitor, bookkeeper, salesman and advertising man—*all at the same time!* The company could not afford any other employees so C. C. Spaulding really *was* the company—and he had to support himself by selling insurance policies.

In spite of ridicule in those days that black men

could not operate an insurance company, salesman Spaulding, with proof that the company had paid a $40 claim, was able to sell policies which produced $800 in premiums within a year.

Then, year after year, Charles Clinton Spaulding traveled the highways and byways of North Carolina, patiently and persistently selling his company's insurance.

He began to build a sales organization. First, he enlisted Negro school teachers in each district as part-time agents. Then other ambitious Negroes joined his growing sales force until hundreds of black insurance agents were bringing the security of insurance to Negroes throughout the east coast of the nation.

By 1923, C. C. Spaulding had advanced from janitor to president and continued to expand the company. When he died in 1952, he left his company a legacy of progress based on proof that *it is not skin color and race, but* INTENSE BELIEF and *success methods persistently and patiently applied, which produce success.*

As proof: In 1969, the North Carolina Mutual Life Insurance Company had nearly 2,000 employees and assets of almost $95,000,000—the nation's largest Negro owned and operated business.

It was co-founded by John Merrick, who never even attended school, and built by Charles Clinton Spaulding, who was born in poverty, one of a family of fourteen children.

They INTENSELY BELIEVED that *they* could succeed.

What do *you* INTENSELY BELIEVE that *you* can do?

Chapter 36

He BELIEVED He Could Be A Writer—So He Won The Nobel Prize!

One of the most distinguished writers of English plays, books and articles (he was awarded the Nobel Prize for Literature) *had only five years of schooling!* He was a poor Irishman who had to go to work as a clerk when he was fifteen—at a wage of four and a half dollars a month.

He wanted to be a writer. *He INTENSELY BELIEVED he could be a great writer,* so he quit his job and started to write. It was *nine years* before he could make a living from his writing. *In fact, his total income for those first nine years was only thirty dollars!*

Still he INTENSELY BELIEVED he could become a great writer—and he DID! *He became one of the most famous of all writers and made millions of dollars from his plays, books and articles* . . . because he continued to INTENSELY BELIEVE he could SUCCEED The great G. B. S.—George Bernard Shaw!

Chapter 37

He BELIEVED He Could Find Land. He Did. He Discovered America!

Some historians have stated that the discovery of America by Columbus was the greatest single feat of courage in history.

I doubt that.

Columbus was not the only one who believed that the world was round. All intelligent people in his day believed it. The schools and universities taught it. One could even buy globes of the world although the land masses shown on them were inaccurate.

Columbus was an expert chart and map maker. He knew mathematics and astronomy. And he was probably the greatest navigator of his time—so good that he seldom used an astrolabe but sailed by dead reckoning and arrived confidently in each harbor.

So while his discovery of America (probably after several others) certainly was courageous, it was not the "greatest feat of courage in history."

It was the greatest triumph of PATIENCE maintained by INTENSE BELIEF.

Christopher Columbus devoted almost all of his life to trying to get someone to financially back his INTENSE BELIEF that lands and fortunes could be gained by sailing west.

His wife insisted that he settle down and stay at home—but he still held deep within him the INTENSE BELIEF that he should sail west.

Finally he interested John II, King of Portugal, who referred Columbus' idea to a committee. *Like many ideas which are referred to committees, it was discussed and discussed*—and turned down. But King John II kept Columbus waiting around for six years before saying a final: "No." (*There is a lesson in this for others who don't know how to get a definite answer—"Yes" or "No"—and get on to the next prospect.*)

Finally Columbus went to King Ferdinand and Queen Isabella of Spain. They referred his proposal to a committee. *This was a fast-acting committee, dedicated, as all committees are, to expediting matters. It only took them two years to say: "No."*

And Columbus, being a typical optimist, hung around three more years, hoping they would change their minds. Meanwhile his red hair had turned white, he got arthritis, his clothes became tattered and worn.

He left for France and, fortunately, on his way he met a man who knew something about getting action. The man said, "*You've got to get in to see the 'boss' and don't let her refer you to any more committees.*"

He got Columbus back in to see Queen Isabella. She bought the idea, outfitted Columbus with three good ships and it was a cinch (in spite of what the poets say) for an expert navigator like Columbus to sail due west from Spain until he came to land. It is a feat which since has been duplicated many times with less seaworthy ships and less able navigators than Columbus.

But to Christopher Columbus goes the honor of having done it *first* (at least by the southern route).

What is much more important is that he had the *patience,* the *perseverance* and the INTENSE BELIEF which kept him ASKING for the opportunity!

It was INTENSE BELIEF and ASKING which finally got him his opportunity—just as they will for YOU. Then, you can follow the words which the poet attributed to Columbus: *"Sail on, sail on . . . and on!"*

But you must do more than sail courageously into the blue yonder. You must have a *definite course*—and *stay on it.* This is the greatest lesson taught by Columbus. Each night he wrote in his log book: "This day we sailed west—*because it was our course.*"

Again and again, night after night, he wrote, "This day we sailed west—*because it was our course.*"

Everyday he proceeded directly and perseveringly *toward his goal—because it was his course.*

Do YOU have a course—a goal?

Do YOU proceed *directly* toward it—*every day?*

Chapter 38

He Gave Himself To His BELIEF That He Should Help Others!

When you say Doctor Albert Schweitzer you can emphasize the title "DOCTOR." By the time he was twenty-six he had a Doctor's Degree in Philosophy, a Doctor's Degree in Theology and a Doctor's Degree in Music.

ALL this in spite of the fact that he was a sickly child who was slow to read and write, and was graded a poor scholar! To overcome these handicaps he made himself master very difficult subjects, like Hebrew, just to train his mind. *When I hear about our increasing school drop-outs who find it too boring to get enough education to make a living, I think of Dr. Schweitzer, his own handicaps, and his three Doctor's Degrees by the time he was twenty-six!* He INTENSELY BELIEVED he could learn!

When he was twenty-five, he became Curate of St. Nicholas Church in Strasbourg. He also began his career as one of the greatest concert organists of all time. He also wrote vast numbers of books.

Then, when he was thirty, he suddenly was filled with an INTENSE BELIEF that his mission in life was to be a medical missionary in the most primitive part of equatorial Africa!

So now he had to get a *fourth* Doctor's Degree, this time in Medicine. Getting a modern medical education is difficult enough in itself—but Albert Schweitzer also continued to be Curate of St. Nicholas, also continued to teach philosophy, also continued to give organ concerts, and also continued to write scholarly books!

You see, he INTENSELY BELIEVED—*and when you INTENSELY BELIEVE you can do it, nothing is too difficult, nothing is impossible!*

So in 1912, at the age of thirty-eight, Albert Schweitzer became a Doctor of Medicine. He went to Lambarene in steaming, tropical Africa where his small group made a clearing in a giant forest where they were treatened constantly by pythons, gorillas, crocodiles and wild savages. There he built his "hospital."

Dr. Schweitzer has been criticized by some in the medical profession and by others because his "hospital" wasn't really a hospital at all. There was no running water, no X-ray and no electricity except in the operating room. The main part of the "hospital" was a long, one-story building divided into small, dark rooms, each opening on a courtyard, where over a small smoky fire, the patient's family cooked all the meals because the savages were suspicious of being poisoned if their food was cooked by a stranger. The patients lay on wooden bunks covered with matting. Certainly not a sanitary, modern hospital! And, perhaps Dr. Schweitzer could have, and should have, done better, as his critics insist.

But let's say this for Dr. Schweitzer: *The conditions under which he worked were the most disagreeable, the most primitive, and the most dangerous in the world!* Modern hospital equipment could not be maintained under the steaming jungle conditions, even if it could have been obtained and people trained to operate it. Metal clips rusted at once. Rubber hot water bottles rotted in a week. The suspicious and superstitious native savages never would have even gone near a modern hospital. Dr. Schweitzer felt that he had to maintain an environment which was acceptable to the primitive natives whom he treated.

The really important thing is that Dr. Schweitzer turned away from the comforts, the pleasures, the fortune and the greatness which so easily could have been his in many fields—to fulfill his INTENSE BELIEF in the sacrificial way he chose to help the most needy of all humanity.

And Dr. Schweitzer—because of his INTENSE BELIEF in his holy mission—found the more divine greatness of a life based on the eternal lesson: *"It is more blessed to give than to receive."*

Chapter 39

He BELIEVED He Could Win Freedom For 400,000,000 People By Nonviolence!

In 1947, the mighty British Empire declared India an independent nation—*and 400,000,000 people had won their freedom without war or incited bloodshed—because of one little seventy-eight year old man who had no worldly possession except a dollar watch!* He had a greater possession—his INTENSE BELIEF *that violence* (*in rehetoric or action*) *produces no permanent solutions, and is counter-productive in attempting to force compliance!*

Mahatma Gandhi *was* India! He was so much a part that he lived in public 24 hours a day. He even slept on a mattress in public. All day long he saw his people of all classes, gave them advice, helped them with their problems. He had no secrets. Anyone could come and listen to the wisdom which the Mahatma spoke so freely.

Gandhi was born a caste Hindu but he identified himself with the Untouchables to encourage other Hindus to do likewise. One of his ambitions was to lead the Hindus to stop their cruel mistreatment of the Untouchables. He ordered sacred Hindu temples, which had been closed to the Untouchables for centuries, to open their doors to them and accept them.

But most of all, Mahatma Gandhi will go down (or perhaps I should say "up") in history *for teaching nonviolence as a way of life and proving its power by using it to free 400,000,000 people!* He so INTENSELY BELIEVED in the spirit of *nonviolence* that he staked the future of his vast country on it—and WON!

It is not the purpose of this chapter to tell the entire, remarkable story of Mahatma Gandhi's life, nor to record once again the history of India's independence movement. Those are matter for historians. This is a book on *how to get WHATEVER you want* by using *Personal Influence Psychology* and other success methods.

So, having just recounted one of the many remarkable achievements of *nonviolence,* I want to urge violence-prone individuals and groups to use only *nonviolent* methods which will get WHATEVER they want—*easier* and *faster* than if they use *pressure* (with real or implied *threats*), or if they use *varying degrees of violence—in words or action.*

It is a psychological fact that violent acts or threats of violence are immature, ignorant attempts *to reassure one's ego* (*self*) which for some reason has been *frightened* or *degraded*—and those who resort to violence are *over-compensating for inferiority.*

This leads to two obvious conclusions:

(1) If people are violent or threaten violence, they are trying to reassure their *frightened* or *degraded* egos (selves). Therefore, their *violence* or *threat of violence,* and even their *thoughts of violence* are evidence that *they inwardly feel frightened or degraded.* And, to the extent that *they inwardly feel* frightened or degraded, *they* actually *are* frightened or degraded . . . and, therefore inferior.

In any situation, especially in a competitive one, *the worst thing people can do is to expose their weakness*—and when they are violent or threaten violence, they clearly show that *they inwardly feel* (and, therefore, *are*) *frightened* or *degraded—and admit their inferiority by resorting to violence.* This puts them at a disadvantage which no show of violence by them can overcome!

(2) Furthermore, the *intended purpose* of violence or threats is to *intimidate others* in the hope *they* will become frightened and submit. This only compounds the problem because, if those who are threatened *do* become frightened, they will take some action (instant or deferred) *against* the person *causing* their fear. And, if they are not frightened, they will be *angered* by violence and strike back in anger.

People cannot win by violence! They may *seem* to win, but their "victory" will be *temporary*—because *they will have made an enemy* who simply is waiting for the most advantageous time for *him to retaliate!* And, in the meantime, those who have threatened violence will live in fear of the retaliation *which they know will come eventually!*

Now, let's consider several common actions

which are related to violence—and which also cause people trouble.

We have been considering violence as a form of *attack* on others. There are less violent forms of *attack* on others, and, being less violent, are more frequent—often daily—occurrances. Nevertheless, they are *attacks* on others and should be identified as such.

ARGUING is an *attack* on the opinions of others. And, an *attack* in any form incurs *instant resistance and hostility. You simply cannot benefit by incurring resistance and hostility!* Not in *any* way! *Ever!*

So . . . NEVER ARGUE! Never! Never! *Never!* No matter how *wrong* the other person is . . . no matter how *right* you are . . . NEVER ARGUE!

There are many *psychological* methods of presenting differing points of view without being *argumentative—without attacking* the opinions of others, *without incurring resistance and hostility.*

We shall devote an entire chapter to these *psychological methods* later in this book.

CRITICIZING is another method which commonly is used to *attack* others—and which, similarly, *incurs their resistance and hostility* . . . so do not use it!

NEVER CRITICIZE! Never! Never! *Never!* No matter how "*necessary*" it is to correct others ("*for their own good,*" *YOU think!*) . . . NEVER do so in the form of CRITICISM which is an *attack* on another's ego (self-esteem, self-pride, self-honor).

There are many *psychological* methods of improving others, "correcting" them, teaching them—which do not require the personal *attack* of CRITICISM—and we shall devote a later chapter to the effective use of such *psychological methods which accomplish better results without incurring resistance and hostility.*

To summarize: If Mahatma Gandhi could win from the powerful British Empire the freedom of the vast nation of India with its 400,000,000 people—by nonviolence—surely YOU can more easily attain YOUR life goal by *not attacking others and thus incurring their resistance and hostility* by threatening, arguing or criticizing.

Simply make *nonviolence* a way of life, by *always* observing these *Rules of Secure Success:*

(1) NEVER use *violence* of any kind!

(2) NEVER threaten *violence* in any way!

(3) NEVER even think *violent* thoughts!

(4) NEVER *argue*—which *attacks* another's opinion! Arguing creates resistance; incurs hostility

(5) NEVER *criticize*—which *attacks* another's ego! Criticism causes resentment—*always*.

People's egos (self-esteem, self-pride, self-honor) are their most treasured possessions. Any attack on people's egos or threat (real or implied) to people's egos incurs their instant hostility—and immediate or subsequent retaliation.

Most of the hostility and violence in this world —between nations, races, groups or individuals—is the result of attacks upon, or threats to, or degrading of other people's egos (their self-esteem, self-pride, self-honor—their *total* selves).

The tragic fact that this goes on, in some degree, *millions of times every day,* day after day—is why we live in an angry, hostile, violent world.

The cure is obvious.

It can start with YOU!

Chapter 40

She BELIEVED She Could Become The Greatest Woman Scientist!

Her maiden name was Manya Sklodowska. Perhaps no one has worked so hard, has been so dedicated to a seemingly impossible goal and has reached that goal *in spite of more privations and difficulties* than this poor Polish girl who became one of the greatest benefactors of mankind.

All because she INTENSELY BELIEVED that ultimately she would SUCCEED in her chosen task.

First, she had to study many years at a university. When I read about the antics of many of the "students" of our colleges and universities of today, I think of this Polish girl *who was so eager to learn that she was willing to live in a garret with no windows, no gas, no electric light and no heat! She could afford to buy only two sacks of coal all winter! She could afford so little food that she often fainted from starvation!*

She had virtually nothing but her INTENSE BELIEF that she would LEARN and SUCCEED!

Learn, she DID—*she became the greatest woman scientist in the world!*

Succeed, she DID—she *twice* won the Nobel Prize, once for outstanding achievement in physics and again for outstanding achievement in chemistry.

Why? Because she and her husband, working in a miserable shed under almost insurmountable difficulties, discovered and produced a new element—RADIUM—*and changed the course of science, medicine and the world!*

The greatest woman scientist in history—Madame Curie! She INTENSELY BELIEVED.

How can YOU complain of handicaps and hardships after reading about a life like that?

Do YOU *live in a garret with no windows? . . . No gas? . . . No electric light? . . . And no heat?*

Can YOU afford so little food that YOU often faint from starvation? *How many times have YOU fainted from starvation lately?*

Just what *is* YOUR complaint?

Do YOUR hardships compare with the hardships endured—and *triumphantly overcome*—by Madame Curie?

Then why have YOU not accomplished *more* than you have?

Is it because YOU have *not* INTENSELY BELIEVED that YOU *could* accomplish *more? Much more?*

Would YOU be willing to learn how to BELIEVE SO INTENSELY *that YOU would get WHATEVER you want?*

This book will teach you HOW to do it!

Chapter 41

She Was Deaf, Mute And Blind . . . But She INTENSELY BELIEVED!

Her INTENSE BELIEF accounts for the miraculous achievements of Helen Keller. *She had been deaf, mute and blind since early childhood. Yet, because she INTENSELY BELIEVED she could, she learned to speak!* So amazing were her accomplishments in all fields of learning and so dramatic was her ability to encourage and inspire the handicapped throughout the world that she and her teacher received the Roosevelt medal for "Cooperative Achievement of Unique Character and Far-reaching Significance."

Her mastery of speech had been called the "*greatest individual achievement in the history of education.*" *She INTENSELY BELIEVED she could!*

So great was her achievement that she was known around the world and her books were translated into many languages long before she frequently went to

Europe, then to the Orient—*always to inspire others to INTENSELY BELIEVE they, too, could overcome their handicaps!*

Her teacher and constant companion for a half-century, Anne Sullivan, deserves *equal* acclaim for Helen Keller's accomplishments. So justly great is Helen Keller's fame that it may be impudent for me to say that *Anne Sullivan, the teacher, was equally great!* Yet Anne Sullivan spent fifty years working THROUGH Helen Keller to reach and teach the handicapped. *And, after all, aren't each of us merely EXTENSIONS of those who have taught us?* Helen Keller would have been the first to say, "Yes!".

It is not my purpose to try to add to the well-known facts of the miracle of Helen Keller and her teacher, Anne Sullivan. Those facts are available in many books. I simply want to point my finger directly at YOU and say, "If Helen Keller, starting life as a blind, mute, deaf child could so INTENSELY BELIEVE that she could achieve inspiring greatness—*what do YOU, with your lesser handicaps, INTENSELY BELIEVE that you can accomplish?*

I have briefly described in this and the preceding chapters only a few of the thousands of lives that have been made great because of INTENSE BELIEF. You have been reading about *others* and how *they* succeeded by INTENSELY BELIEVING that they could succeed. *Now it's time to tell YOU how YOU can open the door to the Treasure Room of Success—how YOU can easily have everything you want in an abundant life here and now—by INTENSELY BELIEVING you can!*

Get ready to get *doing*—in the next chapters . . . which tells you HOW.

Chapter 42

INTENSELY BELIEVE
You Can Succeed!

In the previous chapters you learned how people who lived in different centuries throughout recent history SUCCEEDED.

In every great life there was ONE common ingredient—ONE quality which each person had: the INTENSE BELIEF that he or she could succeed! This INTENSE BELIEF enabled each person to succeed to the height of greatness in WHATEVER field he or she chose, whether it was creating lightning or being a medical missionary in primitive Africa or becoming the greatest woman scientist!

It doesn't matter *what* YOU choose to succeed in doing and obtaining. You can do and get WHATEVER you want! But you MUST do *these* things:

(1) You must decide *exactly* WHAT you want as *your* life-goal.

(2) You must INTENSELY BELIEVE *you will get it.*

(3) You must want it ENOUGH to *pay the price* to get it.

(4) You must use *proven success methods.* By using the proven success methods in this book, YOU can get WHATEVER you want!

Well, if success is that easy, why don't *more* people succeed? Simply because *they don't know how!* They are not *using* proven success methods—they are using failure methods which surely GUARANTEE their failing, just as using proven success methods will surely GUARANTEE their succeeding!

For example: Most people do not INTENSELY BELIEVE they can succeed. And unless they BELIEVE, hey can't possibly succeed! Yet they don't have confidence n themselves and they openly admit it.

In a survey, 600 university students were asked o name their biggest problem. Three out of four replied, *"Lack of self-confidence."*

Think of it! Three out of every four university tudents admitting that *lack of self-confidence* was their *iggest* problem! I wonder where the remaining fourth ated their lack of self-confidence. Second? Third? Wherver they rated it, if they lacked self-confidence *at all,* their niversity training would do them little good, because reember what psychologist Dr. Walter Scott, President of orthwestern University said, "Success or failure is caused ore by MENTAL ATTITUDES *than by mental capaties."* What kind of *attitude* do *you* have?

All the formal education in the world will not

help you *unless* you INTENSELY BELIEVE that *you will succeed.*

If you do INTENSELY BELIEVE that you will succeed—*even if you do not NOW have the necessary education—you will get it,* sometimes from unexpected opportunities which you never even imagined were available to you until you began to INTENSELY BELIEVE you would succeed. Not only the necessary education, but *everything necessary to your success will progressively become available to you* as you more INTENSELY BELIEVE you will succeed!

It is a Law of Life that BELIEF attracts to it all of the elements which make its realization possible.

Yet, for some stupid reason, *people continue failing to believe in themselves!* In another survey almost *nine out of every ten people* confessed that they suffered from *feelings of inferiority and inadequacy!*

Psychiatrists say that lack of self-confidence is perhaps the most common psychological complaint in America today.

Psychologists have found that people do not solve their problems—*not because their problems can't be solved*—but because people GET DISCOURAGED!

They get *discouraged!* WHY? Because they were not *born* rich? Because they were not *born* in an affluent neighborhood? Life didn't *give* them a break? They are *underprivileged?* They are *handicapped?*

Wasn't Helen Keller *handicapped? Deaf, mute, blind from childhood!* Go back and re-read the previous chapters in this book. Weren't the people whose lives were described in the previous chapters *underprivileged?* Yes,

ALL of them (with the possible exception of William Penn) *started life more underprivileged than anyone who will ever read this book!* Did their parents or a benevolent government send them to college? Only *one* of them! Yet their INTENSE BELIEF that they could succeed *opened the doors of education and training in their chosen fields* and they became the greatest in the world.

Difficulties didn't stop *them* from becoming great successes. They did not despair because they were handicapped or underprivileged! They didn't sit around and complain that life had not given *them* a break. And difficulties need not defeat YOU, if you are underprivileged or handicapped or haven't gotten a break.

Listen, life doesn't *owe* you a break! You've got to go out and *make your own!* How? By using the success methods you're holding in your hands right now!

The first job you have to do is to sell YOU on YOURSELF. If YOU aren't sold on YOURSELF – you never will be able to sell others on yourself or on your ideas!

Get in front of a mirror and give yourself a pep talk! *Some of the world's most successful people do that every day!*

Write a *commercial* about YOU and read it to yourself many times every day. That's another self-confidence-building method many successful people use.

Always WALK and ACT as though you had JUST CLOSED A MILLION DOLLAR DEAL!!! *This will change your whole attitude! You will walk, act and talk like a big success!* Everyone who knows you will immediately notice the improvement. It's the fastest, surest way to get and express the all-important "*success attitude.*" Try it—starting right now! Always WALK and ACT as though you had JUST CLOSED A MILLION DOLLAR DEAL!

LOOK like a SUCCESS! . . . TALK like a SUCCESS! . . . ACT like a SUCCESS! . . . THINK like a SUCCESS! . . . INTENSELY BELIEVE you *are* a SUCCESS! . . . And you will *be* a SUCCESS!

Radiate so much of the "*success attitude*" that other people will feel that *they* have to impress *you!*

Use the proven advice of Mrs. Reginald Fellowes, acclaimed as the "smartest woman in the world." She has been quoted as saying that before going into a big party or a big meeting, you should pause for a moment on the threshold and remind yourself that *you must enter that room as though you knew everyone there.* Then you will go in with the proper friendly and *self-assured* attitude.

You cannot succeed without radiating ASSURANCE—because radiating ASSURANCE is the *outer* expression of your *inner* BELIEF!

Memorize it! Make ASSURANCE a part of all your planning, all your thinking, all your attitudes, all of your talking, all your actions.

Here's how:

(1) You must PLAN with ASSURANCE. If you don't, your plans will be uncertain. You won't have the necessary confidence that they will succeed. You can't put all your driving force behind an uncertain plan.

(2) You must THINK with ASSURANCE. This will give your thoughts power, decisiveness, confidence, authority.

(3) You must always maintain the ATTITUDE of ASSURANCE. Remember that everyone radi-

ates an aura of magnetic vibration which reaches and impresses the subconscious minds of all other persons nearby. With a strong ATTITUDE of ASSURANCE, you impress everyone with *your certainty of success.*

(4) You must TALK with ASSURANCE. *This is the only way to be convincing!* The principal and usually the only reason a person will not do what you ASK him to do is that he is not absolutely SURE that what you ask him to do will *definitely benefit him.* So you must constantly ASSURE him that *he cannot lose* and that he SURELY *will benefit.* As taught previously in this book, don't pressure him with argumentative statements, but ASK him leading questions so that he will ASSURE himself by his own answers. Help him *convince himself!*

(5) You must ACT with ASSURANCE. Then all your actions will be forceful, direct, decisive.

And how do you get this ASSURANCE which is so important to your success?

You get ASSURANCE by INTENSELY BELIEVING *you will succeed* and by expressing ASSURANCE in all your planning, all your thinking, all your attitudes, all your talking, all your actions.

By INTENSELY BELIEVING, *you will express and you will have the ASSURANCE necessary for your success!*

And when this book—this SUCCESS COURSE—says "*success,*" it means: "*Success in getting WHATEVER you want.*"

So, having read, in preceding chapters, some remarkable examples of the unlimited POWER of INTENSE BELIEF, let us now apply that power to *your own life* . . . beginning in the next chapter.

Chapter 43

How You Can Get WHATEVER You Want—By INTENSE BELIEF

The power of INTENSE BELIEF is the basis of all the "miracle cures" and all other miraculous happenings throughout history. There have been many, and they cannot be explained except in terms of INTENSE BELIEF, *which truly can produce miracles!*

The power of INTENSE BELIEF has been the motivation and the sustaining strength of every important, successful, remarkable life that ever has been lived!

Preceding chapters have described how INTENSE BELIEF produced great lives. There is no point in recording further documentation here. The miraculous POWER of INTENSE BELIEF simply is beyond question.

So the only question for YOU is: how can YOU use this miraculous POWER of INTENSE BELIEF in *your own life?*

How can YOU use INTENSE BELIEF to *assure your own success?*

How can YOU use INTENSE BELIEF *to get WHATEVER you want?*

Learning how YOU can use the miraculous power of INTENSE BELIEF is so important to you—is so *vital* to your getting WHATEVER you want—that you will be given a *number of methods;* each method will be simply but thoroughly explained in one of the following chapters.

We shall start in this chapter by explaining the basic method of developing and using INTENSE BELIEF through *Personal Improvement Psychology.*

You use *three* "stages" or "levels" of Mind Power. These three levels of Mind Power are *described separately,* however, they *are not separate* but actually blend into each other; are inter-related and really are three parts of *one* Universal Mind.

These three levels of Mind Power as used in *Personal Improvement Psychology* are:

(1) Your *conscious mind.* This is your brain. It can be exposed by brain surgery and examined directly, or it can be studied indirectly through psychological tests. Your *conscious mind* (brain) is remarkably structured almost beyond description, but its functions are generally well known. It is that part of your mind with which you *consciously* think.

(2) Your *subconscious mind.* This is the part of your mind which operates regardless of your conscious control, which works every second, 24-hours-a-day, throughout your entire life to direct all of your bodily functions: heart-beat, breathing, digestion—*everything* which your living requires.

If you had to depend upon your *conscious mind* to think: "Now I instruct my heart to beat . . . now I instruct my lungs to breathe . . . now I instruct my stomach to digest food . . ." your *conscious mind* could not possibly manage, even for a minute, the *trillions* of sensorium nerve impulses required just to maintain your life and your activities. You would be dead in a minute.

So Nature, with an intelligence which we cannot even begin to comprehend, has provided each of us with an *unconscious mind* which most psychologists prefer to call the *subconscious mind,* because the word "unconscious" has a connotation of being inert and unaware—definitions that are the exact opposite of the amazingly total, continuous awareness and activity of the *unconscious mind* which, therefore, we shall hereafter call the *subconscious mind.*

In addition to controlling your bodily functions and performing many other services beyond your *conscious mind's* capability, your *subconscious mind* retains, throughout your entire lifetime, every thought and belief which you ever have had!

Not only does your subconscious mind retain every thought and belief you ever have had, but it uses them to build your character, your personality, and your actual life!

That is a fact worthy of your most serious attention. It means that *what you are now* (your character your personality, the kind of life you have) *is the RESULT of everything you ever have thought and believed!* If you don't like what you ARE now, you can blame only YOUR-

SELF and what you have thought and believed throughout your life to this very moment! Your *subconscious mind* has converted your thoughts and beliefs into YOU!

The supporting evidence—from the great religions, the great philosophies, the great thinkers, the great achievers—is quoted elsewhere in this book so we shall not repeat it here. It is enough merely to re-state that it is SO . . . it is conclusively PROVEN . . . it cannot be changed . . . you must build your life on this eternal principle: *You ARE the RESULT of everything you ever have thought and believed!*

Your *subconscious mind* has created YOU in the image of your total thoughts and beliefs. *It will continue to do so.*

There is another fact which has great bearing on the continuing process of your thoughts and beliefs in shaping and building your character, your personality and your entire life. That important fact is this: Your thoughts and beliefs influence your *subconscious mind* in *the exact degree of their INTENSITY.*

This means that a constant, violent hatred will influence your *subconscious mind,* and therefore your life and your future, much more than a mild, casual dislike. The difference is in INTENSITY.

Timidity is no virtue, but it will not kill you. But a terrifying, overwhelming FEAR *will kill you!* Because of its INTENSITY!

But let us continue our exploration of your *subconscious mind.*

Your *subconscious mind* is your own personal contact with the *Infinite Mind* (or *Universal Mind* or *Mas-*

ter Mind—whichever name your prefer). The author thinks that the name: *Infinite Mind* best defines it, because it actually is *Infinity: all knowledge* (past, present and *future*) . . . *all power* (unlimited and everlasting) . . . *all time* (eternity) . . . EVERYTHING . . . EVERY-WHERE . . . ETERNALLY. That's INFINITY.

Of course, our own little, inadequate human minds cannot begin to comprehend such vastness and we shall not attempt to describe what we cannot. We shall refer to the "mind" part of Infinity as the "*Infinite Mind*" in explaining the relation of your own *subconscious mind* to it. It is *your* source of *unlimited power!*

It has always been recognized that man is not sufficient unto himself; that to live in any meaningful way, man must be able to draw upon a greater Source of knowledge and power.

Infinite Wisdom has provided that channel of contact and supply through man's *subconscious mind*. It is through your *subconscious mind* that you can draw upon the *Infinite Mind* to materialize your INTENSE BELIEFS into the reality of your own life.

We shall discuss the three levels of Mind Power in more detail later. Our purpose here simply is to list them and their functions—so that you can start now to get WHATEVER you want through INTENSE BELIEF.

The three levels of Mind Power—or the *Three Minds*—through which you can channel your INTENSE BELIEFS to attain their materialization in your life, are:

(1) Your *conscious mind*
(2) Your *subconscious mind*
(3) The *Infinite Mind*

Your INTENSE BELIEF must start in your *conscious mind* because that is the mind which you *consciously*, knowingly, deliberately control.

Your *conscious mind* is your *thinking* mind, whereas your *subconscious mind* is your *producing* mind which can get WHATEVER it needs from the *Infinite Mind* which is the *source* of *infinite knowledge* and *infinite power*.

So, first you must decide WHAT you want in life: *happiness* . . . *love* . . . *success* . . . *wealth* . . . *influence* . . . *power* . . . *popularity* . . . *fame* . . . WHATEVER you want.

Having thoughtfully decided WHAT you want —you then *constantly* INTENSELY BELIEVE that you will *get* it. This takes place in your thinking *conscious mind*.

The object is to *deeply impress* into the receptive channels of your *subconscious mind* your INTENSE BELIEF that you will get WHATEVER you want. The more *constantly*, the more *repetitively*, the more *INTENSELY* you impress your BELIEF into your *subconscious mind*, the more your INTENSE BELIEF will *dominate* the cybernetic (goal-reaching) forces of your *subconscious mind*—and the more it will draw upon the *Infinite Mind* for the knowledge and power *to materialize your INTENSE BELIEF into reality*.

It may help you understand the functions of the *Three Minds* if you think of them this way:

Your *conscious mind* is the management which decides what the manufacturing plant (your *subconscious mind*) shall make of your life.

Your *conscious mind* (the management) gives instructions to your *subconscious mind* (the manufacturing plant) through INTENSE BELIEF. The more constantly and INTENSELY the BELIEF is held in your *conscious mind,* the more rapidly and exactly your *subconscious mind* will produce (materialize) it in your life. Your *subsconcious mind* does not reason; it accepts, *without question,* the instructions of your *conscious mind*—and converts those instructions into realities.

The *Infinite Mind* is the power plant with all the power necessary to convert your INTENSE BELIEF into reality. When properly called upon, the *Infinite Mind* will supply WHATEVER is needed to *fulfill* your INTENSE BELIEF.

The purpose of the preceding explanation of *Personal Improvement Psychology* is to give you a general understanding of how it works—because knowing "how it works" is a powerful motivation to use INTENSE BELIEF to get whatever you want.

However, it is *not necessary* to understand the *processes* of *Personal Improvement Psychology* in order to use the miracle power of INTENSE BELIEF to get what you want.

ALL you really NEED to know is this:

(1) The more INTENSELY you BELIEVE that you will get what you want, the surer you are to GET it. To *want,* to *wish,* to *hope* is *not enough.*

(2) The more you CONCENTRATE on *exactly* WHAT you want, the surer you are of getting *exactly* THAT. You cannot *concentrate* on *many* wants.

(3) The more *frequently* you CONCEN-

TRATE on INTENSELY BELIEVING that you will get what you want, the *faster* you will get it.

SUMMARY: You must INTENSELY BELIEVE you will get *exactly* what you want; you must *frequently* CONCENTRATE to make your BELIEF so much a part of you that *it will actually be YOU!*

There are a number of psychological methods which will enable you to *frequently* and *repeatedly* CONCENTRATE on your INTENSE BELIEF that you will get what you want.

The following psychological success-methods will make this CONCENTRATION *easy* and *fun*—and make your success *certain:*

(1) The "*Silent Chant*" Method
(2) The "*Knotted Rope*" Method
(3) The "*Magic Coins*" Method
(4) The "*Deck of Cards*" Method
(5) The "*Mental Picture*" Method
(6) The "*Repeating Card*" Method
(7) The "*Self-Hypnosis*" Method

We shall devote a brief chapter to explaining each of the foregoing methods—beginning *after the next chapter* which will tell you how to *Make Your BELIEF A Personal Slogan!*—which is the *first step* in each of the psychological success methods listed above.

Chapter 44

Make Your BELIEF A Personal Slogan!

You cannot INTENSELY BELIEVE in some *vague generality.*

You cannot CONCENTRATE on some *indefinate wish* that you will be successful . . . at something . . . some time . . . perhaps!

You do *not* need to impress your subconscious mind with *specific* instructions concerning HOW *it should proceed* in materializing what you want—but you *do* need to impress your subconscious mind with WHAT you want.

When you impress your subconscious mind with WHAT you want, it knows better than you (your conscious mind) exactly HOW to enable you to get it—and will proceed to do so in its *own* miraculous way!

So, first you must decide *exactly* WHAT you want. You must be able to put it into *words*—a brief, clear statement of WHAT you want—a *slogan* to sell your subconscious mind!

As every advertising man knows, a *slogan—frequently* (almost continuously) *repeated over a sufficient period of time*—makes an *intense impression* in the mind.

So, to make the necessary *intense impression* in your subconscious mind, you must word WHAT you want in the form of a *personal slogan.*

It's easy! Here's an example:

Suppose you have decided that you want to be rich; that you want to be able to afford anything money can buy.

You must impress your subconscious mind with WHAT you want: to be rich. But suppose you tried to impress your subconscious mind, by repeating silently to yourself, over and over, the following rambling statement of WHAT you want:

"I want to be very rich and have enough money to buy things I always have wanted but never could afford." That is a statement—*not a slogan.*

Just *try* to repeat *that* long statement—over and over! Then imagine what your subconscious mind will DO about it. I'll tell you: Your subconscious mind will do NOTHING about it!

So, to intensely impress your subconscious mind with WHAT you want: to be rich and have enough money, etc., etc., etc., you have to CONCENTRATE the words into a clear, brief *slogan.*

Try this *slogan:*

Make a million! . . . Make a million! . . . Make a million! . . . Make a million! . . . Make a million! . . . Make a million! . . . Make a million!

Read the above slogan—over and over again—for the *next five minutes!* Read it INTENSELY to yourself. Form the words with your lips to put more *force* into them! Make a *command* of this slogan!

Over and over again—*for the next five minutes* —INTENSELY read (or say) to yourself:

Make a million! . . . Make a million! . . . Make a million! . . . Make a million! . . . Make a million! . . . Make a million!

You can *actually feel* the INTENSE IMPRESSION this slogan makes on your subconscious mind!

Now, let's try another example:

Suppose WHAT you want is *happiness:* to be happy and to make others happy as you joyfully go through life.

You cannot repeat *all of that,* over and over again, to impress your subconscious mind.

So you CONCENTRATE it into a *slogan*—like this:

Have JOY!!! . . . *Give* JOY! . . . *Have* JOY!!! . . . *Give* JOY!!! . . . *Have* JOY!!! . . . *Give* JOY!!! . . . *Have* JOY!!! . . . *Give* JOY!!!

Repeat that slogan—over and over again—for the *next five minutes!* Read (or say) it INTENSELY to yourself! Form the words, silently, with your SMILING lips! Look at your *smiling self* in the mirror and *feel* filled to overflowing with the *joy* you are going to *share* with *everyone*—as you (*smilingly*) continue to repeat—silently or aloud:

Have JOY!!! . . . *Give* JOY!!! . . . *Have* JOY!!! . . . *Give* JOY!!! . . . *Have* JOY!!! . . . *Give* JOY!!!

You can *actually feel* the INTENSE IMPRESSION this slogan makes on your subconscious mind.

Now visualize what an INTENSE IMPRESSION you will make on your subconscious mind when you repeat one of these slogans (or one you write for another desire) . . . *over* and *over* again . . . *for five minutes* when you awake *every morning* . . . and *for five minutes* just before you go to sleep *every night* . . . and as *often* as you can *throughout every day* . . . *day after day* UNTIL YOU GET WHATEVER YOU WANT.

That is how you INTENSELY IMPRESS your life-goal into your subconscious mind!

That is how you COMPUTERIZE your subconscious mind to produce for you WHATEVER YOU WANT.

Your subconscious mind is like a computer. Computers now operate almost all complex mechanical devices. Your life is much more complex than any mechanical device, *so nature equipped you with a computer* (your subconscious mind) *to operate your life successfully* and to *produce* for you WHATEVER you "program" it to *produce*—through your INTENSE BELIEFS.

You COMPUTERIZE your subconscious mind by "programing" it: "feeding" into it the data (INTENSE BELIEFS) which it will use, in its own miraculous way, to produce *exactly* the kind of life *you instruct it to produce* through your INTENSE BELIEFS.

Just as an electronic computer produces whatever it is "programed" to produce by the data "fed" into it, so *your subconscious mind produces in your life whatever it is "programed" to produce* by your INTENSE BELIEFS "fed" into it.

The following chapters teach you how to COMPUTERIZE *your subconscious mind* so that it will *produce in your life:* WHATEVER YOU WANT.

Chapter 45

The "Silent Chant" Method

In the early days of man's development, primitive tribes used chants to intensify and express their beliefs. Chants began almost with primitive speech.

Primitive tribes, recently discovered in remote places, even now use chants just as their ancestors did thousands of years ago, and for the same reason: to intensify and express their beliefs *so that their beliefs would become realities.*

The early savages used chants and today's primitive tribes, living in remote regions, still use chants to increase their strength in battle, to impress their various gods with their needs and desires, and *to bring into reality their beliefs intensified by their chants.*

As civilization developed, *the use of chants continued.* Modern man still uses chants to CONCENTRATE THOUGHT and INTENSIFY BELIEF, *which is the purpose of chants.* In modern-day mass demonstrations, the demonstrators intensify their beliefs and project them by chanting in unison. Chants are used in all modern nations today. The litanies in some church services often are forms of chants, as are the repeated mystic affirmations of secret fraternal societies. Chants, in the form of school cheers, are used by all schools, colleges and universities.

Perhaps there is no form of mass psychology which has as long a history, and as universal an acceptance and use as chants. The use of chants: (1) to *concentrate thought,* (2) to *intensify belief,* (3) to *project belief*—from man's early beginning to *greatly increased use in modern times*—is proof of the effectiveness of chants for those purposes. So many *millions of people,* over a period of *thousands of years,* cannot *all* be wrong!

So let us accept the effectiveness of chants as an established fact and learn how to use chants in our own lives.

Chants do *not* have to be shouted or recited in unison by *groups,* but can be used *with equal or more effectiveness by individuals* (for example: YOU).

Chants do not have to be shouted, or even spoken *aloud.* Chants can be used *silently*—with or without lip movement. You can use a psychological SILENT CHANT anytime, anywhere, alone—or in the *presence of others without anyone knowing or even suspecting that you are using a psychological SILENT CHANT!*

A chant, as generally used, is not a type of song, although some forms of chants are sung in a monotone in some religious and other services.

The chants used in mass demonstrations rarely are sung. Neither are most school cheers. The characteristic which identifies a psychological chant is *rhythm,* or more specifically: a BEAT. The most effective chant, psychologically, is a chant which is a SLOGAN (see preceding chapter) with a BEAT ACCENTING EACH SYLLABLE.

For example: In the preceding chapter: "Make Your BELIEF A *Personal Slogan,*" it was suggested that a *slogan* which could be used to impress your subconscious mind with your INTENSE BELIEF that you would make a fortune, was: "*Make a million!*"

You convert that *slogan* into a psychological SILENT CHANT simply by ACCENTING EACH SYLLABLE, thus: "*Make'-a'-mill'-yun'!*" Try it. Say this chant silently to yourself, ACCENTING (*emphasizing intensely*) EACH SYLLABLE:

Make' - a' - mill' - yun'! . . .
Make' - a' - mill' - yun'! . . .
Make' - a' - mill' - yun'! . . .

Continue to repeat this chant silently to yourself for the *next five minutes.*

Drive this thought deeply into your subconscious mind by ACCENTING (*emphasizing intensely*) EACH SYLLABLE! *Feel the rhythm*—the BEAT—*as you intensely emphasize each separate syllable!*

"*Make' - a' - mill' - yun'!*"

As you repeat this chant, over and over again, silently—but *very intensely*—to yourself, you can *actually feel* this chanted command *being driven forcefully* into your subconscious mind!

You can *actually feel* the *greater intensity,* the *greater psychological force* which you achieve by using your personal slogan as a *chant!*

In composing a slogan to be used as a silent

chant, do not use long words with many syllables which cannot be accented into a forceful rhythm.

For example: While you probably would not want to use it in a slogan or chant anyway, the word "appreciated" does not produce a forceful rhythm when each syllable is accented. So you would *not* want to use "appreciated" in a slogan-chant: "I' - am' - a' - pre' - ci' - a' - ted'!" The word "appreciated" just is not chantable.

However, *some* long, many-syllabled words can be used, especially if you can combine syllables into a single BEAT, thus reducing the number of syllables accented (reducing the BEATS) in the long word.

For example: Suppose you want to improve your personality by becoming more enthusiastic. You could use the slogan-chant . . . *"I' - am' - enthus' - iastic'!"* Try that (as shown) by accenting only the first part and last part of "enthusiastic": *I' - am' - enthus' - iastic'!* . . . *I' - am' - enthus' - iastic'!* . . . *I' - am' - enthus' - iastic'!*

You will find that the preceding slogan-chant, *intensely repeated* over and over again, silently, but *enthusiastically*—will make an INTENSE IMPRESSION on your subconscious mind which will change you into an exciting, *enthusiastic* person!

Another example: You will find that some words which technically have two syllables, really "sound" better in a slogan-chant if you accent the *entire word* as *one forceful* BEAT.

Such a word is "power." Suppose you want to greatly increase your personal power. You would use the slogan: "I have power!"

But when you use this slogan as a chant, you *not* accent both syllables in *pow'er'* because the final *"er"* is distractive. So you would accent your chant: *"I' - have' - POWER'!"* Make the word *"POWER"* a *single,* explosive BEAT in your chant. Try it for *five minutes:*
I' - have' - POWER'! . . . I' - have' - POWER'! . . . I' - have' - POWER'! . . . I' - have' - POWER'! . . . I' - have' - POWER'!"

If you silently, but *intensely,* repeat the preceding chant over and over again—it will DEEPLY IMPRESS into your always receptive subconscious mind your INTENSE BELIEF that *you have POWER!* You will notice a feeling of increased confidence and personal power almost at once! As you continue your daily *frequent* repetition of this "POWER chant," you will INTENSIFY your awareness of *an increasing personal confidence and power.*

You *expand* your feeling of POWER by including the word "TOTAL" (*as one explosive beat*) in the rhythm of your POWER CHANT, thus:

I' - have' - TOTAL' - POWER'! (Repeat 10 times.)

Of course, when it improves the rhythm of the chant, you *can* use POWER as two syllables with a beat on *each* syllable: *POW'er'!* Then you can repeat the following "PERSONAL POWER" two-word chant, using *two beats* to each word:

PERS' -nul' - POW' -er'! . . . PERS' -nul' - POW'-er'! (Repeat 10 times.)

Get the *rhythm,* get the *beat*—by VOCALLY VERBALIZING. Here's how:

While you can use your slogan-chant silently—

even without moving your lips—so that nobody can see or know that you are using this psychological method, it is easier and more effective to VOCALLY VERBALIZE (chant aloud or at least in an *intense whisper*) *while you are perfecting the chant* you are going to use.

Be sure to go through all of the impulses and motions of speech (*using your breath, tongue, lips, etc.*) while speaking your chant *aloud* or in an *intense whisper.*

VOCALLY VERBALIZING (*aloud* or in an *intense whisper*) makes it much easier to get the *rhythm,* to get the *beat,* and to divide each word into *chantable syllables.* This is very important in composing your own slogan-chant or even a personal slogan.

Try VOCALLY VERBALIZING the following slogan-chants (which have *different* rhythms) until you *feel* the rhythmic beat of each chant. *Emphasize each beat* by tapping your fist into the open palm of your other hand. Imagine you are a cheer leader and *emphasize each beat!*

Repeat each slogan-chant ten times—or more until you *feel* the rhythmic beat like a school cheer.

Slogan-chants for HAPPINESS:

Have' - JOY'!!! . . . *Give'* - JOY'!!! (Repeat 10 times.)

or . . .

All'-ways' - HAP'-PY'!!! (Repeat 10 times.)

Slogan-chant for LOVE:

I' - LOVE'! . . . *I' - am - LOVED'!* (Repeat 10 times.)

Slogan-chant for SUCCESS:

Yes' - in'-deed' . . . I - SUC'-CEED'! (Repeat 10 times.)

Slogan-chants for WEALTH:

Make' - a' - MILL'-yun'! (Repeat 10 times.)

or . . .

Make' - a' - FOR'-chun'! (Repeat 10 times.)

Slogan-chant for INFLUENCE:

I' - *INFLU'*-ence' - *every'-body'!* (Repeat 10 times.)

Slogan chants for POWER:

I' - have' - *POWer'!!!* (Repeat 10 times.)

or . . .

PERS'-nul' - POW'-er'! (Repeat 10 times.)

or . . .

I' - have' - *TO'tal - POW'er!!!* (Repeat 10 times.)

Slogan-chants for POPULARITY:

I' - LIKE' - every'-body'! . . . They' - LIKE' - ME'!)Repeat 10 times.)

Make' - FRIENDS' - every'-WHERE'! . . . Make' - FRIENDS' - every-DAY'! (Repeat 10 times.)

Slogan-chant for FAME:

FAME' - and - (H)ON' - ors'! (Repeat 10 times.)

Note that the rhythmic timing of the different beats depends upon the emphasis you put on the various syllables in the word combinations.

In establishing the rhythm-beat of any of the preceding slogan-chants or in composing slogan-chants, yourself—it will be much easier and more effective if you VOCALLY VERBALIZE them (*aloud* or in an *intense whisper*), going through all of the impulses and motions of speech: *using your breath, tongue, lips, etc.*

Repeat each slogan-chant until you *feel* the

rhythmic beat. *Emphasize each beat* by tapping your fist into the open palm of your other hand! Imagine you are a cheer leader and that each slogan-chant is a school cheer! *Emphasize each beat!*

IMPORTANT: While we have used a *variety* of psychological *silent chants as examples,* you must decide WHAT YOU WANT MOST and then *concentrate* on *that*—and *only on that ONE objective—until you get it.*

Decide on ONE silent chant and continue to repeat that ONE silent chant . . . over and over again . . . for *five minutes* after you awake *every morning* . . . and *as often as possible* throughout *every day* . . . and for *five minutes* just before you go to sleep *every night. CONTINUE TO DO THIS UNTIL YOU GET WHATEVER YOU WANT.*

Then—and *only then*—should you begin a *different* silent chant.

At first, you may find it hard to CONCENTRATE on repeating your silent chant and your mind may be stimulated to think of something related to it, and wander away from the *exact words* of your silent chant. So the author has devised a number of psychological methods, each of which will enable you to CONCENTRATE INTENSELY on silently repeating your slogan-chant, over and over again, *for as long as you have time to do so.*

You may choose one or you may use any number of the different psychological methods of INTENSE CONCENTRATION described in the following chapters.

We shall start with "The *Knotted Rope* Method". . . in the next chapter.

Chapter 46

The "Knotted Rope" Method

The psychological technique which you must use to INTENSELY IMPRESS your slogan-chant into your subconscious mind is CONSTANT CONCENTRATION. *Intense constant concentration!*

It is desirable that you *constantly concentrate* on the *exact words* of your slogan-chant for periods of at least *five minutes.*

At first, you may find this difficult. Your slogan-chant, not only will be intensely impressed into your subconscious mind, but it also will stimulate your conscious mind, causing it to think about ideas related to your slogan-chant. This is desirable at all times *except when you specifically are concentrating on your slogan-chant.*

During your "concentration periods" of five minutes or longer, you must think of *nothing except the exact words* of your slogan-chant, repeating them over and over—without *any* other thoughts distracting your concentration.

So, to assure your complete, uninterrupted CONCENTRATION on your slogan-chant, the author has devised and will teach you various methods of *Psychological Concentration Control* beginning, in this chapter, with the "Knotted Rope" Method, as follows:

(1) Obtain a four-foot length of light-weight rope, such as a clothes line or window-sash cord.

(2) Tie simple knots in the rope at spaces of every two inches.

(3) Hold the end of the rope with your right hand.

(4) Grasp the first knot (nearest your right hand) between the thumb and forefinger of your left hand.

(5) While holding the first knot: silently but *intensely* repeat your slogan-chant *four times.* CONCENTRATE INTENSELY on each word of your slogan-chant *to impress it into your subconscious mind.*

(6) After you have silently, *intensely* repeated your slogan-chant four times while holding the first knot (nearest your right hand) between the thumb and forefinger of your left hand, slightly release your hold on the knot, and by pulling the end of the rope with your right hand, slip the rope through your left hand until your thumb and forefinger grasp the second knot.

(7) Hold the second knot firmly between the thumb and forefinger of your left hand, as you silently, *intensely* repeat your slogan-chant *four* times, CONCENTRATING INTENSELY on each word of your slogan-chant *to impress it into your subconscious mind.*

(8) Continue the foregoing procedure, pulling the knotted rope with your right hand and, as the knots

pass through the grasp of your left hand, *stop each knot* by gripping it between the thumb and forefinger of your left hand; hold it firmly, as you *intensely* repeat your slogan-chant *four times.*

(9) After you have pulled the knotted rope through your left hand, *stopping at each knot* as you *intensely* repeated your slogan-chant *four times,* continue to hold the unknotted *end* of the rope in your left hand *and grasp the last knot in your right hand.*

(10) Now, *repeat the procedure* by using your left hand to pull the rope slowly through your right hand, and stopping at *each knot* by grasping it firmly between the thumb and forefinger of your right hand, as you *intensely* repeat your slogan-chant *four times.*

(11) Continue to pull the knotted rope back and forth, stopping to grasp each knot as you silently, but *intensely,* repeat your slogan-chant *four times* as you hold each knot. Continue doing this for at least *five minutes* at a time.

The preceding "Knotted Rope" Method is a psychological CONCENTRATION INTENSIFIER, devised by the author to help you *focus your full concentration* on impressing deeply into your subconscious mind the slogan-chant which you have chosen to use to *get WHATEVER you want.*

It is most important that you *intensely concentrate* on your slogan-chant for at least *five minutes* after you awake *every morning* . . . and as often as possible throughout *every day* . . . and for at least *five minutes* just before you go to sleep *every night. CONTINUE TO DO THIS UNTIL YOU GET WHATEVER YOU WANT.*

Of course, it may not be convenient for you to carry your knotted rope with you throughout the day. Yet there are many "empty spaces"—unused minutes of time—every day which could *and should* be used to impress your silent slogan-chant more deeply into your subconscious mind.

So make a miniature reproduction of your knotted rope by substituting a two-foot length of cord, twine or heavy string. Tie simple knots in it, spaced one-inch apart. This will fit conveniently into your pocket or purse. *There is no better way to use minutes which otherwise would be wasted throughout the day and night—than to impress your silent slogan-chant more deeply into your subconscious mind.*

You also can do this by substituting *pocket change* for the knotted rope or cord . . . as described in the next chapter: "The '*Magic Coins*' Method."

Chapter 47

The "Magic Coins" Method

Of course, the coins in your pocket or purse are not magic, but they will *perform like magic* by enabling you to get WHATEVER you want.

Imagine a few coins, probably totaling less than a dollar, enabling you to get WHATEVER you want! Those few coins cannot do it by themselves, but they can help you "COMPUTERIZE" your subconscious mind so that *it* will work *constantly*, day and night, to bring into being the necessary conditions, circumstances, and cybernetic (goal-reaching) forces to *materialize* WHATEVER you *most intensely* and *most continuously* BELIEVE YOU WILL GET.

The psychological methods of INTENSELY IMPRESSING or "COMPUTERIZING" your subconscious mind have been explained in previous chapters. Now might be a good time for you to turn back and review those previous chapters, starting with the chapter: *How You Can Get WHATEVER You Want—by INTENSE BELIEF* (Chapter 43).

Our purpose now is to enable you to CONCENTRATE *intensely* for periods of five minutes or longer *exclusively* on the *exact words* of your slogan-chant expressing WHAT YOU WANT MOST.

You must not let your thoughts wander to related ideas which will be stimulated during your "concentration periods."

To enable you to CONCENTRATE *intensely* and *exclusively* on the exact words of your slogan-chant, you were taught the highly-effective, psychological "*Knotted Rope*" Method in the preceding chapter.

The "*Magic Coins*" Method is exactly the same as the "*Knotted Rope*" Method, except that you use a *different concentration object:* in this case, the coins you have in your pocket or purse.

(1) You should use at least three coins, and it would be better if you could use six or more coins.

(2) Hold the coins in one hand. Then put one coin at a time into your cupped other hand. When you put *each* coin into the other hand, repeat your slogan-chant, silently but *intensely,* four times.

(3) Continue placing coins into your initially empty hand and *each time you transfer a coin,* repeat your slogan-chant, silently but *intensely,* four times.

(4) When one hand is empty, immediately begin transferring coins, one at a time, back into it. And, *each time you transfer a coin,* repeat your slogan-chant, silently but *intensely,* four times.

(5) Continue doing this for five minutes if you have that much time, but use whatever time you have. The act of transferring coins, one at a time, will enable you to CONCENTRATE EXCLUSIVELY on impressing your

slogan-chant into your subconscious mind. Psychologically, you make repeating your slogan-chant *a conditioned response* to your act of transferring a coin from one hand to the other.

You can use this *"Magic Coin"* Method of controlling concentration when you do not have your knotted rope or knotted cord. Almost always you will have coins in your pocket or purse. You can use coins at home, but you will be able to concentrate more intensely by using your knotted rope.

Or you can control your concentration by using a deck of playing cards . . . as explained in the next chapter.

Chapter 48

The "Deck Of Cards" Method

This is another useful psychological method of INTENSIFYING CONCENTRATION.

Your objective is to "*computerize*" your subconscious mind so that it will function as a *cybernetic* (*goal-reaching*) *force* to bring into reality the INTENSE BELIEF expressed in your slogan-chant.

Your subconscious mind is your own private "computer" which functions very much like a space-ship's computer.

A space-ship's computer is its guidance system into which are programed the direction in which the space-ship is to travel and exactly where it is to land. The space-ship's computerized guidance system keeps the space-ship "*on course,*" *heading directly toward its destination until its goal is reached.* This is what you want your personal guidance system to do for you.

Your "computerized" subconscious mind is your personal guidance system. It has been "programed" (given directions) by everything you ever have intensely thought which, in accordance with *subconscious cybernetics* (mental guidance to a life-goal), has brought you to the place you now are in life.

If you do not like where you now are, remember that *your present position in life has been determined by all of your past thoughts* which, in varying degrees of intensity, were impressed into your subconscious mind throughout your entire life to this very second.

Your subconscious mind does not reason; it produces whatever your intense thoughts indicate to it you want in life.

Your subconscious mind does not and can not change the thought-influences which are its *only* instructions, nor can it decide whether or not what it is producing in your life is good or bad for you. Nor, is your subconscious mind in the least concerned about whether or not you like what direction your life is taking. It simply *produces—without questioning anything*—whatever your thoughts and actions *indicate* to it you want in life.

So if you "poison" your subconscious mind with thoughts of fear, failure, hate, violence, sickness, and despair—*your life will be the exact product of those thoughts and of your acts which are based on them.*

But if you direct your subconscious mind to produce your life based on thoughts of self-confidence, determination, courage, faith, love, goodwill, cooperation, and planned effort to reach a worthwhile goal—*your life will be the exact product of those thoughts and of your acts which are motivated by them.* Your subconscious mind will *produce* for you a life of *happiness . . . love . . .*

success . . . wealth . . . influence . . . power . . . popularity . . . fame . . . WHATEVER YOU WANT!

That is why it is so necessary for you to INTENSELY IMPRESS your slogan-chant into your subconscious mind so that WHAT YOU NOW WANT will *completely dominate* your subconscious mind and *forcefully control its future acts.* Thus you can overcome the influence of previous negative thoughts and acts by *dominating* your subconscious mind with your INTENSE BELIEF that *you will get WHATEVER you NOW want!*

That requires that you compose a slogan-chant which *exactly* expresses whatever you want MOST. Then you must cause the exact words of your slogan-chant *to completely dominate* and *forcefully control* the goal-direction of your subconscious mind by INTENSELY IMPRESSING your slogan-chant into your subconscious mind. This requires CONSTANT CONCENTRATION during frequent five-minute "concentration periods."

To enable you to concentrate intensely and exclusively on the exact words of your slogan-chant for periods of five minutes or longer, the author has devised a number of psychological methods, two of which have been taught you in preceding chapters: "The *Knotted Rope* Method" and "The *Magic Coins* Method."

The following *"Deck of Cards"* Method is almost exactly the same as the *"Magic Coins"* Method, except that you use a deck of regular playing cards instead of a handful of coins to maintain constant, intense concentration.

(1) On a table, desk or other flat surface, place *face down,* a deck of playing cards. It is necessary that you

keep all cards *face down* throughout your "concentration period."

(2) You must look at *only* the *backs* of the cards as you concentrate, because the varying numerals and designs on the faces of the cards will distract your attention and completely disrupt your concentration.

(3) Put the entire deck of cards *face down* on the flat surface in front of you. Then remove the top card—*keeping it face down*—and *prepare* to place it nearby to begin a *second* stack of cards. But as you *pick up* the card, CONCENTRATE as follows:

(4) As you pick up the top card, look intensely at the *back* of the card and *repeat your slogan-chant* silently but intensely—CONCENTRATING your full mental power on each syllable (*rhythm-beat*) of your slogan-chant. Intensely repeat your slogan-chant *four times.*

(5) Then place the card *face down* to begin a *second stack* of cards next to the original stack.

(6) Continue the sequence of picking up a card from the first stack, *concentrating on the back of it while you silently but intensely repeat your slogan-chant four times,* then placing it *face down* on a *second stack* of cards near the original stack.

(7) When you have removed all of the cards from the original stack and, having used each as a "concentration object," placed *all* of the cards *face down* in the second stack, then *reverse* the procedure and return each card to the original stack, as follows:

(8) As you pick up *each* card, before returning it to the original stack, look intensely at the *back* of the

card and *repeat your slogan-chant* silently but intensely—CONCENTRATING your full mental power on each syllable (*rhythm-beat*) of your slogan-chant. Intensely repeat your slogan-chant *four times.* Then place the card *face down* to rebuild the original stack of cards.

(9) Continue to transfer cards from one stack to the other, using the foregoing procedure, for *at least five minutes.* If you have time, continue this INTENSE repetition of your slogan-chant *for as long as you can maintain a state of intense, constant concentration.* Discontinue this procedure briefly—after a concentration period of at least five minutes—if your mind begins to wander from the *exact words* of your slogan-chant. But persist in trying to maintain a state of *constant concentration on the exact words for at least five minutes.*

Of course, you can substitute any quantity of *identical objects* for the deck of playing cards. For example: checkers, paper clips, blank 3 x 5 filing cards, or identical marbles (transferred from one container to an identical container, using as containers: cups, small bowls, etc.). You even can use the pages of a book—provided that you concentrate *with your eyes closed* so that you will not be distracted by whatever is printed on the pages.

After you have mastered the three basic methods of maintaining CONSTANT, INTENSE CONCENTRATION ("The *Knotted Rope* Method". . . "The *Magic Coins* Method" . . . "The *Deck of Cards* Method"), then we can proceed to even more effective methods of *ADVANCED Personal Improvement Psychology* . . . beginning in the next chapter: "The *Mental Picture* Method."

Chapter 49

The "Mental Picture" Method

Now you are going to take a big step up the ladder of psychology to SUCCESS!

In recent chapters, the lessons in this SUCCESS COURSE have used the effective techniques of *Personal Improvement Psychology.* If you have mastered them, if you have learned and practiced slogan-chants until you repeat your chosen slogan-chant *automatically* every moment that your conscious mind is not otherwise constructively occupied, then you are ready to use *ADVANCED Personal Improvement Psychology* to turn the words of your slogan-chant into MENTAL PICTURES.

This is one of the most powerful and effective of psychological techniques!

It enables you to transform the words, the verbal ideas of your slogan-chant into MENTAL PICTURES of *whatever* you want, and to *imprint* the MENTAL PICTURES of what you want *permanently* into your subconscious mind so that it will clearly understand *exactly* what you want—and *produce* it for you.

The power of pictures to materialize thoughts into reality must have been understood a century and a half ago by the great English poet and thinker, Samuel Coleridge, who wrote, "*A picture is an intermediate something between a thought and a thing.*"

Now, a hundred and fifty years later, YOU, through *ADVANCED Personal Improvement Psychology*, can transform your desire into a thought (slogan-chant), then visualize your slogan-chant into a MENTAL PICTURE, and *imprint* that mental picture permanently into your subconscious mind which will *materialize your mental picture into reality in your life!*

In the preceding chapters, we have been concentrating on the *words* which you have chosen as your personal slogan-chant to impress into your subconscious mind your INTENSE BELIEF so that you will get WHATEVER you want.

You need to *continue* expressing your INTENSE BELIEF in *words*—in your silent *slogan-chant* exactly as you learned in the previous chapters. *Continue to do this!*

Continue to use your silent slogan-chant exactly as instructed in the preceding chapters.

But now you will use MENTAL PICTURES *in addition* to your slogan-chant.

You will use MENTAL PICTURES to *supplement* your slogan-chant.

Precisely, you will use MENTAL PICTURES to *reinforce* the *intensity of the impression* your slogan-chant imprints into your subconscious mind.

Remember, the more *intensely* you imprint

WHAT YOU WANT into your subconscious mind, the *surer* you are of getting it, and the *faster* you will get it.

As important and necessary as it is to *begin* by putting WHAT YOU WANT into *words*, you will greatly *intensify* their impression into your subconscious mind if you *reinforce* your words (slogan-chant) with MENTAL PICTURES.

As the old Chinese proverb says, "*One picture* is worth a *thousand words.*"

This especially is true of MENTAL PICTURES used to *reinforce* and *intensify* the impression which your slogan-chant imprints into your subconscious mind.

Let's look at some examples of MENTAL PICTURES which can be used with one of the slogan-chants listed in a recent chapter:

Slogan-chant for WEALTH:

Make' - a' - MILL' yun'! . . . Make' - a' - MILL' yun'! . . . Make' - a' - MILL' yun'! . . . Make' - a' - MILL' yun'! (Repeat 30 times.)

Then, *add to the intensity* of that slogan-chant by visualizing the following MENTAL PICTURES of WEALTH—to *reinforce* the slogan-chant.

Visualize, imagine, MENTALLY PICTURE what you WILL do with the WEALTH which you *intensely believe* you are going to get. Imagine that you NOW HAVE your million dollars. *Visualize yourself as a millionaire* . . . successful . . . assured . . . confident . . . secure . . . influential . . . powerful! MENTALLY PICTURE *yourself* wearing expensive clothes . . . driving your favorite luxury car! MENTALLY PICTURE your beautiful, expensive home . . . your big yacht cruising in tropical seas . . . the successful businesses you own . . . your stocks, bonds, jewels, and other investments . . . and more! *Intensify your million dollar mental picture of yourself!*

During every "concentration period" (as described in preceding chapters) . . . *reinforce* and *intensify* your slogan-chant with MENTAL PICTURES of *exactly what* your slogan-chant *will produce in your life! Intensely imagine! Intensely visualize!* MENTALLY *see yourself already having and enjoying what you want!*

Intensely believe that you will get WHATEVER you MENTALLY PICTURE and impress into your subconscious mind by concentrated repetition!

Because *that* is what you *will* get!

How can you visualize *clear, definite* MENTAL PICTURES?

Here are some of the easiest and best psychological methods:

It is easier to visualize a clear MENTAL PICTURE if you look at an *actual picture* of what you want. For example, suppose you want to impress into your subconscious mind MENTAL PICTURES of the WEALTH which you instruct it to *produce* for you with your slogan-chant: *Make' - a' - MILL' yun'! . . . Make' - a' - MILL' yun'! . . . Make' - a' - MILL' yun'!* Then do this:

Make a scrap-book of *actual pictures* illustrating the outer evidences of WEALTH. Get a fashion magazine; cut out and paste in your scrap-book illustrations of attractive, expensive clothes and fashion accessories. *Look at these actual pictures intensely,* then MENTALLY PIC-

TURE *you wearing these expensive, fashionable clothes!* While holding these MENTAL PICTURES before your subconscious mind, intensely repeat your slogan-chant: *Make' - a' - MILL' yun'! . . . Make' - a' - MILL' yun'! . . . Make' - a' - MILL' yun'!* (Repeat 30 times.)

Then go to the showroom of a dealer of your favorite luxury car. Ask for an illustrated folder showing the most expensive models. Cut out the color pictures of "your" car and paste them into your Million-Dollar Scrap-Book. *Look* at these *actual pictures intensely* and MENTALLY PICTURE *your owning this luxury car!* While holding this MENTAL PICTURE before your subconscious mind, intensely repeat your slogan-chant: *Make' - a' - MILL' yun'! . . . Make' - a' MILL' yun'! . . . Make' - a' - MILL' yun'!* (Repeat 30 times.)

Continue to obtain and paste in your Million-Dollar Scrap-Book *actual pictures* of the things you will buy *when you make a million! Look at these actual pictures intensely* as you MENTALLY PICTURE *your owning the expensive luxuries they illustrate.*

Get a magazine which features pictures of beautiful and expensive homes, and paste these pictures in your Million-Dollar Scrap-Book. *Look at these actual pictures intensely as you* MENTALLY PICTURE *your owning such a home!*

Subscribe to or go to the library and *regularly* read a leading financial newspaper, such as the *Wall Street Journal.* Saturate your thinking with money, stocks, bonds, investments. MENTALLY PICTURE *you deciding how you will invest your million dollars!*

Each time you hold a MENTAL PICTURE of

WEALTH before your subconscious mind, repeat your slogan-chant: *Make' - a' - MILL' yun'!* . . . *Make' - a' - MILL' yun'!* . . . *Make' - a' - MILL' yun'!* (Repeat 30 times.)

While the preceding example shows how to create MENTAL PICTURES of WEALTH you can use the "*scrap-book and relevant activities*" principle to enable you to clearly visualize WHATEVER you want. Then use MENTAL PICTURES *of your actually having it* to *reinforce* and *intensify* your slogan-chant instructions to your subconscious mind.

Your use of this miraculously effective method of *ADVANCED Personal Improvement Psychology* several times or more *every day*—combined with *your constant use of the other success methods in this book*—will enable you to GET WHATEVER YOU WANT.

Another technique of *ADVANCED Personal Improvement Psychology* which applies intense concentration to imprinting MENTAL PICTURES into your subconscious mind is the "*Repeating Card*" Method . . . as taught in the next chapter.

Chapter 50

The "Repeating Card" Method

In the preceding chapter, you began to learn how to visualize MENTAL PICTURES of WHAT YOU WANT, and to imprint those mental pictures into your subconscious mind.

This is the same as giving your subconscious mind a blueprint showing how you want it to build your future!

In the preceding lesson you were taught how to transform the *words* of your chosen slogan-chant into MENTAL PICTURES which would *supplement* and *intensify* the exact words of your slogan-chant.

Now you will learn an easy psychological method for *combining* the *words* of your slogan-chant with MENTAL PICTURES of your WHAT YOU WANT as expressed in those words.

Use the following *"Repeating Card"* Method:

(1) Obtain a set of 3″ x 5″ blank filing cards, any quantity from 6 to 20. You may use larger cards. Blank

filing cards also may be obtained in 4″ x 6″ size. The size is not important, just so the cards are convenient to handle.

(2) Obtain a thick-stroke marking pen filled with whatever dark colored ink appeals to you: black, red, blue, purple or green.

(3) With the thick-stroke marking pen, *print the words of your chosen slogan-chant* on one side of *each* of the cards. Try to make the printing on each of the cards as nearly like that on all of the other cards as possible. Be sure none of the printing contains an error—even a corrected error. (What you do *not* want to do, is to imprint an *error* into your subconscious mind!)

(4) Or, to save time and effort—and to be sure each card looks *exactly* like all the rest—have a small printer print your slogan-chant in very bold type on a quantity of 3″ x 5″ or 4″ x 6″ cards. This will cost only a few dollars and you can have an extra supply of a hundred replacement cards printed at very slight additional cost since most of the small cost will be in setting your slogan-chant in type. (However, this method will work just as successfully with hand-lettered cards.)

(5) Whether you personally hand-letter your cards or have them economically printed by a printer, you then will have a set of convenient cards with your chosen slogan-chant identically printed on each card. Use these cards first to impress the *words* of your slogan-chant into your subconscious mind. Place all of the printed cards in a stack—*face up*—so that you can see the slogan-chant in print.

(6) Look *intensely* at your slogan-chant printed on the top card. Read your slogan-chant silently—

but very intensely—10 times. Then place the top card—*face up*—on the bottom of the stack (or deck) and look *intensely* at the *next* card. Of course, it will display exactly the *same* slogan-chant as the first card. Read this *same* slogan-chant *again*—silently, *but very intensely*—10 times. Then place it—*face up*—on the bottom of the stack, and look *intensely* at the *same* slogan-chant printed on the next card.

(7) Continue the foregoing procedure for at least five minutes—preferably much longer if you have the time. Do this as soon as you wake up *every morning* . . . and as often *throughout the day* as you can find the time . . . and just before you go to sleep *every night*.

Why have a *stack of cards*, all with the *same* slogan-chant printed on *each* card? The reason is that, unless you have exceptional powers of *concentration*, you cannot continue to concentrate on a *single* card for a *long period of time*. The monotony will dull the intensity of your concentration and your mind soon will begin to wander along thought-paths which become day-dreams.

But the act of *changing cards* . . . of *beginning to concentrate again* on a *new card* (even though it displays exactly the *same* slogan-chant) . . . *breaks the monotony of looking at the same card* . . . and *thereby renews and re-focuses your intense concentration* as you expose each new card.

This is the same psychological principle used in the "*Knotted Rope*" Method, the "*Magic Coins*" Method, and the "*Deck of Cards*" Method. By thus changing your "*concentration object*," especially to another *identical* object, you *renew and re-focus your intense concentration*.

The next step in the *"Repeating Card"* Method described in this chapter, is to MENTALLY PICTURE what your chosen slogan-chant (printed on each card of the stack of cards before you) will *produce* in your life.

Let's continue to use as an example, as we did in the preceding chapter, the slogan-chant for WEALTH.

(1) Print or have printed on a quantity of 3″ x 5″ or 4″ x 6″ blank file cards the slogan-chant for WEALTH: *Make a MILLION!* Note that you do *not* print it phonetically as a chant: *Make' - a' - MILL' yun'!* You print it as a *command* to your subconscious mind: *Make a MILLION!*

(2) Place the printed cards in a stack in front of you—*face up*—so that you can *look intensely* at the printed slogan-chant: *Make a MILLION!* on the top card.

(3) As you *look intensely* at the slogan-chant printed on the top card: *Make a MILLION!* read this slogan-chant silently but *intensely* 10 times.

(4) After you have read the slogan-chant *intensely* 10 times, *continue to look intensely at the printed words,* while in your mind you visualize MENTAL PICTURES of what *you will do* with the WEALTH which you *intensely believe* you are going to get. Imagine that you NOW HAVE your million dollars.

(5) *Visualize* . . . MENTALLY PICTURE *yourself as a millionaire* . . . successful . . . assured . . . confident . . . secure . . . influential . . . powerful! MENTALLY PICTURE *yourself* wearing expensive clothes . . . driving your favorite luxury car! MENTALLY PICTURE your beautiful home . . . your big yacht cruising in tropical seas . . . the successful busi-

nesses you own . . . your stocks, bonds, jewels, and other investments . . . and more! *Intensify your million dollar picture of yourself*—as long as you can concentrate on it!

(6) As soon as you begin to lose concentration, as soon as your thoughts begin to wander away from your MILLION DOLLAR MENTAL PICTURE, *remove the top card*. Place it, *face up*, on the bottom of the stack of identical cards in front of you.

(7) As you remove the top card, *you expose the identical card which was beneath it*—and you will be looking at the identical slogan-chant for WEALTH: *Make a MILLION!* Repeat the *entire* MENTAL PICTURE sequence for WEALTH, as described in (5).

(8) Continue this procedure, repeating it over and over again, for as long as you have time to do so. Begin with 15-minute "concentration periods" and increase each period to 30 minutes whenever you have time. *Find the time every day*, preferably several times every day, for this MENTAL PICTURE method of impressing instructions into your subconscious mind, directing it to produce WHATEVER YOU WANT.

INTENSELY BELIEVE *that your subconscious mind, having been instructed as described in this and preceding chapters, will materialize (produce) in your life WHATEVER YOU WANT!*

WEALTH has been used as an example, but you do not need to choose *wealth*—you can choose and GET WHATEVER YOU WANT . . . *happiness . . . love . . . success . . . wealth . . . influence . . . power . . . popularity . . . fame . . . . WHATEVER YOU WANT!*

Your chosen slogan-chant and MENTAL PICTURES will "computerize" the cybernetic (goal-reaching) power of your subconscious mind to enable you to get WHATEVER YOU WANT.

Note the words: "enable you"—because they mean that *you* have to do the *getting!* YOU have to do *your part!* That means *you* have to *become involved* in your INTENSE BELIEF! YOU have to *cooperate* with the cybernetic (goal-reaching) power of your subconscious mind!

Your subconscious mind will produce the ideas, the actual opportunities, the exact means of GETTING WHATEVER YOU WANT. Your subconscious mind—with whatever help it needs from the Infinite of which it is a part—will provide all of the power and whatever else you need, but YOU MUST USE IT!

What *exactly* must YOU do?

You must use the success methods given you in this book—this SUCCESS COURSE—chapter after chapter, page after page.

You do not have to wonder about *what* you should do.

Just do what this book—this SUCCESS COURSE—teaches you to do. Use these success methods . . . confidently . . . persistently . . . continuously.

If you do—YOU WILL GET WHATEVER YOU WANT.

Chapter 51

The "Self-Hypnosis" Method

You have been studying psychological methods by which you can give instructions to your subconscious mind so that it will use its cybernetic (goal-reaching) power *to materialize into your life* WHATEVER YOU WANT.

The methods taught in preceding chapters used your *conscious* mind as a *high-intensity instrument* to implant your desires and instructions deeply and permanently into your *subconscious* mind. All of the methods taught are extremely effective!

There is another method, which uses the *opposite* technique, but which is *so very effective* that we must also include it.

Instead of *activating* and *intensifying* your *conscious* mind, you will *lull* it into a state of *deep relaxation* so that you can practically *by-pass your conscious mind* and implant your desires and instructions *directly into your unquestioning, receptive subconscious mind.*

You will remember learning elsewhere in this book that your *conscious* mind is your *reasoning* mind. This, of course, is desirable and necessary—otherwise you could not function at all as a thinking human being.

However, the insistence of the *conscious* mind on *reasoning* can interrupt, delay and impede the concentrated implanting of your desires and cybernetic instructions into your *receptive, unquestioning subconscious.*

Your *reasoning conscious mind* may interrupt by asking, "*Why* should YOU be wealthy?" That may be a subject for philosophical meditation, but we are dealing here—*not with the philosophy*—but with the *psychology* of making you WEALTHY or getting you WHATEVER else you want.

What you want is success—not a philosophical debate with yourself!

So it is desirable to know how you can lull your reasoning, questioning, debating *conscious* mind *into virtual inactivity* so that you can *by-pass* it and implant your WANT (slogan-chant) directly into your *receptive, unquestioning subconscious mind.*

You do this with SELF-HYPNOSIS.

Don't let this method scare you! Actually there is nothing dangerous about *complete* self-hypnosis, but the method you are going to learn does not go even that far. It is only *partial* hypnosis—just enough to by-pass your *conscious* mind and implant your WANT and instructions *directly* into your *subconscious* mind.

The technique is to lull your *conscious* mind into *deep relaxation.* This is a mild and completely harmless form of partial self-hypnosis. While your *conscious* mind is *deeply relaxed* (almost asleep) you can impress your WANT (slogan-chant) and instructions *directly* into your *subconscious* mind and your *subconscious* mind *will do what you tell it to do* (provided that your instructions under full or partial hypnosis are not dangerous, immoral or embarrassing, because *in response to such improper hypnotic instructions, your subconscious mind positively will not act*).

Here's how to use a mild, highly effective form of self-hypnosis to implant your WANT (slogan-chant) *directly into your subconscious mind,* reinforced by instructions to bring it into reality with all possible speed:

(1) Go into a room which has as little light as possible.

(2) Eliminate as much noise or other distractions as possible.

(3) Sit very relaxed in a comfortable chair (it's all right to lie down, but then most people go to sleep when they use self-hypnosis while lying down).

(4) Close your eyes and say quietly to yourself: "I am now completely relaxed . . . every part of my body is completely relaxed . . . loose . . . very loose . . . completely relaxed."

(5) When you feel so completely relaxed that you are almost asleep, say quietly to yourself, "I am now sinking into a deeper state of relaxation . . . deeper . . . deeper . . . down . . . down . . . my legs feel heavy . . . very heavy . . . my hands feel heavier and heavier . . . my eyelids feel heavier and heavier . . . so heavy . . . closed . . . relaxed . . . closed."

(6) When you have reached as deep a state of

relaxation as possible without going to sleep (and this will take some practice) silently repeat your slogan-chant 10 times. Unlike the intense, forceful concentration used in other methods—*when you repeat your slogan-chant under partial self-hypnosis, you should do so with easy self-assurance,* so that you will not re-activate your *conscious* mind which you want to by-pass. Under the deep relaxation of partial self-hypnosis: "*easy does it.*"

(7) Remain *deeply relaxed*—just one level above actual sleep. After you have silently repeated your slogan-chant 10 times, begin to visualize MENTAL PICTURES of WHAT YOU WANT as you were taught to do in the preceding chapters.

(8) Continue visualizing MENTAL PICTURES of *your actually having WHATEVER you want.* Do this as long as you can maintain your state of hypnotic deep relaxation.

(9) Use this "*Self-Hypnosis*" Method at least twice a day—*especially just before you go to sleep at night.* Just before you drift off to relaxed sleep, *repeat* the following hypnotic suggestion to yourself: "I shall *continue* these MENTAL PICTURES while I sleep."

This "*Self-Hypnosis*" Method is easy to learn with a little practice; it is simple to use; and it produces fast, often *miraculous results!*

Chapter 52

PROOF Of The Power Of INTENSE BELIEF

How strong *is* the power of INTENSE BELIEF? Well, it will *multiply* personal power!

Here are some *exact* figures: Three men were given this same test. It was a physical test to measure on an accurate grip-meter the strength of the physical grip in the hands of these three men.

The average grip of these three men under normal conditions was 101 pounds.

Then the three men were put under hypnosis and it was impressed into their subconscious minds that they were "very weak . . . very weak . . . *very weak . . . that their grip was very weak.*" Then, they were given the same grip-test again and their average grip was *only 29 pounds!* Because they BELIEVED (under hypnosis) that they were *very weak*, they actually *lost more than two-thirds of their strength!*

Then, while still under hypnosis, these same three men were impressed—through suggestions to their subconscious minds—that they were men of "great strength . . . very strong . . . super men . . . *with a powerful grip*." They were given the same grip-test again and because they BELIEVED (under hypnosis) that they were *very strong, their average grip was 142 pounds!* BELIEF *alone* increased the strength of their grip 40% ABOVE NORMAL!

BELIEF alone that they were very strong increased the strength of their grip FIVE TIMES MORE than when they BELIEVED they were weak!

This is amazing proof—by actual physical tests—of the power of BELIEF!

If INTENSELY BELIEVING can give you *five times more* PHYSICAL POWER—just think how *much more* your INTENSE BELIEF will *multiply* your POSITIVE PERSONAL POWER! There is no meter, no mechanical means of measuring the *tremendous increase* you will get in POSITIVE PERSONAL POWER when you INTENSELY BELIEVE you will get what you want in life. The definite proof is that *everyone who has ever succeeded* has INTENSELY BELIEVED he would succeed—and the *degree of success* has been in *direct proportion* to how INTENSELY each person really BELIEVED that he would succeed.

How the power of INTENSELY BELIEVING has miraculously improved the lives of well-known people has been described in various chapters in this book. And these examples are but a few. Entire libraries could be filled with volumes describing the successful lives of men and women whose success is the *direct result* of their INTENSE BELIEF in themselves and in what they wanted to achieve.

Then INTENSELY BELIEVE!

BELIEVE with the faith of millions of farmers throughout the world *who take all the grain they have and throw it on the ground!* They have many, many bags of good grain and they scatter it all over the ground until it is all gone. They have nothing left!

Nothing left? Why, *they have the most important thing left*—their BELIEF that the grain will take root and grow! They have their BELIEF that the grains thrown on the ground will produce many more grains in great abundance so that the people of the world will be fed.

You must PLANT before you can HARVEST. There is a great lesson here that applies to life in many vital ways, but, for the moment, we'll pass it by and go on to the other important fact we learn from farmers:

YOU WILL HARVEST EXACTLY THE SAME THING YOU PLANT!

That great fact does not apply only to farm crops. *It applies to the BELIEFS you plant in your subconscious mind!* We discussed that in some detail in preceding chapters, but it is so important I want to emphasize it again.

If you plant in your subconscious mind the BELIEF that you will be a failure—you can only harvest failure! Just as the farmer who plants corn can only harvest corn.

A farmer who planted wheat wouldn't expect to harvest beets! He would know that according to Natural

Law he could only expect to harvest what he planted—wheat. So if you foolishly plant in your subconscious mind the BELIEF that you will be a victim of physical or mental illnesses, this is just as certain as when the farmer plants wheat, he harvests wheat.

Plant, in your subconscious mind, the INTENSE BELIEF *that you will harvest happiness, love, health, wealth, success, popularity, fame,* or WHATEVER *good* things you want. By Natural Law (*which cannot be changed even to the slightest extent*) you will harvest a great abundance of *happiness, love, health, wealth, success, popularity, fame,* or WHATEVER you want, because with INTENSE BELIEF *that* was what you planted in your subconscious mind as your *most-wanted* objective in life.

How do you know YOU are *capable* of obtaining *whatever* you INTENSELY BELIEVE? Again we turn to Natural Law, the Law of the Universe. According to Natural Law: "The INTENSE BELIEF that *you will get a specific thing* or *achieve a specific accomplishment* is Nature's way of telling you that *you have,* or *you will receive, everything you need* for getting or accomplishing WHATEVER YOU BELIEVE you will get or accomplish.

Whatever the mind of man can conceive and BELIEVE, man can achieve!

No obstacle can withstand the enthusiasm and persistence based on INTENSE BELIEF.

I do not believe in magic; I believe in Natural Law. And, yet, there is something like magic in the power of INTENSE BELIEF. Concentrated INTENSE BELIEF in your ability to do a certain thing, *somehow* gives you the *extraordinary* power to *do* it!

It is as though some unseen hand removes obstacles, arranges circumstances in your favor, provides the necessary personal contacts and mysteriously guides you to achieve what you INTENSELY BELIEVE you can do!

I don't believe in magic but I have to admit that *strange, extraordinary happenings inevitably accompany INTENSE BELIEF!* There is too much *proof*. There is too much *scientific evidence*. And, of course, I know the things which have happened to me personally as the result of my own INTENSE BELIEFS.

No, INTENSE BELIEF isn't magic. It's a part of Natural Law—like electricity. And some day perhaps we'll know *exactly* how INTENSE BELIEF works. But for now, let's accept the power of INTENSE BELIEF as we accept the power of electricity. We don't know *all* about electricity. But we do know *how* to use it—so we *do* use it for our own benefit and for the benefit of mankind.

We don't know *exactly how* INTENSE BELIEF, through our subconscious minds, accomplishes its amazing results—but, like electricity, we know *how to use* the tremendous power of INTENSE BELIEF as taught in this SUCCESS COURSE. So, like electricity, let's USE the power of INTENSE BELIEF for our own benefit and the benefit of mankind!

Now, let's take a moment to examine a few more examples of the POWER OF INTENSE BELIEF:

In the entire history of track meets, ever since accurate time records had been kept, it was BELIEVED (based on those time records) that *nobody* could run a mile in 4 minutes because NOBODY ever had done it. And it was BELIEVED so INTENSELY that *nobody did!*

Then, to the astonishment of the athletic world,

one track star *did* run a mile in 4 minutes! So then *everybody* suddenly BELIEVED that a mile *could* be run in 4 minutes or less. And now *every* good miler runs the mile in less than 4 minutes! It is just a matter of BELIEF.

That has been true of all sports records. A record may stand for many years and everybody BELIEVES it represents the ultimate in human capacity. Then someone breaks the supposedly unbreakable record. So *everybody* then BELIEVES it is possible after all—and the old supposedly unbeatable record is broken with such regularity that it becomes obsolete.

That same principle applies to everything in which the power of BELIEF can be brought to bear. Consider achievements in outer-space. Many years ago, here in America, we BELIEVED it would take many years (if ever) to put a space-craft into orbit in outer-space.

Then suddenly one day the world was electrified by the astounding news that the Russians had launched their first Sputnik and that this pioneer space-craft was successfully orbiting the world in outer-space.

THEN WE REALLY BELIEVED it could be done! And spurred on by our BELIEF, we quickly began producing and launching our own space-craft to orbit the world . . . then to land on the moon . . . then to explore the vastness and mysteries of outer-space.

So the new era of exploration of outer-space was begun and accelerated *on a colossal scale* because we KNEW then that it COULD be done—it HAD actually been done—and we INTENSELY BELIEVED we could achieve accomplishments in this new field which formerly were thought to be years in the future, if not entirely impossible.

What really made the difference? Why did all these things *suddenly* become possible? Because we INTENSELY BELIEVED we could do it!

The power of BELIEF is dramatically demonstrated by the fluctuations of the prices of stocks on the stock market. Sometimes the price of a stock will rise or fall drastically *in one day*. The *change* in the total value of a large corporation's *stock* may amount to *millions of dollars in just one day!*

Why? Because investors BELIEVE the price of that company's stock is going to go up or down. Often—more often than not—it is *solely* a matter of mass BELIEF. The *actual* value of that company's stock probably hasn't changed at all, *in that one day*, in terms of the corporation's assets, liabilities, net worth, current earnings, potential earnings and all the other factors which go to make up the *real* value of the corporation itself. Yet the price of that company's stock may *increase or decrease millions of dollars in one day* because the BELIEF gets started among investors that the price of its stock is going to go up or down. *But nothing has changed except BELIEF!*

Such is the great power of BELIEF that it can cause the total value of all stocks to rise or fall BILLIONS of dollars in just one day! *Yet, often, nothing has changed except BELIEF, as is proven by the fact that the stock market—the VERY NEXT DAY—may more than regain its previous day's losses or lose more than its previous day's gains!* And still nothing has changed but BELIEF!

Since BELIEVING is *that* powerful, we had better *handle it with care* . . . as explained in the next chapter.

Chapter 53

DANGER! . . . Handle With Care!

You should be very careful in thinking about your future—especially in holding MENTAL PICTURES of what you expect from life—*because THAT is exactly what you will GET!*

MENTAL PICTURES simply are directives to your subconscious mind to *produce* (materialize) in your life *exactly* what you MENTALLY PICTURE.

Your subconscious mind is not the reasoning part of your mind. All reasoning, all judgment, all deciding is done in your *conscious* mind. Your *subconscious* mind *does not reason concerning the results of its acts;* it does not judge whether its following your MENTAL PICTURE directions will be good or bad for you; it does not decide whether it should or should not cause your MENTAL PICTURES to become your future. Those activities are not the function of your *subconscious* mind. *The function of your subconscious mind is to turn your MENTAL PICTURES (whatever they are) into reality in your life.*

As previously taught in this book, you should think of your two minds (your *conscious* and your *subconscious* minds) as being the management and the factory producing your life. Your *conscious* mind is the management; it *gives the orders,* says *what* to produce, says *what* the final product (your life) must be. Your *subconscious* mind is the *production* part of your life factory. It follows *exactly* the directions given to it through thoughts, chants, and mental pictures in your conscious mind. *It does not—it cannot—question, change or disobey those instructions!* Your subconscious mind (through being a part of the all-powerful Infinite Mind) *produces* in real life *exactly* what your conscious mind tells it to, as explained in preceding chapters in this book.

That is why you have to be so very careful what you *think about*, what you MENTALLY PICTURE—*because THAT is exactly what you will get in real life!*

Take the case of the man who was afraid he would lose his job. Before that fear entered his mind, there wasn't the slightest chance of his losing his job. He was already a minor executive in a large, progressive corporation. He was fully capable, experienced, cooperative, well-liked, and on his way to higher executive positions.

Then his conscious (*reasoning*) mind began to "reason." Suppose he *should* lose his job? There wasn't another job available in his city which required his special qualifications. How could he support his wife and his three children? The mortgage payments on his new, larger home would soon use up his savings. He began to MENTALLY PICTURE his boss calling him in and terminating his job, his banker foreclosing on his home, his applying to a relief agency so he could feed his family. Poverty! Perhaps illness! These fears grew in number. They multiplied in intensity. *And they visualized themselves in MENTAL PICTURES in his subconscious mind.*

So his subconscious mind had its instructions to bring those MENTAL PICTURES into reality in the man's life. *And so it did—just as it always will turn MENTAL PICTURES into reality.*

You can visualize the rest of the story. The man worried. He couldn't sleep at night. He began drinking to "relieve his tensions." He was irritable at work. He became uncooperative. Disagreeable. Disliked. He began making costly mistakes. He just couldn't concentrate on business problems. He developed chronic indigestion which gave him pains around his heart. Maybe the beginning of a heart attack! He should stay home and rest more often. He was so upset that he couldn't handle his job anyway. Just bad luck! Fate! Why fight it? He was licked.

Why? FEAR! *Unnecessary, unreasoning fear!* MENTAL PICTURES of failure—producing failure in real life. It wouldn't have happened if he had read this book—if he had used the success methods taught, chapter by chapter, in this one-book SUCCESS COURSE.

FEAR! More trouble, more unhappiness, more ruined lives are caused by fear than anything else. Why fear? Because fear is one of the earliest and most basic of all emotions. Primitive man had many things of which to be afraid. Some of these were real dangers—wild beasts, enemies, perilous living conditions. Some were imaginary (but just as real to primitive man)—evil spirits behind every tree, superstitions of every kind.

So we inherited from our primitive ancestors an over-awareness of FEAR which can, itself, become a very real part of our lives if stimulated by MENTAL PICTURES of a situation involving fear—justified or imaginary. Do not underestimate *imaginary* fears.

If any intense feeling of fear becomes deeply imbedded in our subconscious minds, we instinctively WITHDRAW from the situation which we have associated with that fear, even though the situation is perfectly normal for others.

As in the case of the woman who began feeling numb:

She was in a large, crowded department store. Suddenly her right leg began to feel numb. She was AFRAID it was the beginning of a stroke! She had a vivid MENTAL PICTURE of having a stroke and lying, unconscious, surrounded by a large crowd in the store . . . with people calling for help!!! . . . doctor!!! . . . everybody move back!!! . . . police!!! . . . ambulance!!! . . . sirens!!!

Of course she didn't have a stroke. She didn't even faint although her fear was so acute that she might have fainted. None of those fearsome things actually happened except in her MENTAL PICTURES. Later, her doctor examined her and found that she was in perfect physical condition although she was emotionally nervous. He said probably her girdle was too tight that day and caused a slight numbness.

But the vivid MENTAL PICTURE of having a stroke with all its consequences *was impressed in her subconscious mind.* She tried going shopping in crowds several times—with longer and longer intervals between each effort. Although she never really felt numb again (she got a larger girdle) she kept having a feeling that she was going to get numb and she became more and more afraid of being surrounded by crowds. Then she couldn't go shopping alone, and finally she gave up personal shopping altogether. Of course, this led to her not going where there were crowds. Then, to not going *anywhere!* Complete WITHDRAWAL!

Your subconscious mind will bring into reality WHATEVER you MENTALLY PICTURE. In the event of a MENTALLY PICTURED circumstance involving FEAR, your subconscious mind will cause you to WITHDRAW from the feared situation. Once this WITHDRAWAL is started, other FEAR situations progressively develop and you WITHDRAW from more and more normal activities.

That's how powerful your subconscious mind is and that's why it is important to include this chapter, titled: "DANGER! . . . *Handle With Care!*"

Your subconscious mind not only acts to bring you the good things of life—it acts in response to MENTAL PICTURES for your benefit *or to your detriment,* depending upon the MENTAL PICTURES you, yourself, impress upon it. You are, in fact, "Master of your fate, Captain of your soul"! *Because YOU control the MENTAL PICTURES!*

The files of every psychiatrist are filled with actual case histories which show the dangers of impressing MENTAL PICTURES of failure, illness and fear into the subconscious mind. However, it is not the purpose of this book to frighten you with psychiatric cases. But it is the purpose of this book to help you and to teach you—*so it is necessary to warn you that your subconscious mind can do you great harm as well as great good.*

In other chapters, I have told you *how to get the good*—now let me tell you *how to counteract the harm.*

(1) Do NOT impress into your subconscious mind MENTAL PICTURES of what you DON'T WANT (failure, illness, loss) because your subconscious mind will produce in your life the exact condition which you constantly MENTALLY PICTURE. Remember, your subconscious mind does not judge what is good or what is bad for you—*it only acts on whatever instructions you give it through your constantly held MENTAL PICTURES.* So if you hold in your mind MENTAL PICTURES of failure, illness, loss, unhappiness, or any undesirable circumstance *that* is exactly what will become a reality in your life. So *don't* do it!

(2) Do NOT impress into your subconscious mind MENTAL PICTURES involving FEAR because your subconscious mind will accept your instruction to make FEAR a *reality* in your life and thus cause you to WITHDRAW from the fear-situation. *You will over-react to FEAR, itself, until it spreads, like cancer, throughout your entire system!* The more situations you FEAR—the more you will WITHDRAW from normal activity, thus starting a psychological pattern of progressive WITHDRAWAL which will be increasingly repeated in other activities until you eventually may become a physical and mental invalid.

In the next chapter you will learn how to cure WITHDRAWAL caused by FEAR—because you will learn how to eliminate FEAR, itself.

Chapter 54

How You Can Conquer FEAR

There is a sure and simple way to eliminate fear from your life.

This is the opinion of the many modern psychiatrists who now use *Behavior Therapy* to "*desensitize*" and eliminate the fear impulse, itself, instead of going through a long, tedious, and very expensive psychoanalysis to seek the early, initial cause, usually rooted in some vague, repulsive childhood experience.

Behavior Therapy (also called *Desensitization Therapy*) simply means confronting and attacking your fear directly—by DOING THE THING YOU FEAR until you desensitize the fear-reaction by exhausting it's response.

This can be begun in the *imagination*. Begin with the mildest possible stimulus. For example, in eliminating the "dirt phobia," one would begin by *imagining* a speck of dirt. Then *imagine* coming into contact with more and more dirt.

When the fear of dirt was "desensitized" in the *imagination,* reality would be substituted for imagination by *actually touching* a real speck of dirt. Then *actually handling* more and more dirt.

By *repeatedly* and *increasingly* DOING THE THING YOU FEAR, you "desensitize" your fear-response.

Actually you *exhaust* your fear—which is why this is called the *Fear-Exhaustion Method* of *Behavior Therapy.*

CONTINUE — INCREASINGLY — TO DO THE THING YOU FEAR — your fear will be eliminated!

I tell you this from personal experience.

When I was a little boy, I stammered so badly I could hardly speak—and then my embarrassed efforts were accompanied by the mimicking ridicule of other children and the unwelcome sympathy of grown-ups. I FEARED being called upon to recite in class. In fact, I FEARED the necessity of speaking anytime, anywhere.

When I graduated from high school I was excused from delivering my senior speech because I stammered so badly that I would have been jeered right off the platform!

About that time, I learned that if you CONTINUE—*INCREASINGLY*—TO DO THE THING YOU FEAR—YOUR FEAR WILL BE ELIMINATED. Since stammering is caused by self-consciousness and fear of speaking, I knew I had to speak at every opportunity.

First I whispered and later spoke aloud at home alone in front of my mirror . . . then I spoke to individuals . . . then to small groups . . . finally to large audiences.

In the beginning, I went through the torments of hell doing it—but I knew *I had to do the thing I feared if I were to overcome it.* The more I spoke, the less I feared to speak—until the FEAR was gone, so the stammering was gone.

I spoke before civic clubs, luncheon clubs, business groups, college graduates, and from the pulpits of churches. I conducted sales seminars for large corporations. I have spoken from the same platform with a member of the Cabinet of the President of the United States. And I have spoken to the world over the *Voice of America* world-wide radio broadcasts.

I increasingly did the thing I feared until the fear was gone!

I learned then—and I have continued to use this method successfully to eliminate *all* fears throughout a lifetime:

CONTINUE — *INCREASINGLY* — TO DO THE THING YOU FEAR—AND YOUR FEAR WILL BE ELIMINATED.

Chapter 55

Beware Of These POISON THOUGHTS!

You can poison your mind!

There are many more people with *sick minds* than there are with sick bodies.

Many sick minds are sick because they are *mentally undernourished.* They are deprived of wholesome thought-nourishment, as provided by the author's 80-chapter book: *Thoughts To Build On* and many other thought-expanding books.

Many sick minds are sick because of lack of *mental exercise.* They are not given enough thought-stimulation to keep them actively healthy.

But most sick minds are sick because they are given a daily dose of mental poison in the form of POISON THOUGHTS!

How do POISON THOUGHTS get into your mind? You THINK them! That's all you have to do to *mentally poison* your mind, to make yourself *mentally sick* —just THINK POISON THOUGHTS. That's all. It's just as simple as that.

And . . . just as *deadly!*

POISON THOUGHTS may or may not kill you *physically*. They may not even kill your *entire* mind—not *all* of it—*they kill the cybernetic* (*goal-reaching*) *part of your mind.*

When POISON THOUGHTS first *sicken* . . . then *weaken* . . . then *kill* . . . the *cybernetic* (*goal-reaching*) *part of your mind*, you become a ship *without a rudder* . . . easily blown off course by the winds of Chance . . . buffeted about by the sickening waves of Fate . . . finally sent crashing, smashing, helplessly into the rocks by the inevitable storms of Life.

The tragedy of insecurity and instability is happening—in some degree—to many people whom you know, or see in person or on television, or about whom you read in the daily newspapers. You may not realize that their *minds have been poisoned*—made *sick* by POISON THOUGHTS—but you *will know* when you read the following list of MENTAL POISONS:

(1) VIOLENCE: We are confronted by a world-wide *epidemic of violence!* There is no need to record the details here because the news media report them in vivid detail every day.

We are concerned here with the *psychology* of violence—not the physical violence, itself, but the *mental-emotional effect* on those who commit violence. And on their victims.

Violence is an *insane form of ego-expression*—

the last mind-explosive resort of those who cannot *intelligently* cope successfully with personal problems. *Violence is the complete collapse of ability to deal rationally with life.*

There are so many forms of violence that we shall not attempt to describe them or even to list them.

We shall consider here only two forms of violence which are not usually recognized as MIND POISONS, and therefore are especially dangerous to most people.

(a) THREATS OF VIOLENCE: You hear threats of violence (real or implied) almost every day, concerning even the most commonplace situations. First there are "*demands*" ("demands" have a built-in threat) . . . then the *insulting challenge:* "Our demands are *non-negotiable!*". . . then the *hostile threat:* "Unless our *non-negotiable demands* are met NOW . . ."

How incredibly stupid! There is no *possible* way to do worse!

Such a threat violates *every principle* of *Personal Influence Psychology!* Even if such a threat obtains some grudging concession, *the concession is merely a delaying tactic*—because no person or group can *threaten* another person or group *without incurring seething hostility* which eventually will *avenge* the insulting, ego-damage of the threat.

The sensitivity of the human ego is such that no other result is psychologically possible. There can be no question concerning *if* hostile retaliation will occur, but only *when* and *how!*

Meanwhile, *all* of the minds involved in the

threat of violence are POISONED! More correctly: INCREASINGLY POISONED . . . *because only a POISONED MIND would make threats as a means of coping with a problem.* Threats are the complete surrender of intelligence; the admission of having a sick mind.

(b) THOUGHTS OF VIOLENCE: This is a form of reaction to a provocation or hostile situation in which most people indulge without being aware that they are POISONING their minds! They are annoyed, irritated, insulted, angered—*so they hope that violence will befall the source of their anger.* They derive pleasure just from *thinking violence!*

This is such a natural, human reaction (which perpetrates no actual physical harm to others) that one might think it harmless—*EXCEPT that it implants in the subconscious mind MENTAL PICTURES of actually engaging in violence.* Even though no *acts* of violence take place, the MENTAL PICTURES of violence are there—*and are implanted permanently in the subconscious mind.*

And . . . each MENTAL PICTURE of violence is just one more dose of MENTAL POISON. *Continued MENTAL PICTURES of violence will accumulate to become an overdose of MENTAL POISON with disastrous consequences to the cybernetic (goal-reaching) guidance part of the mind.*

(2) HATE: Next to *fear* and *violence* the most deadly of the MIND POISONS is hate. *Hate is a mental poison which instantly distorts the mind.* It transforms admirable people into evil demons bent on destruction of the objects of their hate by whatever means their twisted minds devise—the *physical violence* of killing, riot-

ing, bombing, burning, destroying . . . or the *economic violence* of hate-strikes, hate-boycotts, hate-slogans and hate-propaganda . . . or the *mental violence* of sinister plotting, scheming, or just MENTALLY PICTURING harm to others . . . or the *emotional violence* of deeply hurting someone's ego, honor, pride, sensitivity, or love.

It is regrettable that *Personal Influence Psychology* cannot be effective only for doing good. But the grim fact is that *Personal Influence Psychology* is equally effective in transforming naturally good people into evil demons by those who, subversively for secret fortunes, or stupidly for ego-satisfaction, make a career of fomenting revolts or inciting riots; organizing hate-demonstrations, hate-strikes, hate-boycotts; spreading hate-propaganda; shouting hate-slogans and hate-chants.

It is so easy, by using *Personal Influence Psychology* for professional trouble-makers to stir up trouble that they really should not be so well-paid for doing it. It is simple for them to pick the bullies in a dissatisfied group, tell them that they really are "militant activists," and delegate to these pseudo leaders the easy assignment of inciting their followers to use hate in organized revolts, riots, hate-strikes, hate-boycotts, hate-demonstrations through the use of hate-propaganda, hate-slogans and hate-chants.

Thus hate is deeply implanted in the subconscious minds of all of the members of an organized group and the fringe hangers-on. From then on, they are the puppets of push-button psychology, and their hate-actions become an instant conditioned response to the inflammatory hate-speeches of their masters.

Your knowledge of the foregoing method

should prevent your ever becoming involved as a pawn in the hate-mongering racket.

But all hate is not organized. This hate-prone world is a spawning ground for individual, personal hates. There are reasons for this—but there also are psychological methods which you can use to prevent becoming a mental, or emotional, or physical victim of hate—your own hate or that directed against you.

Wouldn't it be wonderful to get rid of hate in your life? Here's how to do it.

Let's begin by getting rid of any hates you may now have, even the "secret hates" you do not want to admit.

Getting rid of hate is so simple, so easy that you will be amazed that you did not get rid of hate long ago. Think of all the self-punishment you could have so easily avoided!

So, beginning now, you will hate no more! Believe that! Feel it locking into your life-controlling subconscious. Permanently. *You will hate no more*! Not anything. Not anybody. *Know it will be so. It will be so*!

Here's why. Hate is an emotion. The more violent the emotion, the more violent the hate. So get rid of the violent *feeling* and the hate *feeling* is gone. So your hate is gone! Doesn't it feel *good* not to feel hate?

When you don't feel hate, you feel *clean inside.* Don't you? Relieved . . . relaxed . . . *free*!

Enjoy feeling free of hate. Take a deep breath. Exhale. Relax. Smile. Laugh. Laugh again. And again. Enjoy your new freedom. *Laugh hate out of your life*!

Know that you never will poison your mind again with hate. Never. *Never*!

Chapter 56

More MENTAL POISONS To Avoid

If you are going to reach your goal in life, if you are going to get WHATEVER you want—you can do so *only* by INTENSELY impressing your goal, your greatest WANT into the *cybernetic (goal-reaching) part of your subconscious mind.*

Preceding chapter-lessons have taught you how to do it. Later lessons will teach you more.

But if you distort your subconscious mind by frequent doses of POISON THOUGHTS, the *cybernetic (goal-reaching) part will be disorganized and will actively produce twisted, poisoned results which will constitute your life.*

If you *saturate* your subconscious mind with an *overdose* of POISON THOUGHTS, you will *kill* its most easily accessible *cybernetic (goal-reaching) part*—and you will become a life drop-out: dully alive physically, but dead mentally, emotionally, and spiritually.

In the preceding chapter, we discussed the

MENTAL POISONS of violence and hate. We separate them from other POISON THOUGHTS because violence and hate are clearly visible—and they are plainly labeled: MENTAL POISON.

But there are other POISON THOUGHTS which are not so easily recognized as *mental poisons* because: (1) they are so widespread and commonplace; (2) they are *slow-poison* mentally, and gradually distort people's goal-reaching capabilities so that their victims are unaware of them until it is too late.

These GRADUAL MENTAL POISONS are:

(1) RESENTMENT: Resentment is our unfavorable reaction to what we consider to be an affront to our precious egos; an insult or attack on our person, relationships or possessions.

Resentment remains imbedded in our subconscious mind where, like cancer in our bodies, it may slowly destroy the vital organs, or it may spread rampant throughout the entire system—uncontrollable and rapidly escalating.

Slow, gradually destructive resentment sometimes turns inward in the form of self-pity and eventual withdrawal to escape further (real or imagined) hurt feelings and to shelter tender egos.

Overt resentment soon becomes a mental-emotional wildfire raging uncontrolled and rapidly escalating from resentment . . . to anger . . . to hate . . . to violence—sometimes even resulting in murder. Many murders begin as resentments which were only "slow burns" until somebody poured on the inflammables of anger, hate and violence.

(2) ESCAPISM: Most people do not realize that escapism is a MENTAL POISON, yet the subconscious desire to escape from an unpleasant reality distorts the *cybernetic* (*goal-reaching*) *function* of the subconscious mind so that *the goal becomes escape, itself*.

Escapism is the primary cause of most "*psychosomatic illnesses*" which are discussed elsewhere in this book but which also must be included here because they are one of the principal results of *escapism*. It long has been known that *more than half* of all patients in doctors' offices and in hospitals are suffering from *psychosomatic disorders*—bodily illnesses, *mentally caused*. And the *mental cause* is the subconscious "goal" of *escaping* a repugnant situation.

A patient with a broken arm certainly feels that his accident was a *physical* happening as, of course, it was. But behind the physical "accident" may well have been a *subconscious escapism goal*—a *mental* desire to *escape* the responsibility of doing something (unpleasant, embarrassing, or dangerous) which he subconsciously acted to avoid. Thus the broken arm provided the *escape*.

The foregoing is a mild example. People go blind; people are partially or completely paralyzed; people develop almost every imaginable illness (although some psychosomatic disorders are more prevalent than others) impelled subconsciously as a means of *escaping* some repugnant situation, or to excuse their withdrawal from some undesirable reality, or even as a subconscious form of self-punishment for a repressed sense of guilt.

Most patients with psychosomatic disorders do not realize that their illnesses or accidents have a primary *mental* cause—and they would not admit it if they did. Nevertheless, the fact is that 50% to 90% of *all illnesses and accidents* have at least *some mental basis!*

That fact should be sufficient warning to the reader to AVOID POISON THOUGHTS: of violence, hate, resentment, anger, fear, escapism, and the MENTAL POISON of *withdrawal.*

(3) WITHDRAWAL: This is the *drop-out syndrome*—and because being partial or full-time *drop-outs* is incapacitating an alarmingly large part of our population, it is important to learn about this MENTAL POISON that deactivates—the *cybernetic* (*goal-reaching*) *function* of the subconscious mind. The drive toward a worthwhile goal *stops—and there no longer is a goal at all!*

No goal . . . nothing to strive for . . . no incentive . . . no motivation . . . no enthusiasm . . . no effort . . . no interest; that is the *drop-out syndrome.*

Another life being wasted because of a *withdrawal psychosis!*

How often we see it happening today! School drop-outs . . . family drop-outs . . . drop-outs from structured society which is the basis of orderly civilization . . . drop-outs from life, itself, into a cozy cocoon of nothingness!

We could devote pages just to listing the various kinds of drop-outs.

Then, we could devote chapters to describing the causes of *withdrawal psychosis* and prescribing ways to deal with each cause and effect.

But we shall do none of that!

We do not *need* to! Because if you will devote

your *full time* to applying the success methods in this book to *everything you think and do*—you will be too busy *succeeding* in GETTING WHATEVER YOU WANT to leave any space in your subconscious for even a drop of MENTAL POISON to seep in.

It is important to know about POISON THOUGHTS and the damage they *could* do to your subconscious mind *if* they could get in—but it is equally important to know that *using the success methods in this book will keep the MENTAL POISONS out!*

And, just for good measure, you now will be given a POSITIVE POWER SYMBOL *which will protect you from MENTAL POISONS,* and which will *multiply* your success in GETTING WHATEVER YOU WANT!

The POSITIVE POWER SYMBOL will be given you in the next chapter . . .

Chapter 57

Special Section:
Multiply Your PERSONAL POSITIVE POWER (× +)

The Symbol "× +" Which Multiplies Your PERSONAL POSITIVE POWER!

All great powers have special symbols.

Great religions have their sacred symbols, for example: the Cross of Christianity.

All nations have their flags and other symbols.

Fraternal orders: the Masons, the Knights of Columbus, and thousands more—all have their symbols.

Many symbols have secret meanings known only to members.

Secret mystic societies have their secret, occult symbols.

Great corporations have their symbols, their marks of special quality, called trademarks, and spend millions of dollars publicizing them. These corporation, or product, symbols (trademarks) acquire such immense value that the trademark symbols, themselves, are worth *millions* of dollars.

You can have *your million-dollar* symbol, too!

It is the symbol of the POSITIVE POWER

PERSON. Because a *Positive Power Person can make a million dollars or many millions of dollars* by *multiplying* his or her PERSONAL POSITIVE POWER, the following symbol is in fact, a *million-dollar* symbol!

The symbol of the POSITIVE POWER PERSON is . . . ×+.

The "×" means "*multiply.*"

The "+" means "*positive power.*" The "+" is stamped into the *positive power* terminal of your automobile battery. The "+" is marked in some way to identify the *positive power* connections of all electrical equipment, accessories and fixtures.

Because "×" means "*multiply*" and "+" means "*positive power,*" the ×+ symbol when used by YOU—specifically means: MULTIPLY (×) YOUR PERSONAL POSITIVE (+) POWER.

The symbol ×+ is the *million-dollar* trademark of the POSITIVE POWER PERSON. Make ×+ your *own* personal symbol!

The "*multiply your positive power*" symbol ×+ not only is a symbol for *multiplying your positive power* to amass *great wealth,* but ×+ is your personal symbol for *multiplying your positive power* to get WHATEVER you want—whether it be great WEALTH to use in helping others . . . or SUCCESS in some worthy cause . . . or LOVE as your fraternal acceptance of the personal worth of every individual . . . or HAPPINESS in service and living . . . or POPULARITY as the result of your positive goodwill . . . or INFLUENCE to increase useful accomplishment . . . or POWER for great achievement . . . or FAME as the reward of benefiting mankind . . . or WHATEVER you want as a *worthy* goal.

Note carefully that the symbol $\times +$ means *multiply your positive power* to get WHATEVER you want as a *worthy* goal in life; you cannot be a POSITIVE POWER PERSON if you seek a *negative* goal!

The symbol $\times +$ is an *instant reminder* to use the success methods in this book—*because they will make you a POSITIVE POWER PERSON.*

Letter your symbol $\times +$ on cards or slips of paper and put these in conspicuous places where you will see them often and thus constantly be *reminded* to be a POSITIVE POWER PERSON.

Obviously, your conspicuously displayed $\times +$ symbol also will be seen by others. So you *must* comply with the following rule:

IMPORTANT: *Do not explain the secret $\times +$ symbol to any other person. Do not discuss it with anybody, no matter how much he or she tries to get you to reveal its secret meaning.*

The symbol $\times +$ is *exclusively* for POSITIVE POWER PEOPLE. If another *Postive Power Person* sees your $\times +$ symbol, he or she will *know* what $\times +$ means. If a person *does not know* what your $\times +$ symbol means, do *not* reveal its meaning. Simply state that it is *secret.* Courteously decline to discuss it further. Be mysterious about it.

This will give you an aura of mystery—and make YOU very interesting.

It also will prove that you are a POSITIVE POWER PERSON because you are resolute and firm.

There are a lot of interesting and curiosity-provoking ways to use your $\times +$ symbol:

(1) Use $\times +$ above your name on your

printed personal stationery, business cards, etc., just as a big corporation uses its million-dollar trademark.

(2) Use × + after your personal signature, just as medical doctors use "M.D." after their names.

(3) Print × + on a card to put on your desk or wherever you work.

(4) Make a list of other ways in which you can display the × + symbol, and use × + wherever it will be a *reminder to you*--and *attract the interest of others.*

Of course, a lot of people will ask you about your × + symbol. That is what you want, because two methods of a POSITIVE POWER PERSON are: (1) *attract attention* and (2) *arouse interest.* Your × + symbol will do both of these instantly!

But you *must not* reveal the meaning of the × + symbol to those who do not understand it. The × + symbol is only for POSITIVE POWER PEOPLE who have studied this SUCCESS COURSE and can use the powerful psychology of the × + symbol.

And the symbol × + *does* have a powerful psychological effect. *It works almost like magic!*

That is because it is a "*psychological concentration object*" and INTENSELY IMPRESSES your subconscious mind with your instructions to *multiply your positive power* and to make you a POSITIVE POWER PERSON.

You also should INTENSELY IMPRESS into your subconscious mind the *personal slogan* (or *silent chant*): "I am a *Positive Power Person!!!*". . . by repeating it twenty times at least twice every day, and preferably much more often—*at every opportunity!*

Remember that your subconscious mind will

accept WHATEVER instructions you INTENSELY IMPRESS into it; then your subconscious mind will use its *unlimited* cybernetic (goal-reaching) power to do *whatever* is necessary to *materialize your instructions into reality.*

So, when you INTENSELY IMPRESS *repeatedly* into your subconscious mind the *personal slogan* (or *silent chant*): "I am a *Positive Power Person*". . . *that is what you will become*—a *Positive Power Person!*

However, you can enormously *multiply* your *personal positive power*, and therefore get WHATEVER you want *much faster* if, *in addition* to using the success methods given you in *previous* chapters, you *immediately begin using* the POSITIVE POWER METHODS in the *following* chapters.

The *following* chapters are the *most important lessons* in this SUCCESS COURSE!

The *preceding* lessons have taught you how to use the cybernetic power of your *own* subconscious mind to become a POSITIVE POWER PERSON.

The *following* chapter-lessons will teach you how you can motivate the subconscious minds of *others* to combine or "fuse" *their* subconscious power with *yours* to enormously *multiply your* PERSONAL POSITIVE POWER—which will enable *you* to get WHATEVER *you* want.

You will discover this tremendous × + *power —and learn how YOU can develop and use it*—in the following chapter-lessons . . .

× +

Chapter 58

Special Section:
Multiply Your PERSONAL POSITIVE POWER (× +)

Your Own Personal World Of POSITIVE POWER

You have your *own personal world.*

It is not geographic, that is, it is not limited by any *area of space.*

Your *own personal world,* as we discuss it in this and following chapters, consists entirely of *people,* specifically *all* of the people within range of *your* PERSONAL POSITIVE POWER—in person, by telephone, by writing, by every form of communication.

This includes in your *own personal world* those whom you reach by *"thought broadcasting,"* a very real means of communication which is explained and taught in Chapter 70.

The purpose of defining your *own personal world* now is to fix in your mind the concept that your *own personal world* consists of "people" or "others": two words which we shall use for brevity in this and following chapters. Through them, you *multiply your positive power.*

As often referred to in this book, the "people" and "others" in your life who comprise your *own personal world* are *all* of the people within range of *your* PERSONAL POSITIVE POWER.

We want to emphasize at the beginning of this Special Section of your SUCCESS COURSE that your *projection* of PERSONAL POSITIVE POWER taught in the following chapters *must radiate equally and impartially to all of the people in your own personal world*—not be limited to a selected few.

The methods of *multiplying* your PERSONAL POSITIVE POWER which you are about to learn—*must* include *every* person and *not be "focused" only to those people whom you specifically hope to influence for your own selfish gain.*

You either are a POSITIVE POWER PERSON —or you are not. *No one can be a part-time Positive Power Person.*

If you are a POSITIVE POWER PERSON, it is a *full-time state of being.* You cannot turn your PERSONAL POSITIVE POWER on and off like a faucet.

Your *projection* and *magnetism* of PERSONAL POSITIVE POWER must be *constant, impartial, nonselective*—like the *Law of Gravity.*

Your PERSONAL POSITIVE POWER must be radiated *equally, constantly* to *everybody* in your own personal world.

It will remain POSITIVE *only* as long as it is

non-selectively radiated to everybody—equally, constantly. If you try to be *selective* in using it for *selfish* gain, it will become NEGATIVE and produce the *opposite* results on the very individuals you are trying to influence for your own gain.

If you try to use your *personal positive power only* on Mr. Big and Miss Charming for *your own selfish influence,* their subconscious insight will warn them that you are a selfish, scheming, conniving person—and you will achieve the business and social obscurity which you thereby justly will deserve. You will be a *selfish* NEGATIVE power which *repells*—instead of a *constant* POSITIVE power which *magnetically attracts all of the people in your personal world.*

Remember *that,* as you study the following chapter-lessons. It is *very important* that you radiate your personal positive power *impartially, equally, constantly.*

This SUCCESS COURSE is *not* a "psychological bag of tricks" which enables you to use some hocus-pocus influence to "master, control and manipulate others."

This SUCCESS COURSE combines *Motivational Psychology, Personal Improvement Psychology* and *Personal Influence Psychology* to make you a POSITIVE POWER PERSON so that by your *projecting* and *radiating* your PERSONAL POSITIVE POWER throughout your entire personal world, you will *magnetically attract*—and through the cybernetic power of your subconscious mind—*materialize into reality* WHATEVER you want in life.

By *projecting* and *radiating* your PERSONAL POSITIVE POWER to *every* person, *equally* and *con-*

stantly—you will fulfill the deep, subconscious NEEDS OF OTHERS, as clearly explained in the following chapter-lessons.

When you fulfill the deep, subconscious NEEDS OF OTHERS, *their* subconscious minds respond with POSITIVE reactions which combine and "fuse" *their positive* subconscious motivation with *yours* to *enormously MULTIPLY your own* PERSONAL POSITIVE POWER.

This combining or *"fusing"* of the *positive* subconscious power of OTHERS with your OWN subconscious power is *so tremendous* that your PERSONAL POSITIVE POWER is much more than increased—*it is MULTIPLIED many times!*

What you can achieve by doing this will seem miraculous—but so are the "miracles" of atomic power, *also generated by the "fusion" principle.*

The next chapter will explain the basic principle, and the following nine chapters will tell you *exactly* HOW YOU CAN MULTIPLY YOUR PERSONAL POSITIVE POWER *in nine different, tremendous ways!*

× +

Chapter 59

Special Section:
Multiply Your PERSONAL POSITIVE POWER (× +)

How Fulfilling The Subconscious Needs Of Others Multiplies Your PERSONAL POSITIVE POWER

You have *two* kinds of vision:

(1) PHYSICAL vision: your *eye-sight*—which enables you to see with your eyes. What you see with your *eye-sight* is *physical:* people and things as you are accustomed to seeing them.

(2) MENTAL vision: your *insight*—which enables you to see with your *subconscious perception.* What you see with your *subconscious perception* reveals an entirely *new dimension of life!* It reveals unlimited opportunities which have remained hidden from your PHYSICAL vision!

This chapter is concerned only with what you see with your MENTAL vision, your *insight,* your *subconscious perception.*

We do not have space in this book to explore the *total new dimension of life* which your MENTAL vision (*subconscious perception*) will reveal to you. We shall confine this chapter to part of what your MENTAL vision (subconscious perception) will see in the *subconscious minds of others.*

What you will see in the minds of *all people* are their SUBCONSCIOUS NEEDS—and their mental attitudes resulting from their needs.

Their deep, insistent SUBCONSCIOUS NEEDS motivate people—*all people*—causing them to do *whatever* they do in their attempts (wise or otherwise) to fulfill their SUBCONSCIOUS NEEDS.

Every time *you* fulfill a basic SUBCONSCIOUS NEED of *any* person, *you multiply your* PERSONAL POSITIVE POWER. *Each* of the next nine chapters will show you a *different* SUBCONSCIOUS NEED which *you can fulfill in others*—and teach you *how to do it.*

The purpose of the present chapter is, in part, to remind you of a fact you already know: that there is much more to every other person than "*meets the eye.*"

Your *physical* vision (eye-sight) sees only the *outer, physical* person.

Your *mental* vision (insight) enables you to see the *inner* person, the *real* person, and the deep SUBCONSCIOUS NEEDS which *crave* to be fulfilled—and which *you can fulfill* by your being a *Positive Power Person.*

When you fulfill a SUBCONSCIOUS NEED of *any* person, you activate a subconscious *positive* response *which combines and "fuses" his or her positive subconscious power with your own*—resulting in *multiplying* your PERSONAL POSITIVE POWER enormously!

This is *easy* when you know *how*.

The next nine chapter-lessons will teach you HOW.

From all of the many—and often very complex—SUBCONSCIOUS NEEDS of people, we have selected *nine* basic NEEDS which *everyone* has, and which YOU *easily* can fulfill.

Each of the following nine chapters will show you a *different* SUBCONSCIOUS NEED—and teach you how to fulfill *that specific need* of the people who comprise *your personal world of positive power*.

Every time you fulfill a SUBCONSCIOUS NEED of *any* person, *you multiply your* PERSONAL POSITIVE POWER . . . so *your opportunities are unlimited* . . . and you now need only to combine the lessons of the next nine chapters with the other success methods in this book . . . to become a *Positive Power Person* and therefore be able to GET WHATEVER YOU WANT.

×+

Chapter 60

Special Section:
Multiply Your PERSONAL POSITIVE POWER (X +)

Fulfill This Subconscious Need With The Goodwill Of ACCEPTANCE

In the preceding chapter, you learned that *all people* have deep SUBCONSCIOUS NEEDS which they constantly, *often desperately*, are striving to fulfill.

To the extent that you help others fulfill their subconscious needs, you enormously *multiply* your PERSONAL POSITIVE POWER.

This is the result of the *positive response* of others to your own *positive action* in helping them.

It has the effect of *combining* their subconscious power with yours in a "*subconscious fusion*" which is the *mental* equivalent of the *physical nuclear fusion* that produces atomic energy. This "subconscious fusion" is as powerful *mentally* as the nuclear fusion which produces atomic energy is powerful *physically*. So, you are soon to learn to use terrific *mental* (subconscious) power!

The "*subconscious fusion*," which occurs when you fulfill the subconscious needs of others, *multiplies* your PERSONAL POSITIVE POWER so enormously that when it is combined with the preceding success methods in this book, it will enable you to get WHATEVER you want.

Beginning in this chapter, we shall devote a chapter to *each of nine basic* SUBCONSCIOUS NEEDS *which everyone has*—and which *you* easily can fulfill. Of course, there are many more than nine subconscious needs, but if you *constantly* fulfill *these nine needs* of the people in your personal world, you will be a Positive Power Person with the *subconscious magnetism* to attract WHATEVER you want in life.

In this chapter, we shall examine the subconscious need of others TO FEEL ACCEPTED . . . and you shall learn how to help them fulfill it.

Every person has a *compelling* NEED TO FEEL ACCEPTED.

When ACCEPTANCE is *denied,* the *rejected* person or group or race or nationality feels *discriminated against*—and responds with resentment, anger, hostility and, sometimes, violence. Every day, you read examples of hostile resentment in your newspaper or see them on TV.

While this hostile response is understandably human, it also is *exactly the opposite* of the way to win ACCEPTANCE—*which cannot be won by hostility or threats or force.* Forced "association" does not produce "acceptance," and it may escalate hostility.

Many civil rights leaders, legislative activists, and ambitious politicians act as though ACCEPTANCE can be *legalized—made legally mandatory*

It cannot.

Legally forced "proximity" and "association" may result in required *physical* "association"—but that is not ACCEPTANCE, which is *mental* and *emotional.*

Real ACCEPTANCE must be *deserved* and, in many cases, must be *earned.* And, as stated later in this chapter, ACCEPTANCE should be *offered* by Positive Power Persons.

But ACCEPTANCE *cannot be deserved or earned by a show of resentment, anger, hostility, or violence,* which further hardens the resistance to acceptance. It is regrettable that these counter-productive tactics have been and still are used—and that they are so widely publicized that *a few militant radicals can delay the deserved ACCEPTANCE of an entire group or race.*

It is equally regrettable that there are racists, bigots, and social, educational and financial snobs. But there are, and there always will be. They are not representative of the majority which would respond with goodwill and ACCEPTANCE if they were not so persistently subjected to unfriendly pressure tactics.

What to do? Two things:

(1) Those *seeking* ACCEPTANCE can *deserve* and, if necessary, *earn* it simply by using the success methods in this book. Re-study this SUCCESS COURSE, applying *every lesson* to the objective of *winning* ACCEPTANCE. This book tells you HOW to do it!

(2) *Positive Power Persons* (already having mastered this SUCCESS COURSE) can greatly *help others* fulfill their deep, subconscious NEED FOR ACCEPTANCE, as follows:

(a) First, by *taking the initiative* and *positively establishing* (if appropriate, by actually stating) that the deserving person, group, etc., is *completely* ACCEPTED and *warmly welcomed.* Often, all that is needed is for a Positive Power Person to "break the ice"—to cause frigid attitudes to thaw and ACCEPTANCE quickly to follow.

(b) By acts and statements of *approval, admiration* and *appreciation* of the ACCEPTABLE *qualities* of another. Acceptance seldom is instant and total. So begin with the most *acceptable quality,* and build acceptability: quality by quality.

(c) By sincere and cordial *invitations* to deserving individuals and groups.

(d) By enthusiastic expressions of *friendliness* and *goodwill*—privately and publicly.

(e) By finding ways to make the other person feel *wanted* and *needed.*

Fulfilling the basic, subconscious NEED FOR ACCEPTANCE is one of the greatest *problems* and one of the greatest *opportunities* of our time.

To the extent that *you can help others* BE ACCEPTED, you will have fulfilled one of their *deepest* SUBCONSCIOUS NEEDS. Their grateful *positive* response to your helpful *positive* action will combine in the "subconscious fusion" previously described—and *multiply* your PERSONAL POSITIVE POWER (× +) to attract *whatever* you want in life.

The *key* to enormously *multiplying* your Personal Positive Power: HELP OTHERS!

The *method:* FULFILL THEIR SUBCONSCIOUS NEEDS!

The next basic SUBCONSCIOUS NEED which *everybody* has and which *you easily can fulfill*—is described in the following chapter which also gives the sure cure for DROP-OUTS!

× +

Chapter 61

Special Section:
Multiply Your PERSONAL POSITIVE POWER (× +)

The Sure Cure For School Drop-Outs, Job Drop-Outs, LIFE DROP-OUTS

Everyone has a compelling, subconscious NEED FOR APPROVAL.

Unless the NEED FOR APPROVAL is *repeatedly* fulfilled, a vacant space is established in the personality. Gradually this vacant space is filled with nagging doubts: fears of inadequacy, incompetency, failure.

Neglect by family, associates or others to provide *positive assurance* of APPROVAL results in the neglected person's losing *positive* motivation and reacting in one of two ways:

(1) *The "I will show you!" over-reaction* in the form of *immature behavior* which often is self-damaging, radical or hostile. (Note: *Mental-emotional immaturity is not limited to the inexperience of youth.* Often adults

express more mental-emotional immaturity than the youths they insensitively criticize.)

(2) *Loss of positive, constructive motivation* —which leads to an increasing *withdrawal* in various forms of *escapism*.

Another drop-out!

Why?

His or her NEED TO FEEL APPROVED by "others" was not fulfilled.

The "others" are dismayed by the irrational freak-outs, the turned-off young people, and the discouraged, the under-achievers, the unmotivated of *all* ages.

The reason is simple enough. When people do not FEEL APPROVED, *they withdraw and defensively turn against the SOURCE of disapproval.*

"*Down the Establishment!*", they shout.

"*Power to the PEOPLE!*" And just who are the "people" for whom instant "power" is sought? They are *similar people who ALSO could not win approval!*

So the withdrawn, escapist and or rebellious disapproved cling together in a sort of sub-culture, seeking such dubious approval as they can eke out of other drop-outs, often by resorting to abnormal or subnormal, defiant, rebellious behavior in a duped (or doped) antisocial cult.

It is a sickening, downward spiral. The more disapproval they incur, the more rebellious acts the "*anti's*" flaunt at the very people whose approval they need in order to achieve any meaningful and worthwhile goal in life.

The *Positive Power Person* can provide the solution which, in these cases, is more than a solution—*it is a CURE for a sinister, character-destroying, life-wrecking, mental-social disease.*

If this *rebellion psychosis* has not progressed beyond possible cure, *it can be reversed* by providing the APPROVAL which was needed in the first place.

This may be difficult because there often is so little left to approve.

But if there is *something—anything*—which can be commended and approved—APPROVE *that!* If you cannot approve the *action*, you probably can approve the *original motive.*

In every *rebellion psychosis,* there usually is a *worthy motive* which has been misdirected. By approving the *worthy motive,* without criticizing the misdirection, you will establish a *point of agreement* which can be expanded in the encouraging environment of continuing approval. Thus you may *re-direct* the *worthy motive* into channels of commendable achievement.

The more deeply the *rebellion psychosis* has become established, the more resentment or apathy you will encounter at first. *But persist!* The subconscious NEED FOR APPROVAL is so compelling and so desperate that your offer of APPROVAL will be almost irresistible.

As you develop your sensitivity to the *subconscious needs* of others, you will discover that people "submit" their commendable qualities for APPROVAL. If you *sincerely* can give your approval at all, *give your approval in lavish abundance!* As long as APPROVAL is genuine and sincere, it is almost impossible to overdo it.

Do not, at the same time, express disapproval. It will be a temptation, in your zeal to apply this newly-learned method of "*managed improvement,*" but resist all statements, implications and attitudes of disapproval while using *approval therapy.*

Approval therapy must be totally positive. It consists of finding more and more qualities to APPROVE —*so that approval becomes a REWARD which is more desirable than the resentment and rebellion which it replaces.*

We have, first, examined the *extreme* and *rebellious* reactions to being *denied* the fulfillment of the subconscious NEED TO FEEL APPROVED—because these withdrawal or defiant responses are so prevalent today, and are causing such great concern among parents, teachers, law enforcement authorities, rehabilitation organizations, and a dismayed public.

Now let us turn to the more simple and normal NEED TO FEEL APPROVED. It is a deep, subconscious need of each of us.

Every person you meet has, not just one, but *many* qualities, activities and accomplishments which *subconsciously* NEED YOUR APPROVAL.

To be a *Positive Power Person,* you will need to develop your *sensitivity* to the *subconscious needs of others.* This "subconscious perception" is especially important in finding what *specific* qualities or activities *each different person* seeks to have APPROVED.

Use the following easy method:

(1) Begin by *openly expressing* your sincere approval of *every* quality or activity or accomplishment which honestly deserves to be commended and approved. Obviously, you cannot recite the entire list in a single conversation or letter—but continue your commendations, a few at a time, at every opportunity.

(2) As a *Positive Power Person,* your sensi-

tivity to the feelings of others will enable you to perceive the *specific* qualities, activities or accomplishments on which your commendation and approval are *most appreciated.*

(3) Having determined WHAT to compliment, *concentrate on those things*—but not to the total exclusion of all other commendable possibilities.

(4) The *more* qualities, activities and accomplishments of others which you sincerely can approve and compliment, the *more* you will *multiply* your PERSONAL POSITIVE POWER.

But remember, as repeatedly emphasized in this SUCCESS COURSE, compliments must be given *unselfishly* and *impartially—and not be selectively "focused" only on those people whom you hope specifically to influence for your own selfish gain.*

Only as long as you use your PERSONAL POSITIVE POWER to fulfill the subconscious needs of *all* of the people within range of your personality—*constantly* and *impartially*—will you continue to be a Positive Power Person.

While it is true that by being a Positive Power Person you will attract WHATEVER you want, you can *only* do that by FIRST *unselfishly helping others*—which is the *source* of your PERSONAL POSITIVE POWER.

You help others *most* when you fulfill their deep SUBCONSCIOUS NEEDS. The next chapter will show you unlimited opportunities to do that for *everybody.*

The next chapter will teach you to: "Give A *Glow!*"

× +

Chapter 62

Special Section:
Multiply Your PERSONAL POSITIVE POWER (× +)

Give A Glow!

In this chapter, we shall study another of the basic subconscious needs of everybody: the NEED TO FEEL ADMIRED.

You will learn to "Give A *Glow!*"

Everybody, beginning in the early stages of life, usually seeks to be ADMIRED for his or her *good* qualities. If *good* qualities are rewarded by the *fulfillment* of the subconscious NEED TO BE ADMIRED, then *positive* motivation results in the seeking of *worthy* life goals.

However, if a person's subconscious NEED TO FEEL ADMIRED is *not* fulfilled by *expressed admiration of good qualities, worthy activities* and *commendable achievements*—then that person will be influenced by the pseudo-admiration of those people *who lure recruits for disruptive "causes" by exploiting the disillusioned* through rewarding them with "admiration" for demonstrating, rioting, disruption, and even violence.

The subconscious NEED TO FEEL ADMIRED can be turned into a life-changing force for good or evil—depending on the qualities and activities which are ADMIRED.

As a *Positive Power Person* you will use the influence of your ADMIRATION to motivate the people in *your personal world* to *worthy goals* and *commendable achievements.*

Obviously, you do this by expressing your sincere ADMIRATION of their *meritorious* qualities, activities, possessions and accomplishments *every time* you talk with or write to *every person.*

You do not just do this occasionally. You do it *every time.* Of course, you cannot recite a long list of compliments each time, but you *always* can sincerely compliment *something.* And you should not conclude *any* conversation with *any* person (or complete *any* letter) without *some* statement of ADMIRATION.

It will be easy for you to learn to do this—and to remind you to express ADMIRATION at *every* opportunity, the author has created the ADMIRATION GAME which you will learn later in this chapter.

First, let us consider HOW to sincerely express your ADMIRATION.

There are *two* ways:

(1) Express your ADMIRATION by what you DO:

You can express admiration just by *visibly admiring.* A charming woman who has attracted the admiring attention of men, does not need to be *told* that she is being admired!

Nor is *visible admiration* limited to charming women, or to attractive men, or to interesting, magnetic personalities of either sex. *Visible admiration* can be expressed by looking appreciatively at *things,* too.

People are proud of their interesting, unusual and beautiful possessions. They always notice, and are pleased and grateful, when any person *visibly admires* their possessions. Your *visible admiration* of the possessions of others is emphasized by the "*go-and-look*" technique. Don't just *sit* there! Get up and *examine* the attractive art object (or whatever) with *obvious appreciation* and *visible admiration.*

(2) Express your ADMIRATION by what you *say* or write.

In addition to *visible admiration,* there is, of course, *spoken or written admiration.* You frankly and *sincerely* say, "I *admire* your (name of possession)". . . or "What a *splendid* idea! . . . or "You do *excellent* work!" . . . or "You have *remarkable* talent!"

You do not have to make a long, eloquent speech. It is better not to. A few, frank sincere words of admiration are more effective—socially *and psychologically.* However, admiration expressed in a letter can be in much more detail—and will be treasured and frequently re-read by the person complimented.

Perfecting your ability to "*give a glow*" to *every* person you talk with or write to—requires that you:

(1) Find at least *something* and, try to find *many* things, to ADMIRE in *everybody.*

(2) *Do not forget* to sincerely and enthusiastically *express* your ADMIRATION to *every* person you talk with or write to.

There are *some* qualities, activities, accomplishments, possessions of *every* person which you *honestly* and *sincerely* can ADMIRE.

Naturally, some people have more *admirable* qualities than others, but you can find *something* (usually *many* things) about which you can express your genuine ADMIRATION.

The problem is that you may *forget* to express your ADMIRATION on *every* occasion. So the author has created a simple, little game to "trigger" your memory.

It is called the ADMIRATION GAME and, if you follow its rules, you *always* will express your sincere ADMIRATION to *every person* on *every* occasion.

Here's how to play the ADMIRATION GAME:

(1) Challenge yourself to find *something commendable* which you honestly ADMIRE about *every* person you meet.

(2) Frankly and sincerely *compliment* that person on what you ADMIRE about him or her. (If you meet a person frequently during the day, only one compliment per day is required by the rules of the ADMIRATION GAME but, of course, compliment as often as appropriate.)

(3) If you *fail* to frankly and sincerely *compliment* ANY person you meet (and are with for several minutes), you must *take a dollar* from your billfold or purse and put it in a pocket money-clip or in some separate place

until you can deposit it in a savings container at home (jar, coffee can, small box) and then subsequently deposit it in a *separate* "PENALTY PAYMENT" *savings account* in your bank.

This savings account will grow quite rapidly until you learn the art of ADMIRING and complimenting. You will *save* while you *learn*—so you gain *doubly*. You actually will be *paying yourself to learn!*

And . . . you will learn *fast!*

The "cost" of *forgetting to compliment* will *quickly* teach you the perception of finding *something* to ADMIRE in *everyone*—and remind you to compliment them on some admirable quality *every time* you meet.

You will learn one of life's most important lessons. *That there is something—and really there are many things—ADMIRABLE about everyone!*

People will look forward to being with you because they will *know* (subconsciously anticipate) that you will give them the *lift of a compliment*—fulfill their subconscious NEED TO BE ADMIRED—*give a glow!*

You will greatly increase your own popularity!

You will *multiply* your PERSONAL POSITIVE POWER.

×+

Chapter 63

Special Section:
Multiply Your PERSONAL POSITIVE POWER (× +)

If YOU Want To Be APPRECIATED . . .

If you want an *instant, favorable response,* express your *appreciation* of someone!

If *you* want to be *appreciated,* then FIRST express *your* appreciation of *another.*

To state fully the scope of your opportunities to appreciate, let's begin this chapter-lesson by completely defining "*appreciate*":

(1) To *appreciate* is to be totally aware of the value and importance of the worth of people and things.

(2) To *appreciate* is to esteem highly.

(3) To *appreciate* is to be keenly sensitive to the admirable qualities of people and things.

(4) To *appreciate* is to show gratitude for . . .

(5) To *appreciate* is to increase the value of people and things.

(6) To *appreciate* is to place a favorable estimate on the worth of people and things.

(7) To *appreciate* is to rise in value (the author likes to think of this *"rise in value"* of a *person* as being a direct result of *"applied appreciation,"* although this is only one of many possible causes).

You instantly will visualize from the preceding definitions, the opportunities to *multiply* your PERSONAL POSITIVE POWER by *sincerely* fulfilling in others their subconscious NEED TO FEEL APPRECIATED.

However, your opportunities are so many and so varied for using the *full extent of Appreciation-Power,* that it is necessary to put them in some organized form.

The author suggests that you prepare an APPRECIATION BOOK. It will so *greatly increase your popularity* and so rapidly *multiply* your PERSONAL POSITIVE POWER that its results will seem miraculous—which only proves again that psychology, properly used, *does* produce *"miracles"!*

Here's how to prepare and use your APPRECIATION BOOK:

(1) Get a notebook. Any kind will do, but you should read the following before deciding what kind of notebook to get. An APPRECIATION BOOK is so valuable that some people use expensive leather-bound notebooks, the impressive appearances of which are constant reminders of the APPRECIATION BOOKS' value. But any kind of notebook will do; the *contents* will be the *real value.*

(2) Beginning with the members of your family, write one name at the top of each page.

(3) When you have written the names of every member of your family—one name at the top of each

page—then write the names of your friends, associates, acquaintances, and anyone you want to add to *your own personal world* . . . one name at the top of each page.

(4) Using the definitions of *"appreciate"* stated at the beginning of this chapter, write on the page under each person's name: *all* of the *ways* in which you *appreciate* him or her, followed by *methods* you can use to *express your appreciation.*

(5) *Then USE them!* Express your appreciation of and to *each and every* person listed in your APPRECIATION BOOK *using each and every definition applicable.* Appreciation, *unexpressed,* is a gift, *ungiven.*

(6) Express your appreciation, in at least one way, *every* time you are *with* each person, but find other ways to do it, too. Write a note or letter. Phone on some other pretext but find or *make* an opportunity to *frankly* and *forthrightly state* your genuine appreciation. Do this in a natural, unaffected manner. Be *sincere!*

IMPORTANT: Know *this!* Just as long as your expressions of appreciation and gratitude are *genuine* and *sincere*—this is a method of fulfilling a basic SUBCONSCIOUS NEED *which cannot be overdone!*

The need—*the craving*—for the FEELING OF BEING APPRECIATED is so great in *everybody* that *it cannot be over-filled* no matter how much appreciation and gratitude you show and express—as long as it is sincere. And your appreciation *must be sincere.*

No one has ever been known to resent any abundance of *sincere* appreciation and gratitude!

Become a constant fountain of outpouring appreciation and gratitude! *Let it flow!*

X +

Chapter 64

Special Section:
Multiply Your PERSONAL POSITIVE POWER (× +)

The Most Powerful MOTIVATION Of All!

We now shall study the *most powerful motivation in the world!*

It has existed throughout the history of mankind. Unchanged. Compelling. Relentless.

It is part of the subconscious root-source of *all* that is *good*—and *all* that is *bad*.

It is not the *only* motivation—but it is the *most powerful*—and it *always* is part of the driving force behind all ego-actions.

Sometimes it is so disguised that you do not recognize it. *But it is there! Always!*

Sometimes it is so deeply buried in the subconscious that no one is aware of it. *But it is there! Always!*

Usually it is so personal—*so closely identified with each person's ego*—that most people will not admit even having it, or being motivated by it. *But it is there! Always!*

It is the NEED TO FEEL IMPORTANT!

And it is the most powerful motivation in the world!

For *good*—or for *evil.*

The good or the evil isn't *in* the *motivation.* The motivation—the NEED TO FEEL IMPORTANT—supplies the power, the irresistible compulsion to DO *something* and, too often, to DO *anything* which will satisfy the starvation pangs of an expanding ego *which no longer can live on mediocrity.*

The good or the evil—and all of the shadings in between—result from the *direction,* the *channeling* and, finally, the *goal* (WHATEVER goal!) which fulfills each individual's compelling NEED TO FEEL IMPORTANT.

We, as parents, as teachers, as advisors, as associates, as leaders—or whatever our contact with, or influence over, another—can supply that guidance, that direction, that channeling, that goal.

Or we can leave it to chance—to fate!

Too often, we leave to chance, the method by which some unguided (or misguided) drop-out chooses his way to fulfill his NEED TO FEEL IMPORTANT. So, the wheel of fate turns and, of a thousand choices, the pointer points to . . . *arson!* It really was not such a "big deal" to burn down a building or a city block! But some poor, misguided kid figured it would give *him* a FEELING OF IMPORTANCE. And now he cannot even feel the heat of that raging fire—*not through the cold, stone walls of his reformatory cell.*

Nobody cared how *he* got *his* FEELING OF IMPORTANCE! Nobody showed *him* a *worthy goal;* nobody told *him* how *he* could reach it; *nobody helped.*

Nobody!

It is incredible that we leave to chance the *all-determining direction of most lives;* that we leave to fate and to unguided (or misguided) minds, the choice of how *they* will attain *their* compelling NEED TO FEEL IMPORTANT.

And we wonder . . . WHY . . .

WHY all the silly or, sometimes, sinister demonstrations? . . . WHY the constant din of embittered threats? . . . the unveiled hostility? . . . the angry riots? . . . the self-defeating boycotts? . . . the strikes which too often are motivated more by the desire to demonstrate IMPORTANCE than by economic strategy.

WHY the thousand-and-one trouble-oriented activities which sicken us with *hate-pollution?* WHY spend billions to clean the *physical* environment while we virtually ignore the *mental-emotional* environment which is much more dangerously polluted with the deadly poisons of hate, anger, resentment, and violence?

It is not enough that we *merely question.* Why don't *we clean up* the polluted *mental-emotional* environment of resentment and hate which sickens our very souls?

What we need is a *solution to hate-pollution!* How do we get rid of the resentment and hate which pollutes our *mental-emotional* environment?

Here's how: Start at the very source—*the most powerful motivation in the world:* the NEED TO FEEL IMPORTANT.

It can be left *undirected*—and cause chaos!

It can be *deliberately misdirected* to incite hate-demonstrations, riots, disruptions and violence.

Or the NEED TO FEEL IMPORTANT can be

directed, channeled, and *guided* to worthy achievements, to personal accomplishments which bring honor to the individual and benefit to all mankind.

Let us direct, channel, and guide the NEED TO FEEL IMPORTANT—*for it is the most powerful motivation of all!*

Having looked at the broad opportunities of variously using the NEED TO FEEL IMPORTANT, let us put aside our wide-angle lens and sharpen our focus on you.

You can *positively* guide this *most powerful motivation of all* by fulfilling in others their compelling NEED TO FEEL IMPORTANT through *your* helping them discover how to *multiply their importance* by becoming a *Positive Power Person!*

Make the giving of a FEELING OF IMPORTANCE one of *your* most *conspicuous* personality traits. Let it be *widely known* that to associate with *you,* even to talk with *you* briefly, *will increase every person's* FEELING OF IMPORTANCE—because you constantly *say* and *do* whatever is required to make *every* person FEEL IMPORTANT.

This really is a lot easier than it may seem. In fact, it is quite simple. The most difficult part is *just remembering to do it* with *every person* you are with even briefly.

Every person—from the already very important to the seemingly unimportant—has in his or her subconscious the *constant compulsion* to reassure or to gratify the NEED TO FEEL IMPORTANT.

This constant need can be fulfilled simply by your treating the other person as being IMPORTANT, or by your implying or forthrightly saying that he or she is IMPORTANT.

You have so many choices that you *always* can find *some* way to increase *everybody's* FEELING OF IMPORTANCE.

But . . . why *everybody?*

Certainly, *everybody* cannot help *you* get whatever *you* want!

So why bother with increasing the FEELING OF IMPORTANCE of *everybody*—and especially of those who cannot be of *any* help to *you* in attaining *your* life-goal?

Here's why:

From the thousands of people you will meet during your lifetime, *you cannot possibly select* the one hundred (or the one dozen) people who—combined with *future* circumstances which you cannot now even foresee—will help you get WHATEVER you want in life.

Your subconscious mind, in its constant cybernetic (goal-reaching) function, will obtain help for you from people and sources of which you now are not even aware!

As I look back over my own life, I find that *almost all of the outside success assistance which I received, came from people and sources I did not even know at the time!*

Every big success "break" I have ever had—came from an *unknown source* and was *unexpected!*

Almost *every day* I receive help from one or more *unknown sources*—from people I do not know and in ways I have not perceived!

Your subconscious mind is a part of the *Infinite Mind* and, as such, is a part of *Infinity.* Your subconscious mind—drawing knowledge and power from the *Infinite* of which it is a part—will cybernetically *combine people and circumstances* to enable you to get WHATEVER you want. *But you must let your subconscious mind do it.*

Even if you *could* (and, again, I assure you that you *cannot*) *select the people* who, combined with *future* circumstances which you cannot now foresee, will help you get WHATEVER you want, *you would destroy your positive personality by trying to seek them out selfishly* as objects of your success methods.

If you try to fulfill the subconscious needs of ONLY those *you think can help you* get what you want—*you will become a warped, twisted, selfish, greedy, grasping person!* And then all of the success methods in this book cannot make you successful!

This book—this SUCCESS COURSE—gives you the success methods of *Personal Influence Psychology* for your use in your personal relations with *everybody* with whom you come in contact.

This SUCCESS COURSE repeatedly has emphasized that the success methods taught here *must* be used with *everybody—impartially* and *unselfishly.*

Only by your being a *full-time Positive Power Person* can you attract WHATEVER you want.

That requires that you *constantly* fulfill the subconscious needs of *all* of the people you meet or write to—and that you do this *impartially* and *unselfishly.*

So, in fulfilling the need of *all* people to FEEL

IMPORTANT, you must treat *every* person with whom you have *any* contact (in person, or by letter, or by telephone) as being in *some* way: IMPORTANT.

Begin by using the proven psychological method of "AS IF":

Always *think, feel, talk* and *act* AS IF the other person *is* IMPORTANT.

No matter how unimportant, insignificant or lowly in position the other person may *seem* to be, *always treat every person* AS IF he or she *is* IMPORTANT.

And, do it with obvious respect, courtesy, and sincerity.

When you perfect your skill in using this "AS IF" technique through *constantly* and *sincerely* using it on *everyone*, you will discover that your sense of perception has become so keen that you can instantly find in *every* person *some* way (perhaps *many* ways) in which he or she *really is* IMPORTANT.

In the meantime, whether or not you perceive anything important about a person, ALWAYS *think, feel, talk*, and *act* AS IF that person *is* IMPORTANT.

How?

If you follow the preceding method exactly—you *naturally* and *automatically* will *treat* every person AS IF that person *is* IMPORTANT.

However, to make your recognition of their IMPORTANCE instantly clear to everybody, always do *at least* these two things:

(1) Treat them AS IF they are IMPORTANT by showing them *obvious respect, gracious courtesy*, and *genuine admiration*.

(2) Sincerely *tell* them that *they* are IMPORTANT; *tell* them by implication or by forthright statement—but *tell* them that *they* are IMPORTANT.

There simply isn't space in this book to illustrate every method by describing a lot of examples. Anyway, the author knows that you will learn more thoroughly if you mentally create your own relevant examples—or by your putting the lessons into practice and actually creating real examples.

However, since there may be some doubt in your mind concerning how you would fulfill the NEED TO FEEL IMPORTANT in a person who may not hold a position of generally recognized "importance". . . here are several examples:

You are driving in a strange part of the city, looking for Blank Street. You see a boy delivering newspapers. You *could* get the directions you need by yelling, "Hey, kid! Where's Blank Street?" (That would serve your purpose: first, attact attention; then ask your question as concisely as possible.)

Or you *could* ask with respect and courtesy—and give the boy a FEELING OF IMPORTANCE by respectfully saying, "Young *man, I'm a stranger* here, and *I'm lost!* I'll appreciate *your helping me.* Will *you direct* me to Blank Street, please?" (You called him a *man.* You were a *stranger, lost* and *in trouble.* You asked him for *his help.* You asked *him* to *direct you.* You had the *courtesy* to say "*please.*")

It only took a few additional seconds to *increase* the FEELING OF IMPORTANCE of that newspaper delivery boy. But by doing so, you *multiplied* your

PERSONAL POSITIVE POWER by *unselfishly* fulfilling another's subconscious need. By constantly doing *that,* you become a *Positive Power Person.*

Another example: You are in an office building, looking for the location of the new offices of a new tenant. The firm's name has not yet been posted on the directory near the elevators. You could disagreeably confront the elevator supervisor and demand, "Where are the offices of Blank and Company? They moved in this morning and aren't listed on the directory board *yet!* How long does it take for you people to find out you have a new tenant?" (You really told the old man off! Of course it wasn't *his* responsibility to post the names and office numbers. But he was the only employee in sight. And in response to your criticism, he curtly gave you the run-around: "I only check on the elevators. You'll have to see the building manager.")

You would have saved time and temper if you had respectfully approached the elevator supervisor and courteously said, "Sir, I see that *you* are *in charge* here. *I* have a *problem* and I'm sure *you can help me. You* have a new tenant, and since they have just moved into *your* building, *there hasn't been time* to list them on *your* directory board. Would *you please* give me the office number of Blank and Company?"

You addressed him as "*Sir.*" You acknowledged that *he was in charge.* You admitted that *you* had a *problem.* (*Your* inferiority.) You asked for *his help* and expressed *confidence* that *he could provide it.* (*His* superiority.) *You volunteered a reasonable excuse* for the name not yet being posted. You *confidently* and *courteously* asked for the office number. (Which he "officially" and promptly read to you from the notebook *which he took from his pocket!*)

A final, and different, example: This time the man you call on is one of a number of vice-presidents of a large corporation. He already *is* important

After an informal and cordial introduction, you say with casual, good-nature: "I understand that you are known around here as the *'Vice-President In Charge Of GETTING THINGS DONE!'* Well, I've got something that needs to be done—*so I came to YOU.*"

That would make even an important vice-president feel a little *more* IMPORTANT. And, because IMPORTANCE is dependent, in part, on the opinions of others, even the most important people need to be reassured, from time to time, of their established importance.

The preceding examples only serve to emphasize what you already have learned in this chapter. It would be helpful for you to re-read the entire chapter *very thoughtfully*—right now.

It puts you in command of *the most powerful motivation of all*—others' NEED TO FEEL IMPORTANT!

To the extent that you *constantly* and *unselfishly* fulfill the compelling subconscious needs of others. you *multiply* your PERSONAL POSITIVE POWER.

Then, as a *Positive Power Person—using the success methods in this book*—you will attract WHATEVER you want in life!

×+

Chapter 65

Special Section:
Multiply Your PERSONAL POSITIVE POWER (× +)

The Way To Be AGREEABLE . . .

The way to be *agreeable* is to *agree!*

That fact seems obvious enough. It is *so* obvious that few people pay any attention to it. Most people rush to disagree even with another's *inconsequential* comments!

To most people, another's debatable opinion invites verbal war!

It isn't really that they want to be disagreeable —they only want to disagree. Usually, the results are the same.

Why, then, are so many people so eager to disagree and thereby, often unintentionally, be disagreeable.

Because it is their way of flexing their own egos; of demonstrating their own importance, even their superiority. They hope, by disagreeing, to attract the spotlight, if only briefly. It is their unwitting way of attracting attention.

What does blatant disagreement get them? It gets them the reputation of being disagreeable. It is no way to win friends and influence people.

One way to *multiply* your PERSONAL POSITIVE POWER is to be *agreeable.*

And the *best* way to be *agreeable* is to *agree!*

The *next best* way to be *agreeable* is NOT to *disagree.*

It is not required that you express verbal judgment on all statements made by others. *Unless you agree. Then* it *is* necessary, because by expressing your hearty agreement, *you increase your popularity rating in proportion to the conviction and enthusiasm of your expressed agreement.*

Do not miss *any* opportunity to *agree!* Even if your opinion is not directly requested—*agree anyway!* It makes you *agreeable.*

But *disagree* only when the population of the entire world is waiting in hushed attention—waiting for *your* verdict to be handed down to rectify or prevent an *irreparable* wrong!

You seldom will be confronted with such a momentous occasion to be disagreeable. And since few lesser occasions warrant your being disagreeable, you may get through life without being disagreeable at all! *An accomplishment worthy of your constant effort!*

This does not mean that you must *instantly agree* with all statements made by others or to all of their requests. Certainly not!

It simply means that *you must not INSTANTLY disagree.* Or *POINTEDLY disagree!*

In most instances, you may never *need* to *express* your disagreement at all. If you do not *immediately* precipitate or join in an argument, you most likely will not be *forced* into disagreeing. Few people *invite* open disagreement. And, again, let me emphasize: you are *not required* to *express* your judgment or opinion on *everything.*

You simply can remain a *silent*, interested observer. You do not have to appear bored and inattentive. Indeed, if you are *clever,* you can *participate* in a discussion without *definitely disagreeing*—or even *taking sides* in an argument (which would require your disagreeing with one side or the other).

But you can only manage this if you are *clever.* If you are not *that* clever, *then remain silent.* It is better to be quiet than to be vocally disagreeable.

Of course, there are those *rare* instances when you *must* take an adverse position and *state your disagreement.* Do not *instantly* join the fray *with vigorous or violent dissent.* Delay as long as courtesy permits. Thoughtfully (*silently*) consider all of the points—especially those with which you disagree. Finally, if you still *really* must *state* an adverse opinion, do so *not as an argument* and *not even as a disagreement*—but simply as a *thoughtful statement,* not intended to be a part of any debate.

There is a real art to doing this. There is not space to discuss it in detail here. But one or more of five general methods should be used:

(1) Use the *"Other Persons Method":* Do *not* disagree *yourself.* Do *not* state that *you* disagree. Instead, thoughtfully suggest that: "Possibly, *some people* might

disagree by saying (put *your* disagreement into the words of the '*some people*')." By doing this, *you* never openly disagree, *yourself*, but attribute your disagreement to what "Possibly, *some people* might say, etc." Thus *you* never take an adversary position.

(2) Use the "*Question Method*": Do *not directly* disagree. Put your disagreement in the form of a thoughtful *question*, as though you were assisting in the preparation to "meet any objections," like this: "Suppose *somebody* would raise the *question* that (state *your* disagreement in the form of a *hypothetical question* attributed to 'somebody')." By disagreeing through *impersonal hypothetical questions* which "possibly might be raised," *you* never take an adversary position, *personally*.

(3) Use the "*Disassociation Method*": Make your statement of disagreement as far apart from the main argument as possible. As previously suggested: delay it; defer it; take time to give it long and thoughtful consideration. Remember, when you disagree with another, you attack and deflate his or her precious ego. *Handle with care!* Be very slow to disagree. *The slower, the better!* Then disassociate your disagreement as far as possible from the main argument.

(4) Use the "*Sandwich Method*": First, *agree* freely and enthusiastically with *every* relevant point on which *you possibly can agree,* and introduce *other agreeable* points which may not even have been discussed. That is the first layer of the sandwich.

Now for the meat: You casually *mention* some other points (your disagreements), "*which also ought to be considered*"—but do *not argue* them or *emphasize* them; simply *state* them as a *continuing part* of what began as an agreement. Do not be argumentative. Just suggest that there are at least *two sides* to every proposition; and that *all* sides should be given *fair* and *equal* consideration.

Then the final layer of the sandwich: Conclude your comment with a *re-statement of your agreement with as many points as possible* and *suggest a thorough reconsideration of ALL of the points.* (*That keeps your disagreement in the discussion* without *your* being *too* directly associated with it.)

This "*Sandwich Method*" enables you to *unobtrusively state your points of disagreement* and at the same time maintain an *agreeable personality*. Those who have used this "*Sandwich Method*" have written the author that the results have been most effective, without causing any resentment—in fact they have won admiration for "open-mindedness."

(5) Use the "*Substitute Method*": This is the best method to use when your *disagreeing* also *denies* another person something for which he or she has asked. For example: Junior argues that he must have the family car tomorrow night to take his buddies to the football rally. You have plans for using the family car yourself tomorrow night. You do not argue or express heated disagreement. Nor do you assert your authority with a flat, unexplained "NO!".

You calmly state the facts. More than a week ago, you accepted an invitation which requires your use of the car tomorrow night, and no other transportation is available. (This is reasonable, but it does not soothe Junior's disappointment.)

So you provide an *agreeable substitute.* You had planned to use the car next Saturday night, but you can make other arrangements so that Junior can use the family car then—*which is the night of the school dance.*

You cannot always offer a substitute as agreeable as *that,* but you always should offer the best possible substitute—never a flat, arbitrary, disagreeable "NO!".

Being agreeable is the *art of accommodation.* While the *best* way to be *agreeable* is to *agree,* this is not always possible. What *is* possible is that you *agreeably* seek to *accommodate* your points of view with those of others—and that you do so in the most *agreeable* manner which you thoughtfully can devise.

Everyone has a compelling subconscious NEED TO BE RIGHT—because to be *wrong* deflates the precious ego.

To be *right,* to be *correct,* provides a pleasant glow of *self-satisfaction.* It increases *self-confidence,* strengthens the feeling of *self-importance.*

If, by disagreeing, you challenge and even undermine another's feeling of being right, of being correct, of self-satisfaction, of self-confidence, of self-importance—you create a subconscious resentment.

Of course, you also may provoke conscious, unconcealed resentment and dislike.

Few disagreements are worth it.

But, although conscious resentment may fade in time, *subconscious resentment* will remain as a *permanent ego-damage*—hidden, sulking deep in the other person's subconscious—and *no disagreement is worth that!* Find *some* way to avoid *disagreement.*

But remember, *avoiding disagreement*—as important as that is—*does not make you agreeable.* The only way to be agreeable is to *agree.*

So make it one of your notable personality characteristics to *agree.* Find *some* way—*many* ways—to openly, enthusiastically, vocally (or in writing) express your *agreement* with as many people as possible—as often as possible.

Do not wait for others to ask you for an expression of agreement. *Volunteer your admiring and enthusiastic agreement at every opportunity.*

You can become an engaging conversationalist and a much-sought companion just by sincerely and enthusiastically saying, "I *agree* with you completely," every time another expresses an opinion!

The way to be *agreeable* is to *agree*—and being AGREEABLE will *multiply* your PERSONAL POSITIVE POWER.

×+

Chapter 66

Special Section:
Multiply Your PERSONAL POSITIVE POWER (× +)

People Riot To Get This!

Ask the leader of any mass (or even small) demonstration *why* the marching, the chanting, the scrawled signs, the disruption—and he will tell you (or grab a microphone and tell *everybody* within range): "We are demonstrating to CALL ATTENTION to our (cause . . . plight . . . grievances . . . demands . . . etc.)."

The key words are "CALL ATTENTION."

People *demonstrate* to "CALL ATTENTION."

People *riot* to "CALL ATTENTION." Ask anyone who has listened to the explanations of convict-participants in a prison riot. The prisoners rioted, destroyed property, captured and held hostages. Why? To "CALL ATTENTION" to "conditions," "bad food," "guard brutality," etc.

And they *demanded* the ATTENTION of the

highest authority, usually the governor. But also they wanted the ATTENTION of the *public.* Of course they wanted to make demands, but the "demands" were often vague and even the rioting prisoners couldn't agree on the "demands" for which they were rioting.

What they did agree on was that they wanted ATTENTION!

And they rioted, destroyed, even threatened murder to get it!

People will do almost *anything* to attract ATTENTION. Not only in groups (as in demonstrations and riots) but as individuals. You read about them every day in your newspaper. You see them on television.

Desperate individuals stand for hours on the upper-story ledges of skyscrapers, to be pleaded with by the clergy. Usually, they are "talked back" to safety—to read about themselves on the front pages. (If they had been *intent on suicide,* they would have *leaped instantly* to their death.) Thus their damaged egos are "healed" by the ATTENTION. And, hopefully, by subsequent mental therapy which can provide a permanent cure.

Other individuals seek to satisfy their subconscious NEED FOR ATTENTION by engaging in almost every conceivable antic from the *ridiculous* to the *hazardous.* This brief paragraph is all the "attention" they shall receive here.

However, there are individuals and groups of *attention-seekers* among us whose methods of fulfilling their NEED FOR ATTENTION are a constant source of disruption, annoyance and concern.

They are the radical, activist trouble-makers.

I do not need to describe them or their activities; you read and hear about them every day.

To the extent that they are the result of poverty, deprivation, racial bias, lack of education, unemployment, harassment, and the countless other disadvantages *to which organized assistance too often has responded so ineptly*—we owe them our sympathetic understanding and effective help.

To the extent that they presist in *expanding their distorted egos in disruptive search for attention, importance, and the admiration of fellow-radicals*—we must use every legal means to put an end to their trouble-making; and *then* help them find *worthy* activities for fulfilling their compelling NEEDS FOR ATTENTION AND IMPORTANCE.

If we but look about us, we shall see that the *radical, activist trouble-makers* have infiltrated every level of our society. Most of them fulfill their NEED FOR ATTENTION by relatively unimportant but annoying, disruptions.

Here's a typical case history: He dropped out of school because of lack of interest. Got a job on a factory production line in a big industry. Even though he *voluntarily* dropped out of school, he says that he represents the "educationally *deprived.*" Proudly calls himself a "*radical activist.*" Is constantly initiating all sorts of work-disruptive innovations to cause his employers trouble—for which he has been disciplined (usually laid off) more than twenty times so far. This attracted the ATTENTION and *admiration* of his fellow-workers who elected him their union committeeman!

There is something wrong with a business system in which the employees reward the fellow-employee who causes management the most trouble.

As for the radical activist, he explains, *"I have a monumental ego! I'm quite a show!"*

Well?

What have mass demonstrations, and prison riots, and trouble-making employees got to do with *your getting WHATEVER you want in life?*

Quite a lot!

They prove the *tremendous power* of the NEED FOR ATTENTION. They show that people will do almost *anything* to ATTRACT ATTENTION to themselves or to their "cause."

So now you know that you are dealing with—*and have available for your own constructive use*—one of the most powerful of all psychological forces!

Like all powerful psychological forces, the NEED FOR ATTENTION can produce good or evil *depending upon how it is used.*

This is no Pollyanna book.

This is not like a book about electricity which tells you that electricity will light your home and provide countless beneficial services—*without also telling you that the same electricity, improperly used, will electrocute you!*

This book tells you how to use psychology to GET WHATEVER YOU WANT. But it would be a dangerous book, if it did not *also* tell you that *psychology, improperly used, can damage or ruin your life.*

Therefore, one more example: *Psychosomatic illness,* which has been mentioned often in this book, but which is discussed again here because it is ***extensively used*** to fulfill the NEED FOR ATTENTION.

Many people develop a psychosomatic illness in order to fulfill their NEED FOR ATTENTION and their DESIRE for SYMPATHY. These people feel *neglected* by their families or friends. The only way they can get the ATTENTION and SYMPATHY which they *subconsciously need* is by having fainting spells, or symptoms of a heart attack, or symptoms of other alarming illnesses, or even just "general weakness." Many psychosomatic illnesses become quite serious and can be fatal if not properly treated.

Although sometimes these illnesses are consciously and deliberately contrived, *more often they are the result of the subconscious mind cybernetically fulfilling an unsuspected desire* for ATTENTION, SYMPATHY and CARE—and *the patient is aware only of the illness* and not that it originated as a subconscious NEED FOR ATTENTION.

As repeatedly emphasized in this book, your subconscious mind will *materialize* in your life WHATEVER you want and INTENSELY DEMAND by *concentrated thought.*

Remember, your subconscious mind cannot "reason." It cannot decide what is good for you or bad for you. Its function is totally *cybernetic:* to *materialize* in your life WHATEVER YOU INTENSELY DESIRE.

So, if you *intensely desire* ATTENTION, and *if you do not fulfill your desire through normal channels,* then your *subconscious mind* will be impelled to fulfill your *intense desire* through some *abnormal materialization, which certainly will not be of your conscious choosing*

—such as a psychosomatic heart condition or other illness.

That is why it is so important to use the psychological methods, taught in previous chapters to INTENSELY IMPRESS into your subconscious mind your POSITIVE LIFE GOAL, and to *constantly fill* your subconscious mind with mental pictures of your POSITIVE LIFE GOAL being *materialized* in your life.

Completely *saturate* and *dominate* your subconscious mind with *positive* thoughts and *positive* mental pictures so that there will be no *"thought-time"* left for *negative* thoughts of anxiety, fear, failure, or illness.

Two opposite (positive vs negative) thoughts cannot occupy your subconscious mind at the same time. So if you keep your subconscious mind constantly saturated with *positive* thoughts, then *negative* thoughts cannot enter and, therefore cannot affect your life.

This will make you a Positive Power Person!

Then, *multiply* your PERSONAL POSITIVE POWER by fulfilling the subconscious needs of *everybody* in your own personal world—as taught in this Special Section of your SUCCESS COURSE.

In this chapter, you are studying the compelling subconscious NEED FOR ATTENTION. We have observed that this basic subconscious need is the motivation for many of the problems of our times—from demonstrations and riots to psychosomatic illnesses.

In addition to preventing or redirecting the *negative* adverse activities of people who seek to fulfill their NEED FOR ATTENTION, you can use *your own personal positive power* to fulfill this impelling need of others in an almost *unlimited* number of *positive,* helpful ways. Let us examine some of the most important.

Obviously, the basic way to fulfill the NEED FOR ATTENTION is simply to *give the attention wanted.*

However, it is important to give *exactly the kind of attention* which is wanted.

Just giving ATTENTION *in general,* will not fulfill the need. You must give *exactly the kind* of ATTENTION which is needed by each individual.

For example:

(1) The convicts who rioted in prison, took over a prison area, and held a number of guards hostage—wanted the ATTENTION of the governor (also the press and public) so that they could explain their grievances, their complaints of guard brutality, poor food, filthy living conditions, etc. ONLY *that kind* of ATTENTION would *satisfy* them. When *that kind* of ATTENTION was provided, the riot ended, the guards were released, and the prisoners voluntarily returned to their cells.

It is not the purpose of this book to condone such extreme methods of getting ATTENTION, but it is within the province of psychology to point out that if *that kind* of ATTENTION had been regularly given the prisoners *in the first place,* the riot never would have occurred. There obviously would have been no NEED for it.

(2) Many public demonstrations, regrettably, are organized by ambitious, publicity-seeking people, who are interested primarily in obtaining SELF-ATTENTION to feed their own insatiable egos, and who use the dubious method of promoting the latest popular "cause" by recruiting the naive to march doggedly behind them, holding up crudely scrawled signs which advocate the "cause" selected by the self-appointed demonstration "leaders."

There is little we can or need to do about such

ego-promotion, except ignore it, and if it is too disruptive, prosecute the *leaders*, and credibly inform their misguided followers.

However, some demonstrations are genuine, broadly-based appeals for ATTENTION to *consequential conditions* in which the *conditions, themselves,* not self-promoting leaders, are the justification for ATTENTION and these deserve serious consideration. Such orderly demonstrations are the public expression of a pent-up *need* which the demonstrators honestly feel has been unfairly neglected. The *demonstrators* and the *need* should be given *exactly the kind of attention* which is *wanted*—and which is justly deserved.

It cannot be assumed that *every objective* of every meritorious demonstration can be granted. But the ATTENTION which is sought *should be given*—and *should be continued while a satisfactory solution is sought.* Thus the need for *demonstrating* for ATTENTION will be eliminated. Then the problem can be given calm, rational, sympathetic consideration.

However if the real purpose of a demonstration is not merely to seek ATTENTION, but is, in fact, a *threat of mob violence*, then it is a case for *firm law enforcement* with prompt and severe penalties which will deter future attempts at intimidation and mob rule.

(3) The subconscious NEED FOR ATTENTION of every individual naturally varies with each person. Just because it is not as violent as a prison riot or as dramatic as mass demonstration, does not mean that the individual's NEED is less compelling. Often an *individual's* NEED FOR ATTENTION is *more severe!*

As a *Positive Power Person,* you can and should fulfill the NEED FOR ATTENTION of *every* individual in your own personal world.

The first requirement is to give each individual the *exact kind of attention* which is wanted by *that individual.*

The second requirement is that you pay *interested, undivided* attention when your attention is expected. You inflict a serious subconscious wound when you reward enthusiastic expectation with indifference.

Not only must you *look* attentive and *be* attentive—but you should *emphasize your attention by action.* One of the best ways to *emphasize your attention* is to *do* something appropriate to *show* it.

Inactive interest is a lazy way to express attention. *Doing* something with *active enthusiasm* to express your attention is many times more appreciated!

And, never treat a complaint with indifference. It is especially important that you express your *undivided interest and concern by listening with sympathetic attention to all complaints.* Do not interrupt. Do not argue. Let the aggrieved person completely "*talk out*" his or her complaint. Do not look bored or indifferent. Maintain an interested, attentive, sympathetic attitude for as long as the other person feels the "*need to talk.*"

The "*need to talk*" is often a very compelling psychological need. It provides the mental-emotional therapy which psychiatrists call "catharsis." Sympathetically encouraging an upset person to "*completely talk out*" a problem, a complaint, a grievance, is one of the most effective ways of treating many mental-emotional illnesses.

It also is the way to de-escalate grievances, prevent many demonstrations, work stoppages, and even riots. Completely *"talking it out of one's system"* permits emotional fires to consume themselves.

In the foregoing ways—and in the many others which they will suggest to you—you will discover the enormous value of fulfilling the NEED FOR ATTENTION of *all* those in your own personal world.

Thus, you will continue to *multiply* your PERSONAL POSITIVE POWER.

Only by becoming a *Positive Power Person* can you be sure of attracting WHATEVER you want in life!

×+

Chapter 67

Special Section:
Multiply Your PERSONAL POSITIVE POWER (× +)

Help Others FEEL NEEDED!

Perhaps the greatest sadness of growing old begins with the realization, or maybe only the feeling, that one is NO LONGER NEEDED.

Because no longer being NEEDED, often is the beginning of no longer being WANTED.

There is much logic in the "*compulsory retirement age.*" And much illogic. And much heartbreak. Much *self-imposed* heartbreak!

Being retired need not mean a rocking-chair existence. Being retired really means that you have the time and the opportunity to choose a SECOND CAREER. It is the time when you can do what *you* always have *wanted* to do—without the time-clock, quota-striving, success-demanding pressure and regimentation of big business—or worse, of little business trying to compete with big business.

There are many advantages in the increasingly popular SECOND CAREER concept for retired persons. If you are retired, you can choose any SECOND CAREER within the range of your finances and ability—and then use the quick, simple and easy success methods in this book to succeed at *your own chosen pace,* without running in the "rat race."

This book—this SUCCESS COURSE—enables you *to choose your own speed and degree of success.* It is like owing a powerful automobile. You can step down on the accelerator and race ahead to your life-goal, or you can drive ahead leisurely and enjoy the scenery along the way. In either case, you will be successful. But *you* choose the speed and degree.

Giving a copy of this book to a retired person, or to a person whose retirement is only a few years away, is one of the most *positive* ways of saying, "There is much which *you can do,* and *do successfully! You are NEEDED!*"

At the other end of the spectrum of those who do not feel NEEDED, is *youth.* Especially youth seeking employment, or a few years before seeking employment.

All of those adolescent wise-cracks about the "square" Establishment just don't seem quite so funny to the Third Assistant Personnel Director who shows so much more interest in *how many years of practical experience* the applicant has had in automated programing of mechanized production than in the student "'leadership" he or she demonstrated in taking over the university adminstration building and dumping out the contents of the files.

Suddenly, in the strange, new world of big business, youth sees all those "square" adults competently performing complex operations with the confidence of years of experience—and youth has that sickening feeling of NOT BEING NEEDED.

Of course YOUTH IS NEEDED.

Business has been employing, teaching, training, encouraging, promoting—yes, and *seeking* YOUTH—since the first primitive businesses began. BUSINESS NEEDS YOUTH!

And business *wants* youth! Business, and the professions, and the services—the whole organized adult world *needs* the very special qualities which youth has in such exuberant abundance. Youth is the transfusion of life-blood without which business could not continue to exist.

In every youthful job-applicant, the employer is looking for *one special quality*. That is the ability to make the *employer* MORE SUCCESSFUL. That is *why the employer is in business:* to be SUCCESSFUL. So naturally, what every employer is looking for in each job applicant is: can he or she increase the *company's* SUCCESS?

Obviously, a youth seeking his first job cannot be expected to know very much about his prospective employer's business—or *any* business. *But he can know how to be SUCCESSFUL*—and *that* is what the *employer wants!* Because when the employees know how to be SUCCESSFUL, themselves—naturally they will make the business that much more SUCCESSFUL.

And . . . knowing how to be SUCCESSFUL is just as quick, simple, and easy as reading this book—mastering this SUCCESS COURSE.

If you want to make a youth FEEL NEEDED

in the business world, give him or her a copy of this book. Because this SUCCESS COURSE enables youth to bring to business the *only* thing that business wants *and must have*—SUCCESS! Specific job-skills will need to be learned. But, SUCCESS, *the most important job-skill of all,* must be learned, too. And SUCCESS can be learned *in advance*—from this book.

That does not apply *only* to *youthful* job applicants but to job applicants of *any age*.

A lot of clever managers are going to give copies of this book to their present employees, because they know that the more their employees learn about SUCCESS, the more *successful* their businesses will become.

Because SUCCESS is what business is about!

And SUCCESS is what this book is about!

They *belong together,* don't they? This SUCCESS COURSE and every successful business!

But there is more to FEELING NEEDED than *second careers* for retired persons and *new careers* for youth and *successful careers* for those of all ages.

FEELING NEEDED is one of the basic psychological needs. When a person no longer FEELS NEEDED, that person's ego begins to shrivel; the *reason for being* no longer exists.

It is a heartbreaking tragedy which can occur at *any age*—for so many different reasons that we shall not even attempt to list but several examples.

Instead, we shall diagnose the basic cause, and prescribe the basic cure.

The dull feeling of NO LONGER BEING

NEEDED occurs when a person thinks of *being NEEDED in the same way* that he or she *previously has been needed*—and that *same need* no longer exists.

For example:

A widow whose children have grown, married, and moved to a distant city. She is alone—and lonely. There no longer are loved ones to help take care of, or seldom even to see. The daily household chores seem meaningless. And so does life. NO LONGER NEEDED.

The survivor of an elderly couple whose lives had been a constant and devoted companionship. Now only one is left . . . alone . . . and lonely. NO LONGER NEEDED.

The youth who, for whatever reason, has turned off and dropped out. For a while, a shabby sort of seeking; a few highs, always with lower lows. The *lost* following the *lost* to . . . *nowhere* . . . and *nothing*. The vacant feeling of NOT BEING NEEDED.

The old worker who, day after day, year after year, has done his job. It wasn't the most important job, but . . . well, *every job* that needs doing is important. Unfortunately, *every worker* isn't. Especially *old workers*. The *job* is still there, but the *old worker* no longer is. He is home . . . and NO LONGER NEEDED.

Each case a heartbreaking tragedy: the FEELING OF BEING NO LONGER NEEDED.

There is a cure!

There is a glorious, exultant, triumphant cure!

We cannot change the Past. We only can accept it. It is done. It cannot be otherwise.

We *can* change the Present!

We begin with the realization that EVERYONE IS NEEDED! Urgently needed! Now!

There is so much to be done that if each of us worked at it twenty-four hours every day for the rest of our lives—we still could not do it!

Let us look again at the *cause* of the feeling of NO LONGER BEING NEEDED—because it is in the *cause* that we find the *cure.*

"The feeling of NO LONGER BEING NEEDED occurs when a person thinks of *being NEEDED in the same way* that he or she *previously had been needed*—and that *same need* no longer exists."

Since the person no longer is needed in the *same way* as *previously*—it only is necessary to be *useful* (and therefore, NEEDED) in some *other* way!

There are *millions* of persons who need *help* in some way!

Surely, out of *millions* of persons needing *help, every* person—of whatever age, condition, and skill—can find *many* or, at least, *someone* to *help* . . . in *some* way!

And . . . to HELP is to BE NEEDED!

When Fate closes one door, Faith opens another. That doorway leads to the glorious, exciting, satisfying life of HELPING OTHERS!

That is the message *you* must give to those who feel that they NO LONGER ARE NEEDED. You must help them find a way in which *they can help others!* Then *they* will be NEEDED!

You must help them find the *open* door to

helping others . . . some way . . . any way . . . using *whatever* talent and skill they have!

You must help them walk through that *open* door into a world of *new* HELPFULNESS—into a *new, glorious, triumphant life* of feeling that THEY ARE HELPING and, therefore, THEY ARE NEEDED.

It is the noblest use to which you can put your knowledge of psychology.

It will *multiply* your PERSONAL POSITIVE POWER.

It will establish you as a *Positive Power Person* with *compassion equal to your power.* And, *that* is greatest of all!

×+

Chapter 68

Special Section:
Multiply Your PERSONAL POSITIVE POWER (X +)

Get On The "MOST WANTED" List

The FBI publishes and distributes a "MOST WANTED" list of the most sought criminals.

It is not recommended that you get on the FBI's "MOST WANTED" list—because it terminates careers with as much certainty as the habit of criticizing others.

The people in your own personal world also have *their* own "MOST WANTED" list. It is a mental list of *those to whom they could turn* when confronted by a situation with which they are unable to cope—*alone.* It is in such situations that *you* should be "MOST WANTED."

And so we come to the last of the nine SUBCONSCIOUS NEEDS of others which you easily and surely can fulfill—and thereby *multiply* your PERSONAL POSITIVE POWER.

There are many other subconscious needs, of

course, but we have selected the nine which are the least complex—*and which every reader of this book easily can fulfill.*

Fulfilling the nine subconscious needs, as taught in this and the eight preceding chapters, will be quite sufficient to make you a *Positive Power Person* and enable you to get WHATEVER you want!

This chapter concerns the compelling subconscious NEED FOR OUTSIDE HELP which, on occasion, becomes tragically desperate.

This need, not only is psychological, but is physical and spiritual. However, here we shall deal primarily with the *subconscious feeling of being unable to cope with the personally overwhelming problems and conditions* which sooner or later confront everybody.

There is a wise proverb: "*The wind and the ocean quarrel. He who pays the price is the sailor in a boat.*"

Like the "sailor in a boat," we are at times the victims of circumstances *not of our making* and *beyond our control.*

At such times—which may be occasional, frequent, or constant—we have a subconscious and, often, a spiritual and physical NEED FOR OUTSIDE HELP which takes two forms:

(1) The NEED FOR HELP from a SUPERNATURAL POWER: God, Infinity, or whatever Deity-name you use.

To the author, the religious and spiritual beliefs of each reader are personal and sacred to the individual. It would be presumptuous for this book to intrude into the holy realm of religion, and it shall not do so. But, neither shall this book preclude this source of help.

The NEED FOR SUPERNATURAL HELP has been included because it is universal; however the term "OUTSIDE" has been eliminated from the description "OUTSIDE HELP," since it would be inaccurate to list God as a source of *"outside"* help; God, being infinite and everywhere, not only is *outside,* but *also inside,* each of us. Here is help *unlimited.* "Ask, and ye shall receive."

(2) The NEED FOR OUTSIDE HELP from HUMAN SOURCES:

If you have thoroughly mastered this SUCCESS COURSE, you have at your command a powerful system of proven success methods and the psychological techniques of *Motivational Psychology, Personal Improvement Psychology* and *Personal Influence Psychology.*

If you have mastered these, as taught in this book, you will have become a *Positive Power Person* with *tremendous capabilities for helping others!*

You will have *multiplied* your PERSONAL POSITIVE POWER and become (× +) times more powerful—*to the extent that you continue to use your positive power to help others.*

The key: HELP OTHERS!

That is the *source of positive power!* As long as you use your power to *help others,* your power will be *positive* and, in addition to helping others, your power, being *positive,* will *attract* WHATEVER you want in life.

But, if you try to use your power *only for your own selfish purposes,* it will become *negative* and *repel instead of attract.*

Of course, you now have learned *never to use your power selfishly*. So you are a *Positive Power Person.* This gives you unlimited opportunities, but it imposes great responsibilities for using your positive power to help others.

"*To whom much is given, much shall be required.*"

What have you *received?* What is *required* of you?

You now have learned the success methods, and have developed the subconscious cybernetic power to *get WHATEVER you want.* And, of course, you will—by *doing* what you have learned.

But it is your *responsibility,* as a *Positive Power Person,* to *help others,* who cannot cope with events and conditions which are beyond *their* individual capabilities.

When others are confronted by situations which they cannot *individually* manage, they have an urgent NEED FOR OUTSIDE HELP.

This is the *ninth* NEED of others which is given you to fulfill as a means of *multiplying* your PERSONAL POSITIVE POWER.

Since every person has so many and varied NEEDS FOR OUTSIDE HELP, it is not practical to attempt to list all such needs. Nor would a long list be useful because each need of another person requires a specific solution.

Therefore, we shall list *general* procedures and leave the *specific* actions for you to apply according to each individual problem.

You greatly *multiply* your PERSONAL POSITIVE POWER simply by *saying* to *all* people within the range of your influence:

"If you ever need my cooperation, you can count on me!"

That simple, sincere statement of *advance positive assurance* of your ready and willing cooperation in time of serious need—will establish you as a POSITIVE POWER SOURCE.

Then others will *feel* your *assurance* of *positive power.* They will seek *you* as an *associate.* They will seek *your influence* and *your leadership.*

You will experience the great forces of psychology in action!

When you affirm to others—*everybody* in your personal world—the *confident* statement which gives them *your advance positive assurance: "If you ever need my cooperation, you can count on me!"*. . . here are some of the powerful psychological forces you use:

(1) You use the tremendously effective psychology of "AS IF." You *look, talk* and *act* AS IF you are a POSITIVE POWER SOURCE. So you *are!*

(2) You use the infinite, subconscious power of INTENSE BELIEF in your *positive power.* So you *have* it!

(3) You fulfill another's subconscious NEED. So you *multiply* your PERSONAL POSITIVE POWER.

We could almost endlessly continue this list, but you will find the powerful psychological success methods throughout this entire book—so you can review them in more detail.

Use them constantly and you will establish yourself as a POSITIVE POWER SOURCE.

You will radiate the *assurance* of PERSONAL POSITIVE POWER with the result that others will seek *you* as an *associate;* they will seek *your influence* and *your leadership.*

You will be on their "MOST WANTED" list.

This chapter is the last of the nine chapters, each describing a different, basic subconscious need of others—which you can fulfill and thereby *multiply* your PERSONAL POSITIVE POWER.

Every time you fulfill a compelling SUBCONSCIOUS NEED of any person, you give him or her a GIFT of priceless value!

To have a deep SUBCONSCIOUS NEED fulfilled, is one of the most important and satisfying of all possible GIFTS which others can receive from you.

The subconscious *gratitude* for such a GIFT is so deeply felt as to be beyond description.

You now have learned *nine* different SUBCONSCIOUS NEEDS which you can fulfill as your priceless GIFTS to *everybody* within the range of your personality. As you *give*, you shall *receive.*

It is so important to you—and to your future as a *Positive Power Person*—that you give one or more of these nine GIFTS to *everyone* . . . *wherever you go* . . . *always* . . . that, as a concise reminder, these nine priceless GIFTS have been listed as "*Your* POSITIVE POWER *Gift List*". . . in the next chapter.

X+

Chapter 69

Special Section:
Multiply Your PERSONAL POSITIVE POWER (× +)

Your POSITIVE POWER Gift List

The preceding nine chapters of this SUCCESS COURSE have *each* described a *different*, basic SUBCONSCIOUS NEED which *everybody* has.

Of course, there are many more than *nine* basic subconscious needs. The *nine* needs described to you in the preceding chapters were selected because:

(a) *Every person you talk with or write to, has these nine basic, compelling, subconscious needs.* Therefore you have the unlimited opportunity of fulfilling them for *everybody*.

You never should talk with or write to anyone —without fulfilling one or more of these nine subconscious needs!

(b) Many other subconscious needs are very complicated and involve an entire tangled network of neuroses, complexes, compulsions, sublimations, obsessions and repressions, to mention a few.

Obviously these require psychoanalysis, psychiatric therapy or similar professional services—and are not within the province of this book, the purpose of which is to teach *uncomplicated*, but nevertheless *very powerful*, psychological methods which the average reader can use *constantly* in his or her dealings with *everybody*.

As stated, one or more of the nine subconscious needs selected, can be fulfilled by *every reader* of this SUCCESS COURSE *every time he or she talks with or writes to anybody*.

(c) The selected nine subconscious needs, described in the nine preceding chapters may be fulfilled by every reader of this book—*easily* and *directly*. For example: The subconscious NEED TO FEEL ACCEPTED is fulfilled by providing ACCEPTANCE; the subconscious NEED TO FEEL APPRECIATED is fulfilled by providing APPRECIATION.

It is just that simple. Anybody can do it.

And, fulfilling the nine basic subconscious needs described in the preceding chapters is more than sufficient to *multiply* your PERSONAL POSITIVE POWER so surely and so enormously that your *positive power, through the cybernetic forces of your subconscious mind*, will attract to you WHATEVER you want in life.

Every time you fulfill a compelling SUBCONSCIOUS NEED of any person, you give him or her a GIFT of priceless value!

The *subconscious gratitude* for such a GIFT is *so deeply felt* and *constantly remembered* that it is vital to *you*, as a *Positive Power Person*, that you give one or more of these nine GIFTS to *every person* you meet, talk with, or write to—and that *you remember* to give one or more of these GIFTS *every time!*

So, as a concise reminder, these *nine* basic SUBCONSCIOUS NEEDS, these nine priceless GIFTS are listed and briefly described in the following:

POSITIVE POWER *Gift List*

GIFT #1: Make others FEEL ACCEPTED!

When the NEED TO FEEL ACCEPTED is *denied*, the rejected person or group feels *discriminated against*—and becomes resentful, angry and hostile.

Most racial problems have as their subconscious center the *denial* of BEING ACCEPTED by a *different* race. This *implication of inferiority* naturally is resented.

However, *denial* of ACCEPTANCE is *not limited* to differences in *race*.

Denial of ACCEPTANCE also occurs because of differences in wealth, in social status, in education (where "intellectual snobbishness" too often exists), and in any level of society which will not ACCEPT—and, in fact, boorishly rejects persons considered belonging to a *different* (and despotically defined: "inferior" level).

There is *denial* of ACCEPTANCE because of *differences* of creeds and because of *differences* in nationality—and because of *differencs* between geographic, political, and tribal segments of the same nationality.

The key word is: DIFFERENT.

Being *"different"* regrettably—and *often falsely*—implies that one or the other is *"inferior"* and not fully ACCEPTABLE to those who feel that they belong to a *"superior"* class.

But the inescapable fact remains: The NEED

TO FEEL ACCEPTED is one of the most basic and compelling subconscious NEEDS. Now it has surfaced as a *threatening demand.* Its continued and arrogant *denial* assures resentment, ill will and hostility.

To the extent that the ACCEPTANCE BARRIER can be lowered and subsequently eliminated, we shall be that much closer to the goal of *goodwill toward ALL—which will bring peace on earth.*

As a *Positive Power Person,* you have the opportunity—and the responsibility—to lower the ACCEPTANCE BARRIER, *to assert that "different" does not mean "inferior," and that "inferior" does not mean "unacceptable."*

When *you* give people the sincere assurance that *you* ACCEPT *them,* and when you help them attain increased ACCEPTANCE *by others*—you give one of the most appreciated and valuable of *Your* POSITIVE POWER *Gifts!*

GIFT #2: Make others FEEL APPROVED!

Everyone has a subconscious NEED TO FEEL APPROVED. This need is so basic and so compelling that, if it is not fulfilled, its absence leaves a vacant space in the personality. Vacant spaces tend to fill with something. When APPROVAL is withheld or withdrawn, the vacant space it leaves is filled with nagging doubts: the fears of inadequacy, incompetency, failure.

To the immature of *all ages* (immaturity is not confined to youth), the denial of APPROVAL constitutes a subconscious ego-rejection, the rejection of the person or his actions, which destroys his self-confidence, and leads to his over-compensation in one of two directions:

(a) Radical, character-destructive behavior

(b) Loss of motivation and ultimate withdrawal. *Another drop-out!*

So your GIFT of making others FEEL APPROVED can provide emergency benefits and prevent personality disasters—*thus making it one of the most urgent of all gifts!*

You may review HOW to fulfill the compelling NEED TO FEEL APPROVED by re-reading chapter 61.

GIFT #3: Make others feel ADMIRED!

The gift of expressing your ADMIRATION of *everyone* within the range of your personality is an art and a skill which you must perfect and constantly use in being a *Positive Power Person.*

The compelling urge to BE ADMIRED is conspicuously expressed by the expenditure of *billions of dollars* on cosmetics, clothes, jewels, hair styling and all the things which people do to win ADMIRATION.

So fulfilling the universal NEED TO BE ADMIRED is potentially a *billion-dollar* GIFT—which you now have and can give without cost . . . just by following the simple suggestions in Chapter 62.

GIFT #4: Make others feel they are APPRECIATED!

One of the distinguishing (*and most popular*) characteristics of a *Positive Power Person* is his or her ability to make others feel that they, their activities and/or their possessions are APPRECIATED. *You cannot overdo it!* So be a fountain of APPRECIATION! *Let it flow!*

Of course, APPRECIATION is a gift which is literally *craved* by almost everyone. *Unfortunately, the very people whom APPRECIATION would help most, receive it least—or not at all.* They are the very old, the very young, and those anxious people of all ages who, for a wide variety of reasons, *feel subconsciously insecure.* Be certain *always* to include *them* on your *Gift List* of APPRECIATION.

And be sure to *review* HOW to fulfill the NEED FOR APPRECIATION: Chapter 63.

GIFT #5: Make others feel IMPORTANT!

One of the most powerful motivations of all is seeking a secure FEELING OF IMPORTANCE.

As a *Positive Power Person,* you should establish your ability to make *others* FEEL IMPORTANT as being one of your most *conspicuous* personality traits.

Let it be widely known that to associate with you, even to talk with you briefly, will increase every person's FEELING OF IMPORTANCE—because you have the *Positive Power Person's* ability to *say* and *do* wha ever is needed to make *everyone* FEEL IMPORTANT!

This is an asset which will attract others to you, and enormously *multiply* your PERSONAL POSITIVE POWER to get whatever you want!

To *review* HOW to fulfill, in others, their compelling NEED TO FEEL IMPORTANT: re-read Chapter 64.

GIFT #6: Be AGREEABLE . . . *agree!*

Other people want *agreement*—not disagreement and arguments.

They want to be RIGHT. They want *your agreement* that they *are* RIGHT.

There is a subconscious NEED TO FEEL "AGREED WITH."

Being right, being *"agreed with"*—supports the ego. It sustains confidence. It maintains the satisfying feeling of security. *You challenge it at your own risk!*

Others may not be right *all of the time*. Of course not! But as a *Positive Power Person*, you will not *disagreeably* disagree *any of the time!*

If you are clever, and if you have learned the valuable psychological techniques in Chapter 65, you may not have to *openly* disagree at all. *And there is no limit to the popularity you will attain!*

Naturally, your constantly giving the GIFT of ego-support, reassuring confidence and satisfying security —will *multiply* your PERSONAL POSITIVE POWER.

So . . . be AGREEABLE! . . . *Peace!*

GIFT #7: Give others the ATTENTION they crave!

A *few* people can instinctively attract ATTENTION. But they want *much more attention* than they can attract.

Give them the *extra attention* they crave!

Most people do not attract *much attention*, yet subconsciously they deeply want *much more attention*. They are suffering from "ego-starvation," to state it psychologically.

So, as a *Positive Power Person*, give them *much more attention* than they ever have had before!

Sadly, there are people who do not get *any attention at all!* They are often the old, the lonely, the poor, the deprived. Why are *they* denied the attention for which they are starving? *Because others don't care!*

Well, as a *Positive Power Person, you* care! You will give them your GIFT of priceless value—your sincere, sympathetic, helpful ATTENTION.

And . . . "*As ye have done it unto any of the least of these* . . ."

To *review* HOW to fulfill, *in all others,* their own special NEEDS FOR ATTENTION, re-read Chapter 66.

GIFT #8: Make others feel NEEDED!

To make others FEEL NEEDED is the noblest use to which you can put your knowledge of psychology.

To make others FEEL NEEDED is the GIFT of LIFE, itself! What good is life, if one is not needed? Because not to be *needed,* often means not to be *wanted.*

Yet, many of the old feel no longer needed. And many of the young can find no meaningful place in a social structure grown rigid. And the under-motivated, the undereducated, the deprived, the poor . . . *who NEEDS them?*

WE need them!

In a world of *Positive Power People—everybody* is NEEDED!

There is more to be done than all of the people on earth can do for generations to come! The NEED is *now!* The people are *here!*

But it will take Positive Power People to put it all together!

YOU can begin by reviewing Chapter 67.

GIFT #9: Fill the NEED FOR OUTSIDE HELP!

No one is sufficient unto himself.

"The wind and the ocean quarrel. He who pays the price is the sailor in a boat."

Often, because of circumstances far beyond their control, people find themselves, like the "sailor in a boat," being tossed helplessly about in the unforeseen storms of life.

They cannot cope with their problems—*alone.*

They *must seek help* from two sources:

(1) SUPERNATURAL HELP: From God, Infinity, or whatever Diety-name each person uses. Here is help *unlimited!* But it is beyond the province of this book. We shall leave it to the theologians.

(2) HUMAN HELP: Which *is* the teaching of this book, and the responsibility of every Positive Power Person.

You establish *yourself* as a POSITIVE POWER SOURCE by providing *advance positive assurance of help to others* in times of serious need—by assuring everyone in your own personal world: *"If you ever need my cooperation, you can count on me!"*

When you radiate the confidence of a POSITIVE POWER SOURCE, others will seek *you* as their associate; they will seek *your influence* and your *leadership.*

This concludes the list of nine compelling SUBCONSCIOUS NEEDS which you can fulfill in others and motivate *their positive subconscious response* which will *multiply your* PERSONAL POSITIVE POWER.

These nine subconscious needs of others comprise *Your* POSITIVE POWER *Gift List.*

To constantly remind yourself to fulfill these nine subconscious needs of others, list the *key word or words* identifying each on small cards or slips of paper, then place these reminders wherever they will remind you to fulfill one or more of these subconscious needs *every time* you talk with or write to *anybody*—regardless of whether or not you think that person can help you get WHATEVER you want in life.

To be a *Positive Power Person,* you must *impartially, unselfishly* and *constantly* use your PERSONAL POSITIVE POWER to help *everybody.*

Your POSITIVE POWER *Gift List*

GIFT #1: Make others feel ACCEPTED
GIFT #2: Make other feel APPROVED
GIFT #3: Make others feel ADMIRED
GIFT #4: Make others feel APPRECIATED
GIFT #5: Make others feel IMPORTANT
GIFT #6: Make others feel AGREED WITH
GIFT #7: Give others your *enthusiastic* ATTENTION
GIFT #8. Make others feel NEEDED
GIFT #9: Give others your COOPERATION and HELP

You will *multiply* your PERSONAL POSITIVE POWER to the extent that you give the *nine* GIFTS in this chapter's *Gift List.*

And you will attract through your subconscious mind and its *Infinite Source of wisdom and power* —WHATEVER YOU WANT.

So . . . the time is NOW!

TAKE COMMAND OF YOUR LIFE!

MAKE it happen!!! Begin by *mentally broadcasting* your GOODWILL to *everybody!*

Chapter 70

How To Mentally Broadcast Your GOODWILL To Everybody!

What you are about to learn will have a profound and miraculous effect on your life—from the first minute you start to use it!

Your mind broadcasts your intense thoughts and feelings to others. It does so now—whether you will it or not. This is a well-known, undisputed fact.

There is no doubt about the established fact that *everyone* mentally broadcasts his or her intense thoughts and feelings *to all persons* (and animals) *within range of sight or presence.* Constant scientific experiments are taking place (at the Institute of Extrasensory Perception at Duke University, for example) to determine if thoughts and feelings can be broadcast great distances. *Astronauts are testing mental broadcasting from outer space!*

This psychic radiation or mental broadcasting of thoughts and feelings is known as an *aura.*

Persons who are intensely afraid of dogs, mentally broadcast their *aura* of fear to dogs which then instinctively growl or bark at or even attack the frightened persons. Persons who genuinely like dogs are not molested but are welcomed with tail-wagging affection by the same dogs which attack persons who mentally broadcast fear of them.

If you can *mentally broadcast* your intense thoughts and feelings to a dog—obviously, you can *mentally broadcast* to a person. And this is an established, proven, scientific fact.

Mental broadcasting can have a miraculously beneficial effect on your life! Here's how:

Always—whenever you are near or even within sight of a person or a group of people—*think intensely: "I am broadcasting GOODWILL to him* (or her, or them, or my fellow workers, or whatever name or description by which you can identify them in your mind)."

Then, follow your *mental broadcast* of GOODWILL with a GOOD WISH.

For example: You see your friend, Joe, walking toward you. You *think intensely: "I am broadcasting GOODWILL to Joe. I hope I can make him happy!"* (Then you will greet Joe with the attitude of GOODWILL and the goal of making him happy. And Joe will *receive* and *favorably respond* to your *mental broadcast* of GOODWILL and GOOD WISHES.)

It is not necessary that you confine your *mental broadcasts* of GOODWILL and GOOD WISHES only to those whom you know personally—or even whom you expect to meet.

Mentally broadcast your GOODWILL and

GOOD WISHES to the policeman on the corner, the crippled boy across the street, to all the people in the elevator, to all of the people in the office, store or factory, to *everybody . . . everywhere!*

There is not space in this book to discuss to what extent more remote and unknown persons will be aware (consciously or subconsciously) of your *mental broadcasts* of GOODWILL and GOOD WISHES to them.

It is sufficient, for the present, that you know the psychological fact that *your mentally broadcasting GOODWILL and GOOD WISHES to everyone, every day, is a proven method of CONDITIONING YOUR OWN ATTITUDE; multiplying your personal positive power* (× +).

Mentally broadcast GOODWILL and GOOD WISHES before you write a letter, or dial a telephone call, or make a personal visit, or talk to an individual or a group.

It will give you a radiant personality!

It will make you a POSITIVE POWER PERSON (× +). So . . . *mentally broadcast goodwill!*

Chapter 71

Take Command! MAKE It Happen!

You now have at your personal command—through this SUCCESS COURSE—the success methods to enable you to GET WHATEVER YOU WANT . . . *Happiness!* . . . *Love!* . . . *Success!* . . . *Wealth!* . . . *Influence!* . . . *Power!* . . . *Popularity!* . . . *Fame!* . . . WHATEVER YOU WANT!

Your ownership of this book certifies that *you have bought stock in yourself;* proves that you have confidence in yourself—which is the first step in GETTING WHATEVER YOU WANT.

Investing in *yourself* is the most profitable investment you can make because *you were born to succeed.* Success is Nature's Law. Plants, animals and people have a *natural success instinct.*

Failure results only when the *natural success instinct* is NOT USED. People fail simply because *they do not know* HOW TO SUCCEED!

In order to *use* your *natural success instinct,* you must know HOW. It is the purpose of this SUCCESS

COURSE to teach you HOW to use your *natural success instinct* to GET WHATEVER YOU WANT . . . simply, easily, quickly.

If you *constantly* USE the success methods in this book, YOU WILL GET WHATEVER YOU WANT.

YOU—yes, YOU—will succeed . . . *whoever* you are . . . *wherever* you are . . . *whatever* your *age* . . . *whatever* your *skin color* . . . *whatever* your *present education* (or *lack* of education) . . . *whatever* your *present situation* (whether you are *now employed* or *unemployed*) . . . whether you are *rich* or *only in the middle income bracket* or *poor* . . . whether *you live in a ghetto* or *wherever you live* . . . IF YOU CONSTANTLY USE THE SUCCESS METHODS IN THIS BOOK, YOU WILL GET WHATEVER YOU WANT.

That is *all* there is to being successful: (1) Knowing HOW to do it . . . and (2) DOING it!

This SUCCESS COURSE teaches you HOW to use *all three* simple, easy, sure kinds of *Success Psychology* to GET WHATEVER YOU WANT:

(1) *Motivational Psychology* will turn you into *one-person spectacular!* It will *turn you on!* You will *come alive!* Be a *shaker* and a *mover! Light up! Heat up* an *inner glow* so that you *radiate* an *outer glow* (personal magnetism)! Be *something!* Be a *happening!* Be *somebody!* CONSTANTLY USING the *Motivational Psychology* and other sure success methods in this book will make the difference between your being a *one-person volcano*—or a *cold fish!*

(2) This SUCCESS COURSE teaches you how to use *Personal Improvement Psychology* which is the simplest, easiest, fastest way to *improve yourself*. If you

CONSTANTLY USE the instant improvement methods in this book—your family, your friends, your employer, and everyone you want to impress will notice your personal improvement beginning with the *very first time* you start USING the amazingly quick methods of *Personal Improvement Psychology.*

(3) Then, *to positively assure your success,* this SUCCESS COURSE teaches you the powerful methods of *Personal Influence Psychology* which—if you CONSTANTLY USE them—*will enable you to smoothly influence others so that they willingly and enthusiastically help you GET WHATEVER YOU WANT.*

Everything you need to know about *Success Psychology* is in this book—but you cannot learn *all* of it (perhaps not even *much* of it) by *just reading* this book once. To get the *full* benefit of this SUCCESS COURSE, you *must re-read this book over and over again.*

Read at least one chapter of this book *every* night. The success method of getting the most out of this book is: *never finish it!* This means that as soon as you have read the *last* chapter, you *immediately* read the *first* chapter. Thus, instead of having *finished* this book you will, in fact, have *just begun* it. This simple psychological technique will automatically cause you to continue re-reading this SUCCESS COURSE over and over again.

Be sure to *underscore* every success method you especially want to impress into your subconscious mind —so that it will be an *automatic response* which you will use whenever necessary.

Make check marks or draw arrows to attract your attention to success methods which you especially want to emphasize in your daily activities.

This SUCCESS COURSE is to be *used—not just read.* Use it *constantly.*

If you USE the success methods in this book, *you will succeed*—even if you have "handicaps." This book contains the real life stories (see Chapter 10) of how poor boys became multimillionaires, how cripples became world champions, how weaklings became the strongest men in the world, how a deaf man composed some of the world's greatest symphonies, how "old" men past retirement age amassed huge fortunes! *Handicaps are challenges, not excuses!*

There simply is *no excuse* for YOUR not getting WHATEVER YOU WANT as your own worthy life goal.

This SUCCESS COURSE explains the "*Hollywood and T.V.*" *Key to Success* so you can use the success methods which have made the movie and television stars rich and famous.

This book is a treasure chest! It contains the "*Make Friends and Use Influence*" *Key to Success* . . . and the "*Overwhelming Service*" *Key to Success* . . . and the "*Human Dynamo*" *Key to Success* . . . and the "*Mind Power*" *Key to Success* . . . and the "*Will Power*" *Key to Success.*

And those proven success methods are *just the beginning!* You now have in your hands—ready for *your* instant use—*hundreds* of simple, easy, sure success methods! So . . . *USE them!*

For example, you *constantly should use* the very simple—but almost *irresistible*—method of *successfully* ASKING which is so thoroughly taught in this SUC-

CESS COURSE. The dependable *Law of Averages* guarantees its success.

But suppose, when you ASK—the answer is "No!" This book teaches you *exactly* what to *do* and what to *say* when you ASK for what you want—and get a "No!" reply. And it teaches you *How To Discover and Remove The HIDDEN REASON For Refusal* (Chapter 21). It teaches you how to change "No!" to "Yes!"

Of course, review *all* of the chapters in this SUCCESS COURSE—but especially be sure you learn *How to FAIL Your Way to Success* (Chapter 24).

An entire *Special Section* of this SUCCESS COURSE is devoted to teaching you *The Miraculous Power Of INTENSELY BELIEVING That You Will Succeed* (beginning with Chapter 26). *It consists of fifteen of the most inspirational real life stories of all time!* A brief chapter is devoted to each life story. Here is proof positive that *miraculous success was achieved* by men and women who INTENSELY BELIEVED that *they could get whatever they wanted* . . . and they became so successful that they are recognized as being among *the greatest people in the history of the world!*

This SUCCESS COURSE teaches *you* how to develop that *same miraculous power* of INTENSE BELIEF *which made others great and famous!*

To enable *you* to develop this *miraculous power* of INTENSE BELIEF that *you* will succeed in GETTING WHATEVER YOU WANT, this book teaches you easy-to-use psychological methods (many of which *have never been revealed* in *any* book or success course): the "*Knotted Rope*" Method, the "*Magic Coins*" Method, the *"Deck of Cards"* Method, and many more—including the *"Silent Chant"* and simplified *Self-Hypnosis.*

This course teaches you how to *prevent* POISONING YOUR MIND. It lists the most dangerous *poison thoughts to avoid.* This may save your career, your health or your life!

Then, this SUCCESS COURSE has a large *Special Section* on *How To Multiply Your PERSONAL POSITIVE POWER* (×+).

You now are in command! You MAKE it happen! You MAKE it happen . . . NOW!

You enter the realm of the vast SUBCONSCIOUS *where power is unlimited!*

Your subconscious mind *controls* your present and your future because it has the *cybernetic* (goal-reaching) power to *materialize* into your life WHATEVER you *intensely desire*—and this SUCCESS COURSE *teaches you how to control your subconscious mind* so that through its cybernetic (goal-reaching) power YOU WILL GET WHATEVER YOU WANT.

This book teaches you how to fulfill the deep, subconscious NEEDS of *others* and thereby obtain their grateful, positive allegiance so that *others—many others—* will help you GET WHATEVER YOU WANT.

By fulfilling the deep, subconscious NEEDS of *others* (as clearly explained in this book, beginning in Chapter 59), *you enormously multiply your PERSONAL POSITIVE POWER* (×+).

When you enormously multiply your PERSONAL POSITIVE POWER (×+), *you will irresistibly attract success like a powerful magnet!*

YOU WILL GET WHATEVER YOU WANT'